942.

Hert
COUN
Commun

2

1

S
p

R

8

JUL 1999

Portrait of GOWER

WYNFORD VAUGHAN-THOMAS

Photographs by
RICHARD WINSLADE
and others.

ROBERT HALE · LONDON

© *Wynford Vaughan-Thomas 1976 and 1983*
First published in Great Britain 1976
Second edition 1983

ISBN 0 7091 5577 8

Robert Hale Limited
Clerkenwell House
Clerkenwell Green
London EC1R 0HT

Photoset in Century Schoolbook by
Kelly Typesetting Limited
Bradford-on-Avon, Wiltshire
Printed in Great Britain by
Redwood Burn Limited
Trowbridge, Wiltshire
Bound by W.B.C. Bookbinders Limited

Contents

Illustrations

MAPS

PICTURE CREDITS

Acknowledgements

The writer wishes to acknowledge the ready help he has received from the Librarian and Deputy Librarian of Swansea Public Library in checking on the available literary sources; to W. R. Rodgers for advice on the history of the Lucas family; to Dr Peter Lloyd Jones for procuring some of the rarer books on Gower; to numerous members of the Gower Society who patiently answered his queries on many special points; to Jonathan Cape and Mr F. R. Fletcher, the editor, to quote from Kilvert's *Diary*, ed. William Flomer; and to Mrs Gwen Watkins for permission to quote *Ode to Swansea* by Vernon Watkins.

Introduction

A Portrait of Gower! But how do you set about painting a true portrait of this unique part of Wales? Gower does not cover a large area. The peninsula itself is only sixteen odd miles long and about seven miles across, although the hinterland is somewhat larger. Yet into this small space is packed an infinite variety of turbulent history, complicated geology and a landscape of glittering limestone cliffs, golden sands, wild moorlands and crowded industry. You cannot put everything on canvas. A portrait has to be selective and that means it must be personal.

This book therefore embodies my own personal reaction to Gower. It is one man's view of a rare patch of the Earth's surface. I shall write of the structure of Gower, of its history and of its holiday delights as I have discovered them in the course of a lifelong devotion to this delectable land, and in doing so I shall hope to convey something of its quality to the visitor who is seeing it for the first time.

Gower, as marked on most modern maps, is a peninsula running westwards from Swansea and bounded by the Bristol Channel and the estuary of the River Loughor. But it had better be described as that section of the old county of Glamorgan which lies west of the valley of the Tawe. This was the old Welsh commote of Gwyr, whose origin goes back to the mists of the Dark Ages. The present parliamentary constituency still includes the greater part of it. These two sections of Gower offer a sharp contrast, following the old Welsh division of the lands of South Wales into the 'Bro', or vale and the 'Bryniau' or uplands. By this rough and ready division Peninsula Gower can be defined as basically low-lying, English-speaking, sea-girt and agricultural, while upland Gower is high, industrial and Welsh. There are plenty of exceptions to this rule but it will do as a working description.

Our portrait will be mainly concerned with Peninsula Gower.

This is the Gower of golden sands and the splendid coastline—
the tourist 'honey-pot'. Here lie most of the popular and well-
known attractions, the places that every visitor wants to see.
This is the area that has been officially designated as an Area of
Outstanding Natural Beauty. But I have also included two
chapters which describe Swansea, the gateway to Gower, and a
very short note at the end of the book on the hidden surprises of
the uplands behind the city; all part of the old political division
of Gwyr.

Throughout the book I have called the area by what I am
convinced is its correct title—Gower, quite short and simple! In
some parts of Wales you will hear people talking of '*The* Gower'.
"We'll be going down the Gower on Saturday", they will tell you
in the mining valleys. But I note that it is usually the folk from
outside the peninsula—from Welsh-speaking or what used to be
Welsh-speaking South Wales—who tack on 'the'. I may be
wrong but I have a theory that this practice grew up in the late
nineteenth century when Gower became, for the first time, a
place to which you could take the Mumbles train for a day trip.
In the mining valleys they lived in the 'Bryniau'. Below them
lay the fertile Vale of Glamorgan or the 'Bro'. When Gower came
into their holiday ken, what could be more natural for them
than tacking a 'the' onto Gower, on the analogy of 'The Vale'.
People do not take kindly to this practice in the 'Englishry' of
Gower. No one born in Swansea or the peninsula ever calls it
The Gower. And after all the original name was Gwyr and not Y
Gwyr. No medieval manuscript or inscription ever uses The
Gower. I was all the more surprised therefore to find that the
new issue of the Ordnance Survey, which at long last includes
the peninsula in one map, has "Swansea and The Gower" on its
cover. Let it be removed in the next edition, please. Gower,
short, simple and correct it shall be for my portrait.

As for my qualifications for attempting it, I suppose I can
claim technically to be a Gower man. My mother's family
farmed the high moorland behind Pontardulais and I, myself,
was born in Swansea. All my early holidays were spent in that
now far off wonderland of old Gower before the First World War,
when the landscape was still lonely, unspoilt and unknown to
the outside world. Gower was a secret Swansea people hugged to
themselves. I remember long drives in a wagonette over white,
dusty roads to Rhossili; the great adventure of being taken out
crabbing by old Mr Grove on Sedgers Bank; the wild excitement

of watching the practice launch of the Port-Eynon lifeboat with a team of great horses dragging it down through the surf; of listening to Phil Tanner singing, pint in hand, on his bench outside the King's Head at Llangennith and of riding down to Parkmill, perched precariously on the roof of a Pioneer bus, into a Gower that still seemed to belong to the nineteenth century. I saw the slow change of that quiet, settled society in the years between the wars, and then the shatteringly quick break-up of old Gower under the impact of mass tourism.

I talk of a break-up, and such it must seem to anyone who remembers the Gower of even fifty years ago. But, when all is said, so much remains. The caravans and the cars have come, but the wild commons are still there. The gulls still scream around the great cliffs of Paviland, the Llanrhidian marshland is still withdrawn and mysterious and the herons have not deserted Penrice. That Gower remains Gower is surely due to the unremitting efforts of the Gower Society. This strong group of dedicated conservationists was formed under the leadership of Dr Gwent Jones and Stephen Lee in 1947. For over numerous years it has waged doughty battle against developers and the general spoilers of the countryside. But for the efforts of the Society there would be no Gower of which it would be worth painting the portrait. I therefore dedicate this book to the gallant members of the Gower Society.

The Society also published an excellent and handy guide to Gower, as well as a yearly journal. The well-illustrated numbers of *Gower* are invaluable to anyone who is interested in the peninsula, and I have naturally kept a complete series on my shelves. This book could not have been written without them. But there are other books on Gower that anyone who paints its portrait must consult, starting at the fountain-head, the Rev. J. D. Davies's volumes on the history of West Gower, published between 1877 and 1898. This kindly and curious cleric, wood-carver, yachtsman and archaeologist, was the rector of Cheriton and Llanmadoc and an insatiable collector of all sorts of out-of-the-way information about his beloved countryside. Without him Gower history would seem dull indeed. His volumes are long out of print but I had the pleasure of reading them in the comfort of the Swansea Library. I owe a debt to the Deputy Librarian for his hospitality during the many pleasant days of research I spent in the library. There is a vast temptation once you are launched on a scheme of reading for a volume such as this, to turn up every reference in every journal that concerns Gower. I gallantly ploughed through the volumes of the *Archeologia Cambrensis*. I enjoyed finding the elegantly expressed accounts of the nineteenth-century archaeologists on the antiquities of Gower—what an untrammelled world of gentlemanly research they reflected!—"A mediaeval thurible found in Penmaen" (*Arch. Camb.* 1891); "Penny Crick Tumulus" (Arch. *Camb.* 1887); "Pre-Norman sculptured stone and thirteenth century sepulcral slabs at Llanrhidian" (*Arch. Camb.* 1888).

Then there was a vast array of pamphlets, from Clarence Seyler's *Early Charters* to the proposals for a Gower Light railway and the "Appeal to Justice" in the great battle in 1845, between the Rev. Samuel Phillips, Fairy Hill, the Rev. John James, Penmaen, and Major Penrice. There came a time when I had to call it a day. If I had not, I would still be in the pleasant surroundings of Swansea Public Library, deeply immersed in Gabriel Powell's survey and the tour of the Duke of Beaufort. Besides, other and far more competent writers had been before me, experts in their various fields. Professor Balchin, of the University College of Swansea, edited an important collection of articles on 'Swansea and its Region' for the meeting of the British Association in the city in 1971. J. D. Rutter has produced an excellent survey of *Prehistoric Gower*. There is a classic account of the Gower flora by Mr Goodman and the delightful volumes by the late Horatio Tucker cover the old social life of Gower and its folklore. W. H. Jones has collected all the medieval records in his *History of the Port of Swansea*, and the Rev. Latimer Davies did the same for the Pennard area; *Letters from Swansea*, collected by J. E. Ross, are delightful. Olive Phillips wrote a charming and sensitive account of Gower, as it stood in the 1950s. Jeremy Talbot has published a complete guide to Gower as a rapidly developing centre for rock climbers. Clive Gammon has edited an *Angling Guide to Wales* for the Wales Tourist Board which has an excellent section on sea-fishing in Gower. Mary Gillham's *The Natural History of Gower* is a delight and indispensable. And there are many more; above all the *Gower Journal* and the Society's indispensable pocket guide to Peninsula Gower.

But some of these volumes are rather difficult to come by, others are out of print, and many were written some years ago. There is thus a fair reason for producing a new volume on

Gower, aimed at the modern visitor, an up-to-date Gossiping Guide which would also allow the present writer to yield to the long-felt temptation of writing about his favourite part of the fair land of Wales. Inevitably in a volume like this there are bound to be mistakes and omissions, but not I hope too many. There are also bound to have been some changes and new discoveries between the time of writing and publication. I must also explain some seeming inconsistencies in the spelling of place-names.

Gower spelling has, in fact, been inconsistent down the ages, Rhossili is a notorious example. It seems to be spelt differently in the church-porch, the post-office, the signposts, on the car park ticket and on the maps. Is it Rhossili, Rhossily, Rhosili, Rhossilly, or Rhosily? What should be the preferred spelling—Llangenneth, Llangennith, or Llangenydd? Are there one or two 'n's in Pennard? And is there an 'e' in Whiteford? The early Ordnance Survey men made some natural mistakes in recording Welsh place-names, which have rolled happily on through edition after edition, but Welsh orthography has long been fixed by scholars and the form of Welsh names agreed upon. It is no longer permissible to end names with a 'y'. Thus the correct form is now Llanelli, for example and not the old style Llanelly. And Loughor should be written Llwchwr.

I felt that I had to come to some decision in this matter and so I have, with many misgivings, used the forms as printed in the new Ordnance Survey map. This, after all, is now the map that all visitors will buy and use. It is on sale everywhere and is displacing all previous maps. I have already lamented its use of "The Gower" and I am unhappy that it gives "Llangennith" once again for the preferred form of Llangennydd and Llwchwr stays as the anglicized "Loughor". The map uses the new metric scale, 1:50,000 and if you belong to my generation, you will still be disconcerted to find the heights given in metres rather than feet. Somehow Rhossili Downs do not seem very high when you see them marked 193. To keep the best of both worlds I have put the metre heights in brackets after the feet, where I can find them, but only in the section covering Peninsula Gower.

I also plead guilty to another anachronism. I still talk of Pembrokeshire and Carmarthenshire in describing the views from the high summits, although I am only too well aware that these two counties have been thrown in to a shot-gun marriage with Cardiganshire to create the three-headed administrative monster called Dyfed. Again I have done this for the convenience of visitors, who I am sure will use the old county names for some little time to come. Gower, in the new reorganization, is now officially included in the new county of West Glamorgan.

But perhaps these are, after all, small changes and will soon be absorbed into our everyday living. In five years' time metres, Dyfed and the rest of them will be so familiar that we will have forgotten that other forms ever existed. What I hope will never change is the charm and delight of the Gower I now invite you to explore in this book. I know that the pressures on this lovely land are increasing, and every time I look out over Llanmadoc Hill or Worms Head, I breathe a silent and alas, impossible prayer. "Lord, let this Land of Gwyr always look exactly as it looks now, at the moment I lay down my pen in September, 1975."

Swansea, 1975.   W.V.T.

In this second edition of *Portrait of Gower* I have taken the opportunity of noting some of the changes in the Gower landscape that have taken place over the last eight years. Happily, thanks to the continued vigilance of the Gower Society and the ever-increasing concern of the Authorities for the preservation of our natural heritage, these changes have been relatively few. The face of Gower has not been radically altered. There have been important archaeological discoveries at Rhossili and Llanelen which have now been recorded in our text. Imposing new buildings have been erected in the old South Dock area of Swansea, and the Parliamentary boundaries of the Gower constituency may be re-drawn. It is proposed that the Pontardawe area in the Tawe valley, should be assigned to the Neath area, while Oystermouth will leave the constituency of Swansea West and join that of Gower. At the time of writing, these changes have yet to be ratified by Parliament, but no doubt they will take place during the coming years. For the rest, I can only repeat my prayer in my first introduction and hope that the land of Gower will remain as enticing as it now is in 1983.

                                                                                                          W.V.T.

1

Swansea, Gower's Gateway

Swansea City is the curtain-raiser to the Gower scene. Most visitors have to pass through it, and Gower-folk have always regarded it as their capital. "Swansea Market," one old Gower farmer declared to me, "Why, every one knows it belongs to us. It's just a nice patch of Gower in the middle of these damned houses." Indeed Swansea and Gower have always been tangled up together throughout their long history. Swansea Castle held the power that ruled the ancient lordship of Gower, and so in any account of Gower, Swansea must come first.

I was born in Swansea and therefore cannot write a dispassionate account of it. I still see the city through the hopeful eyes of youth, and for me Swansea will always be the unplanned, smokily-romantic town of between the wars, long before it got ennobled with its recent citydom. I remember looking out over it with my fellow-townsman, Dylan Thomas, when we were both in our sardonic twenties. "This town", said Dylan, "has got as many layers as an onion and each one reduces you to tears." There was a deep Welsh layer, a strong English one, an industrial layer, a musical layer full of choirs singing test pieces for the National Eisteddfod and a furious sporting layer of rugby teams and boxers from the Valleys. Old Swansea was a delicious architectural chaos. It was never planned, it was sprayed over the landscape with a flit gun. From the top-storey bedroom of our tall Victorian house on the lower slopes of Town Hill I used to look out over the wonderful architectural mix-up spread below. The builders of old Swansea were masters of the art of surrealist juxtaposition. The enormous back-side of the Plaza Cinema flaunted itself in shameless splendour over the centre of the town. The Town Hall hid from the citizens amongst the docks. The local museum, a fine early Victorian dream of culture, was tangled up with overhead railway arches. The market loomed over the town like the Duomo over Florence, and under its great glass dome they sold everything, from herbal remedies and cockles to laverbread and Welsh flannel shirts for colliers. The Art Gallery stood next to the Working Man's Club. There were chapels and pubs mixed up haphazardly with banks and drapers' shops, while outside the centre the streets shot up the hills at alarming angles. And always, you were aware of the ships making for the docks and the lovely curve of the bay around to the dazzling limestone headland of the Mumbles. And you hugged to yourself the secret knowledge that just beyond the headland lay Gower and all its glory.

The heart of this old Swansea of my far-off youth was obliterated by German bombs in 1941, when Swansea suffered as severely in the Blitz as any town in Britain. The ruins had been cleared by 1945, and soon after this the centre was replanned and largely rebuilt in a brisk, practical modern style with the wide avenue of Kingsway right through the heart of the place, and a pleasant, open garden replacing the maze of narrow, twisting streets. Today the tall G.P.O. Tower dominates this new Swansea. All very proper and sensible but old inhabitants like myself cannot help sighing, occasionally, for that lost, happily unorganized, friendly town of not-so-long ago.

But the rebuilding has brought one advantage. At least you can see clearly from the central gardens the oldest building in the city—the castle, the point where Swansea began. Now Swansea has a long history but is distinctly short of early buildings to bear witness to it. The shell of St David's Hospital, now the Cross Keys Inn, and the fine keep of the castle, are all that remain and both were erected in the early fourteenth century by the greatest of the Welsh ecclesiastical builders, Bishop Henry de Gower. He created the magnificent bishops' palaces at St David's and Lamphrey, with their elegant arcaded decor, and he repeated this architectural trick with great success at Swansea. Thanks to the Ministry of the Environment, the castle has now been cleared of the clutter of old buildings that once housed the local newspaper, and the grey walls rise above a trim, green lawn. The arcades on Henry de Gower's keep can be seen in their true proportions and the ancient castle has become the worthy centrepiece of the new Swansea.

But, then, Swansea Castle is used to these strange changes of fortune. The castle, as was often the case in Wales, was the beginning of the town. No one knows much about any previous settlement on the site—if there ever was one. The pundits have argued long and learnedly about the origin of the name. The Welsh simply called the place Abertawe—the mouth of the Tawe River, and what could be simpler than that! But Swansea? Where did this curious name come from, which has clearly nothing to do with Swans or the Sea although in my boyhood I was firmly convinced it was the reason why the local soccer team was called the Swans, I felt that I was keeping alive a tradition that went back to the Dark Ages as I joined the great rallying cry of the club supporters: "Up the Lily-whites!"

The most plausible explanation seems to be that Swansea is derived from the Scandinavian 'Sveinn'—a personal name— and 'ey', an island. It is therefore Sveinn's Island, and indeed there was a small island at the mouth of the Tawe until the eighteenth century. Who Sveinn was we shall never know, but the Danes certainly sailed continuously up the Bristol Channel leaving a scattering of names behind them from Skomer Island to Worms Head, and it is possible that there might have been a small Norse settlement here.

With the coming of the Normans we are on firmer ground. By the end of the eleventh century these formidable freebooters had started to push deep into the fertile lowlands of South Wales. Gower and the hinterland of Swansea was certainly in the hands of Henry de Newburgh, Earl of Warwick, by 1106, and, like a good Norman he built his castle at Swansea as the centre of his new lordship. It was probably a motte-and-bailey affair and indeed you can still see the mound depicted in the Buck prints of old Swansea in the early eighteenth century. This may account for the fact that we constantly hear of the castle being destroyed by the Welsh in their repeated forays into Gowerland throughout the twelfth century. King John strengthened the castle and a little township began to grow up under the protective shadow of its walls. Llywelyn the Last burnt the town but the castle held and the little town recovered. It had already been granted charters by William de Newburgh and King John, and Henry de Gower certainly kept a protective hand over it. But the castle did not play a dramatic part in history.

Poor Edward II may have used it when he was being hunted through South Wales, for the city possesses one curious and tragic reminder of that sad flight of the king from his implacable wife, Isabella, and her paramour Mortimer. We know that the harassed king reached Neath bringing with him the royal treasure and his personal records. We know, too, that he sent hurried orders to Swansea to provision the castle, but we also know that he had to turn back only to be captured with his young supporter, Despencer, in a dingle near Llantrisant, still called to this day Pant-y-Brad—the Vale of Treachery. So he went to his shameful death at Berkeley Castle.

But the curious thing about the story is that Edward's death set off a grand treasure hunt which, in some ways, has continued right up to our own time. Edward had scattered his wealth for safe keeping in castles and monasteries at Margam, Neath and Swansea. The royal commissioners who hunted for the royal money-chest, armour and valuable documents were still hard at it years after the fall of Edward II. Robert de Penres, Lord of Penrice in Gower, was suspected of illegally removing a hoard of money in 1331. A small hoard of coins of the period was discovered only a few years ago during restoration work on Neath Abbey. But the strangest find of all occurred in the middle of the last century. Dr Nichol of Swansea was called to a case in a remote part of Gower. As payment for his services, the farmer offered him a box which he withdrew from a hiding-place in the thatched roof. The box contained the parchment of the original document recording Edward II's affiancement to his Queen, Isabella. You can see the frail and faded parchment in its glass case in the Royal Institution in Swansea. To me there is something infinitely moving in this relic of royal unhappiness found in a lost corner of distant Wales.

But, then, Swansea Castle never brought luck to its royal guests. The next king to stay there was the equally unfortunate Richard II, who had a most uncomfortable night, for his courtiers complained that the castle was so badly furnished that the king actually had to sleep on straw, poor fellow. And twenty years later the castle had sunk so low that the approach of Owain Glyndwr in 1406 threw the authorities into a panic and they hurriedly commissioned material for "building anew and mending the walls of the bailey of the castle, broken and thrown to the ground ... because of the coming of Owen Glyndourdy and other traitors threatening and rising in these parts". In vain! Owain had an efficient fifth column operating and he overran Swansea and its neglected castle in next to no time.

From then on, the castle fades into the background. By the nineteenth century it had sunk into being a debtors' prison. You can still see the heavy cell doors, and not so long ago could decipher the gay doggerel inscribed on the wall:

> Welcome, welcome, brother debtor
> To this poor but merry place
> Where no bailiff
> Dares to show his frightful face
> But, kind sir, as you're a stranger
> Five shillings you must pay
> Or your coat will be in danger
> You must either strip or pay.
>   By order of the Committee.

But if the castle decayed, the town it had created flourished. By the beginning of the eighteenth century the little port was packed with vessels carrying coal over to Devon, Somerset and Ireland, to the approval of that practical man, Daniel Defoe, who published his *Tour through the whole Island of Britain* in 1724–7. He made the exciting announcement: "There are lately mineral waters found at Swanzey, which are reputed to be of great efficacy in fluxes and Haemorrhages of all sorts. Consumptions if not too far gone, palsies rheumatisms, dropsies and other distempers are said to fall before these styptick and restorative waters." Alas I have never discovered the exact whereabouts of these invaluable "styptick waters". They seem to have been near the present St Helen's. Unfortunately Swansea never developed as a second Llandrindod Wells, but it did have the honour of producing the arbiter of taste in Britain's premier spa, Bath. This was the celebrated Beau Nash, who imposed his rules of gentlemanly conduct on all visitors who came to take the waters, and governed fashionable Bath as the absolute arbiter of good taste for nearly fifty years. In truth, Nash has always seemed to me rather a dull dog and pompous with it all—not a trace in him of the easy friendliness which is the boast of all good Swansea men. Even Oliver Goldsmith had to admit, when he came to write his account of him: "The amours of coxcombs, and the pursuits of debauchees, are destitute of novelty to attract us, as they are of variety to entertain. . . . The life of Mr Nash is incapable of supplying any entertainment of this nature to a purient curiosity." How far away this seems from our permissive age!

When the first Swansea Guide appeared in 1802, the author was loud in his praise of the bathing facilities. "The bay is universally allowed to be singularly beautiful. . . . The Burrows contain many good lodging houses, pleasantly situated; and that of Mr Jordans in particular is fitted up with an excellent Warm Sea-Water Bath, on the following terms: 'Bathing each time three shillings, each napkin if found by the proprietor two pence, with an additional sixpence for bathing in the winter half-year.' "

But if one visitor is to be believed, bathing in Swansea Bay in those days was not without delicious dangers.

As we were strolling along the sands, about a mile above the town, we remarked a group of figures in birthday attire gambolling in the water: not suspecting they were women we passed carelessly on, but how great was our surprise, on approaching them, to find that the fact did not admit of a doubt. We had not paused a minute, before they all came running towards us, with a menacing tone and countenance, that seemed to order us away. Though we did not understand their British sentences, we obeyed, and very hastily too, on finding a volley of stones rattling about our ears. This hostile demonstration, we afterwards found, arose from a suspicion that we were going to remove their clothes, a piece of waggery often practised by the visitants of Swansea to enjoy their running *nudiores ovo*. The girls knew we were not their countrymen, or we should have passed unconcerned, unless indeed, acquaintances who would have made their usual salutation, and perhaps joined in the party's amusement. In our subsequent rambles on the beach these liberal exhibitions of Cambrian beauty afforded us many pleasing studies of unsophisticated nature:

Graceful, cleanly, smooth and round;
All in Venus' girdle bound.

Little of that gay and cosily genteel Regency Swansea remains—a few decaying rows of once elegant houses near the docks, a villa here and there in its own grounds and a terrace on the road along the bay with wrought-iron balconies from which the visitors might have cheered Lord Nelson when he made his celebrated visit to the town in 1802. He received a boisterous welcome for he arrived complete with his Emma and her complaisant spouse, Sir William Hamilton. Emma warbled "God Save the King" and "Rule Britannia" at the Portreeve's banquet, and a crowd of sailors on leave drew the hero's carriage through the streets, joined by Tom Cleaves, the landlord of the Plume and Feathers. Tom had been a boatswain on one of Nelson's ships and blew a series of calls on his boatswain's pipe.

Nelson heard the sound, sprang up in his carriage and shouted "Tom Cleaves' pipe, by Jove". The carriage stopped and Nelson shook Tom warmly by the hand to the delight of the crowd. Nelson had nothing to learn from any modern politician in the gentle art of personality projection and popularity!

The bay has changed, of course, since Nelson's visit but it still has an impressive beauty in spite of all the new industrial plants, from steel-works to petro-chemicals, that now fringe part of the shoreline. It is still worth climbing Town Hill to see it, or walking along the Promenade that runs near St Helen's Rugby Ground. Swansea Bay starts with the limestone islets of the Mumbles—"flashing white", as John Masefield described them as seen from a wind-jammer beating up channel under full sail. Then come the steep cliffs behind Oystermouth and the still wooded curve around to Blackpill. To the east are the high hills of mid-Glamorgan, reaching nearly to the 2,000 foot mark. When the tide is full and night falls, the lights run in a glittering circle around the bay. Then it almost justifies the celebrated comparison made by none other than the irascible and fastidious poet, Walter Savage Landor, when he declared that he preferred it to the Bay of Naples. We must make some allowance for poetic licence here, and maybe the extraordinary chimney that once carried the smoke of the old Cwmavon copper works a thousand feet up the mountain side made the 1210-foot Foel Fynyddau look like Vesuvius! But Landor was certainly deeply impressed by the then unsullied beauty of Swansea Bay.

Until Dylan Thomas arrived on the scene, Landor was the town's most important connection with the poets. The unfortunate Richard Savage, the friend of Dr Johnson, had once been banished to Swansea by his friends to write an unactable tragedy, and Shelley made a brief tragic visit in 1816, when Fanny Imlay committed suicide in the Mackworth Hotel. But Landor actually lived in Swansea for a spell and remembered it with deep affection during his Italian exile. "If it should ever be my fortune, which I cannot expect, and do not much hope, to return to England, I would pass the remainder of my days in Swansea—between that place and the Mumbles."

This is not surprising since it was at Swansea that the celebrated meeting occurred which inspired his most famous poem. He was walking on the sand-dunes of the Burrows in 1796— "how beautiful was the sea-shore covered with low roses, snapdragons and thousands of other plants"—when he met a young seventeen-year-old girl whose beauty made an overwhelming impression on him. He could not pay his formal addresses to her since he was then living at Swansea with his mistress, Nancy Jones, by whom he had a child. Instead he distilled his feelings into perfect verse:

> Ah! what avails the sceptred race!
> Ah! what the form divine!
> What every virtue, every grace!
> Rose Aylmer, all were thine.
> Rose Aylmer, whom these wakeful eyes
> May weep but never see.
> A night of memories and of sighs
> I consecrate to thee.

Strange to think that these lapidary lines were inspired by a meeting on a site which, until recently, was covered by the decaying buildings which surrounded the old South Dock. But now the site is rapidly changing. A big Leisure Centre occupies the place of the old Victoria Station. The handsome loading shed on the side of the dock has been turned, by the Swansea Corporation, into a fascinating maritime and industrial museum, and the dock itself will become a modern marina. To the west rises the gleaming white and impressive new headquarters of the West Glamorgan County Council. The restless shade of Walter Savage Landor has surely been appeased.

Although there was one Swansea 'poetess' who would undoubtedly have fitted in with alacrity to any marina—Ann of Swansea. This rather disreputable sister of the great Sarah Siddons had been relegated to Swansea with an allowance from her relatives. Anything was better than having her hanging around London, giving curious lectures at Dr. Graham's notorious Temple of Health. She boldly announced everywhere that she was the youngest sister of the great tragedienne and became the proprietor of the Swansea Bathing House around the same time as Landor's residence in the town. Perhaps Rose Aylmer patronized her establishment! Ann of Swansea appeared on the stage with results noted by a visitor, J. T. Barber:

"During our stay in this town protracted to several days by its agreeable society, Mrs Hatton, mistress of the bathing house and sister of the English Melpomene, exhibited her theatric powers on the humble boards of Swansea Theatre. But labouring under the misfortune of lameness, and the encumbrance of more flesh than I ever before saw crowded in one female figure, she was obliged to go through her task, the recitation of Alexander's Feast, sitting; notwithstanding which weighty drawback, the lady did not fail to exhibit a vivid tincture of the family genius."

I'm not sure if her poetry showed such a "vivid tincture", but she had an eye for sales in her dedication of her *Poetic Trifles*, published by an Irish gentleman with the improbable name of John Bull.

"Dedicated to the officers of the Royal Western Regiment of the Local Militia. It is not without apprehension Ann of Swansea sends her Poetic Trifles into the world in defence of which she takes the liberty of observing that she has left no useful avocation—neglected no duties—to follow the allurements of the Muse".

The Muse allured her to her best known poem which was dutifully quoted in all Victorian guide-books to Swansea:

> In vain by various griefs oppressed
> I vagrant roam devoid of rest
> With aching heart, still lingering stray
> Around the shores of Swansea Bay. . . .
>
> Then Kilvey Hill, a long adieu
> I drag my sorrows hence from you:
> Misfortune, with imperious sway,
> Impels me far from Swansea Bay.

But there were other influences at work impelling not only poor Ann of Swansea but most fashionable visitors far from Swansea Bay. The city is mainly built on the shore-land and climbs up the Town Hill immediately behind. The River Tawe flows down between the two hills of Town Hill and Kilvey Hill. Town Hill is built over and the inhabitants of the big municipal housing estate have the finest view in Swansea, which includes not only the sweep of the bay towards Gower but the great view northwards over the ever-rising series of hills through which the Tawe—pronounce the "e" by the way—cuts its way to the sea. In the background, twenty-five miles away, is the long, impressive line of summits, rising to over 2,500 feet, which form the range of the Carmarthenshire Vans. The northward view from Town Hill includes the coalfield of West Glamorgan and it was coal that changed Swansea's destiny.

The ease with which plentiful coal could be obtained near at hand brought the copper industry to Swansea and made the place the premier smelting centre in Britain for over a hundred years. The chief sources of copper at this time were Cornwall and Anglesey and the smelting technique was based on charcoal. The ore had to be taken to places where wood was plentiful—the Weald or the Forest of Dean. But by the early eighteenth century the new technique of smelting the ore with coal was rapidly developing, and the copper-hungry industries of Birmingham, the capital of brass, were demanding far bigger quantities of this vital product. It was much cheaper to bring the ore to the coal since the process demanded about thirteen tons of ore to eighteen tons of coal. Swansea possessed the nearest and most easily worked coal deposits to Cornwall, all situated on a river that could accommodate small ships. As a matter of fact, the south outcrop of the coalfield actually crosses Swansea Bay itself and there are coal-measures underneath most parts of the city.

So throughout the eighteenth century the copper industry grew and swiftly changed the whole landscape. The tide could carry the ships up-river as far as the narrow vale between Town Hill and Kilvey Hill known as the 'Hafod', the Summer Dwelling. "Delightful Hafod, most serene abode!" sang the local poet:

> Thou sweet retreat fit mansion for a god!
> Dame Nature lavish of her gifts we see,
> And Paradise again restored in thee. . . .

Hardly Paradise today as you look out of the window as the train runs down past Kilvey Hill into High Street Station.

This is the way everyone came into Swansea before the motorcar arrived, and they usually got a shock. Delightful Hafod, indeed! Tips everywhere, the shells of abandoned factories, the Tawe yellow and struggling past broken bridges, a choked canal—the classic industrial wasteland. Before the war, this back-door entry into Swansea was even more dramatic. Tin-plate and copper works were in full blast. The fumes from the giant spelter works at Llansamlet drifted across the track and sent passengers hurrying to pull up the windows. By the time the train had turned across the viaduct of Landore the visitor was contemplating taking the first train back to London. There has been a strange change in recent years. The vast proportion of the industrial establishments are gone. The impressive Lower Swansea Valley reclamation scheme has worked wonders. Tips have been levelled, trees planted and the bare, brown slopes of Kilvey Hill are changing colour. There is plenty of evidence still left however, to show that this was the place where Swansea first made big money.

Many of the early copper kings naturally were Cornish in origin, the Vivians in particular. Later Vivians lived in Singleton Park, where the university now stands and they took an active part in the practical life of Swansea. John Henry Vivian was the Member of Parliament for the borough from 1832 until his death in 1855, while his son represented Glamorgan from 1857 to 1875. He became the first Baron Swansea and his statue stands before the Patti Pavilion in Victoria Park. One of the most attractive of the new copper masters, however, was a Welshman, John Morris. His father had established copper-works at Landore and the younger Morris ran them in a very progressive way, well ahead of his time. He planned a model village for his employees still called Morristown, and high on the hill above you can still see the gaunt walls of the block of model flats he built to house forty of his workmen in fresh air well away from the copper fumes. They call it Morristown Castle.

But those copper fumes and the reek of all the works that followed them, spelters and tin-plate works, raised that great plume of smoke between the two hills which was Swansea's trademark right up to my own day. There is a vivid drawing of it in the special number of the *Illustrated London News* produced for the British Association's 1880 meeting, showing a long-vanished forest of chimneys clustered around Landore. Swansea is still a great industrial centre but the tin-plate and copper worlds have gone and oil, petro-chemicals and light industries reign in their stead. Yet, thinking back on that black cloud, I remember that out of one of those smoke producers, there came, for a brief moment, objects of transcendent beauty.

Swansea had always possessed important pottery works, but in the early years of the nineteenth century, first George Haynes and then his partner Lewis Weston Dillwyn raised Swansea pottery to higher things. At the Glamorgan Pottery, Dillwyn persuaded artists from Nantgarw like the famous William Billingsley to paint designs for his porcelain, and the brief golden age of Swansea china began. Billingsley excelled in flower painting, and Thomas Baxter in landscape and local

views. There are excellent collections of Swansea china in both
the Glyn Vivian Art Gallery and in the Royal Institution, where
you can inspect some of Baxter's delicate water-colours.
Swansea china is now extremely difficult to come by, and pieces
change hands at astronomical prices. The classic volume on the
subject was written by E. Morton Nance who lived in Swansea
himself for a period. About this massive and scholarly work the
former keeper of ceramics at the British Museum, very justly
declared "I doubt if any ceramic theme has ever been treated
with such thoroughness." Connoisseurs cannot do without it,
with the result that the book has become almost as precious as a
piece of Swansea china. I gaze on these lovely plates and dinner
services in the museum with a certain amount of envy. There
was a time in my early youth when we, too, possessed a collection of Swansea china, and with it a few pieces of greater rarity.
They were displayed on a Welsh dresser which stood on a floor of
highly polished Welsh slate. Alas, one morning our maid,
tugging at a reluctant drawer in the dresser, gave a loud
scream. The dresser tottered and tipped over with the most
expensive crash I have ever heard in my life! And the broken
pieces were swept into the dust-bin! I was six at the time and the
next week the First World War broke out! There must surely
have been a connection between two such cosmic events.

The Swansea of the Hafod, Morriston and the Tawe valley
was basically a Welsh Swansea, much of it Welsh-speaking and
a great fountain-head of male voice choirs. Morriston Orpheus
have been one of the premier choirs of Wales for many years,
and one of the best-selling Welsh records has been the disc of the
great Gamanfa Ganu (Hymn-singing festival) held in the
presence of Prince Charles in Investiture Year at the 'Cathedral
of Nonconformity', Tabernacle Chapel, Morriston. The houses
may cling in rows to the hillside but this is no joyless, un-
cultured centre. It has always had a vigorous life of its own, and
this industrial Swansea created the second Swansea—the port
and its dockland.

Swansea was always a busy little port, since the mouth of the
Tawe was much easier to sail into than that of its neighbour
stream, the Neath. The latter had a bad reputation reaching
back to the Middle Ages. Geraldus Cambrensis (Gerald the
Welshman) vividly describes the difficulties of crossing the
Neath in his account of his tour through Wales with Archbishop
Baldwin when they were preaching the Second Crusade. The

adventurous ecclesiastics nearly sank in the quicksands and
sighed with relief when they got safely to Swansea Castle. But
the big expansion of the port began in mid-Victorian days. The
North Dock was created in 1852 by diverting the Tawe into a
new cut. It is now filled in and in process of being built over. The
South Dock opened in 1859 and is suffering the same fate. But
the other docks on the east side of the Tawe, the Prince of Wales,
the King's and the Queen's Docks, are still in vigorous being.

The most romantic period in the story of Swansea Docks
stretched from the 1870s to the First World War. In the first
section of this period the copper works were still important and
demanding new sources of ore. A whole fleet of windjammers
sailed from Swansea around Cape Horn to Chile. I remember
many of the sailors who manned these ships for, in my early
youth, there were plenty of old men left who were proud to call
themselves Cape Horners and could fix you with endless stories
of their adventures beating around "Cape Stiff" in a howling
gale, as certainly as Coleridge's Ancient Mariner fixed the
Wedding Guest. There were still a few sailing ships around in
the twenties, most of them from the celebrated Aaland Islands
fleet, sailing with greatly reduced Scandinavian crews on the
Australian grain trade. They brought the wheat to the old
Weaver's Flour Mill on the North Dock basin—the gaunt shell
of the mill is still there at this moment of writing. And I am glad
that I saw something of the old glory of sail as the *Pamir* came
up to the Mumbles light with all sails set, to pick up the pilot and
the tug. No more beautiful ships were ever created by the hand
of man and I am proud that Swansea can claim connection with
some of them.

Sail did not entirely disappear until the closing of the North
Dock, for the Breton onion men came over to sell their wares—
and still do. The lock-gates of the North Dock were opened to let
them in, as well as the swing bridge which then carried the main
road. Any boy attending the grammar school from St. Thomas
had what he thought was a cast-iron excuse for being late: "The
bridge was open, sir." This worked well until one spoil-sport of a
master smashed this cunning ploy completely. He bought a
tide-table.

Along the North Dock ran the Strand. From the early days
this had been the centre of Swansea's sea trade, where the
eighteenth-century merchantmen unloaded against the steep
bank at the foot of the castle. When the river was diverted to

make the North Dock, the Strand sprung into a vigorous life of its own, with warehouses interlaced with pubs and seamen's lodging houses, including the celebrated Seaman's Home From Home of Dai Vaughan, where rumour maintained that the ends of the beds were fastened to a rope, which was briskly let down in the morning to tumble the bemused guests into the street.

Even in my young days it was always a daring adventure to "go down the Strand" and one never to be undertaken after dusk. The curious juxtaposition of the eminent respectability of the streets that ran parallel and up above—Castle Street and Wind Street—added to the thrill. Wind Street was the business street, with its banks, the statue of Sir Henry Hussey Vivian in the centre and the trio playing in the palm court of the Metropole Hotel, where all the important visitors stayed. Castle Street had the most modern shops, while nearby was the celebrated emporium of Messrs Ben Evans—"Bens"—a delightful maze of a shop, supported on plate-glass windows, in which "the change sang on wires".

But once you slipped down the steep alleyways that led behind the castle into the Strand you rocketed into another world. The sailors swayed out from the back door of the Cornish Mount, the coal trucks rumbled overhead and through the dark arches poked the bowsprits of the small French sailing vessels. There were delicious glimpses through open doors of mysterious piles of ships' chandlers stores. All has changed. The North Dock is filled in, the arches are abandoned, the sailors are gone and the Strand has collapsed into decayed respectability.

The docks over the eastern side of the river are in full swing. The oil tankers use the Queen's Dock and the oil is pumped up to the first oil refinery to be built in Britain at Llandarcy, just outside the old Swansea borough boundary. The refinery started in 1917 and the name chosen for it caused lifted eyebrows in Wales. Was the name of d'Arcy, the oil tycoon, a proper one to be linked with the Welsh "llan" which usually means a church? The worship of Mammon can surely be carried too far!

As for coal, there are very few coal-hoists left, for although there is still a demand for anthracite, the great days of coal are over. I remember the last glories before the Depression of 1921, when war-wearied Europe still needed coal desperately, and great fleets of colliers waited off the Mumbles Head for their turn to enter the docks and load. On a still night, the roar of the coal-hoists working all out echoed through the town. Then came the Strike and the Great Depression and coal ceased to be a power at Swansea. Today the docks have succeeded in seeking other cargoes. As a symbol of the new dockland you will see, outside the pier-head, the powerful new pilot boat and the great ore-carriers on their way to Port Talbot. There is plenty of life in Swansea's dockland today.

I always feel that the link between Swansea Docks, Industrial and Residential Swansea is forged by that remarkable building, the Royal Institution of South Wales. It survived the Blitz and stands in somewhat lonely dignity on the edge of dockland but within sight of Wind Street, leading towards the centre of the city. It is now under the aegis of the University College of Swansea. It began in the 1830s when Swansea had a group of brilliant scientific men of the calibre of de la Bêche, the great geologist, Lewis Weston Dillwyn and Dr Thomas Williams, physician and zoologist, who was the centre of the great Copper Trial of 1833, when the effect of the copper fumes on the countryside was meticulously argued—one of the first cases concerning pollution in British Law.

The classical façade, with its portico supported by columns, gave the Royal Institution the right look of earnest research proper to an organization devoted to the spread of knowledge among the people. Swansea at this time was the intellectual capital of Wales. It was the first place to publish a weekly newspaper and then a daily one. Maybe the Royal Institution has lost a little of its early lustre but it still holds an important collection of objects from the local past. Here are the finds from the local bone caves, Swansea china, geological specimens and examples of industrial archaeology. Local museums have a charm of their own and a visit to the Royal Institution before you visit Gower can be very rewarding.

As the nineteenth century developed Swansea naturally equipped itself with all the institutions proper to a growing, successful town. It had a variety theatre, the Empire, now demolished, where I remember seeing many of the great names, even though the sands were running out for variety after the First World War. Still, it is something to boast that you saw Harry Tate in his motoring sketch, Sir Harry Lauder, Albert Wheelan—yes, and dear old Nellie Wallace. "If you don't go in Swansea," said Nellie Wallace to me, "you'd better give up, because you won't go anywhere."

The Grand Theatre is still happily with us. It has the friendly air of the 1890s, with florid decorations and columns framing the proscenium arch, which once had a shield above it which once proclaimed in Welsh Shakespeare's confident assertion, "All the world's a stage". Maybe it is no theatre-in-the-round, no super-modern art centre of the Coventry or Nottingham type, and the accommodation back-stage may not be on a big enough scale for modern times. When the Welsh National Opera arrives for its annual season the Grand fairly creaks in its efforts to accommodate *Don Carlos* or *Don Giovanni*. Swansea has plans, of course, for a new theatre and arts centre, to be created during the coming years. In the meantime the city supports the Grand, and for a short time yet, I can sit in the Grand Circle and remember the lost pleasures the old theatre gave to me. For like everybody else born in Swansea, it was at the Grand that I first saw great acting and was introduced to the delights of theatre-going. At ten years old, I sampled the frenzied excitement of the annual 'panto'. The Puss, in *Puss in Boots*, actually came around the Grand Circle at the interval, to the fearful joy of the children. Later on we saw some of the stars, not perhaps at their prime for I do not think that the Grand was ever on the major touring circuit for plays. But we got the second best companies with the London successes. Then there was the Carl Rosa Opera Company, which introduced us to grand opera in the old-fashioned grand manner. We could also take pride in the knowledge that one of the legendary stars of the operatic world had chosen Swansea—or at least the Swansea Valley—as her home.

I was recently talking to a well-known TV producer who had once played Swansea in her early repertory days. She told me a curious story. She was rehearsing one morning on the empty stage when she looked up at one of the boxes. She saw a beautiful lady in rich Edwardian costume lean forward and give polite applause to the act. She turned to a stage hand to ask who was in the box but when she looked again the lady had vanished. Said the stage hand, "We all know her—it's Madame Patti." Indeed the great Adelina Patti used to occupy this box when she came down to Swansea to grace charity concerts with her presence.

Patti had been born in Madrid but was brought up in New York. She dazzled nineteenth-century Europe with her voice, her beauty and her loves. She made a fortune out of her singing but found no harmony in her love life. She looked for some secure, out-of-the-way refuge, to which she could retire in between tours with her leading man, the tenor Signor Niccolini,

who she married. Lord Swansea was a great admirer of her
talents and he persuaded her that Craig-y-Nos, at the top of the
Swansea Valley, was her ideal hide-out. The choice could not
have been bettered. At Abercrave the River Tawe leaves the
northern edge of the coalfield and turns to cut its way through
the glittering limestone hills. Beyond rise the high summits of
the Carmarthenshire Vans. In this landscape of white crags,
clear streams and green mountains Patti built her pseudo-
Gothic castle of Craig-y-Nos, the Rock of the Night, complete
with trout pools for Signor Niccolini who developed into a keen
fisherman in between arias. She also built a private theatre
where she entertained her guests with scenes from her favourite
operas. Craig-y-Nos is now a hospital, but the little theatre is
still there, with the curtain painted with a representation of the
Diva, black tresses floating in the wind, as she drives a four-
horse chariot in her famous role of Seramide in Rossini's opera
of the same name. Her private sitting-room at Penwyllt station
also remains to remind us that, when the Queen of Song
travelled, she did so in regal style. Sometimes her carriage
progressed through the streets of Swansea with a mounted
escort, and no charity concert could end without Patti being
persuaded to come onto the stage to sing "Home, Sweet Home"!
    Patti died in 1920 and Swansea re-erected the great con-
servatory from the gardens of Craig-y-Nos in Victoria Park in
her memory. I wonder if the youngsters of today, who attend the
Saturday-night dances, remember who Patti was, and her
strange romantic connection with Swansea.
    The Grand Theatre, it must be confessed, does not stand in
architecturally distinguished surroundings, and there are still
open spaces left behind by the Blitz in the neighbourhood.
Nearby is the parish church of St Mary's, which was left an
empty shell after the German raids. Its few medieval remains
suffered damage in the fire, although the fifteenth-century
sepulchral brass to Sir Hugh Jonys of Landimore, and his wife,
Dame Maude, remains. The reconstruction has created a light,
airy interior with modern glass by John Piper, who also
designed the fine ceremonial vestments.
    Three main avenues run westward from the centre of
Swansea. Oxford Street still follows the line of the pre-1941
street. In it is the reconstructed market, which was such a
pleasure of the Old Swansea. On Saturday nights, in the old
days, Oxford Street was entirely given up to the shoppers, the

miners and their families and everyone who was out for a good
time. The market stayed open as long as anyone wanted it, and
the street was simply abandoned by any wheeled vehicle—the
walking crowd happily took over. Within the vast, glass-roofed
hall the Gower farmers' wives sat at their stalls and sold everything from fresh butter to tender chickens, home-raised with a
taste now forgotten in these days of the battery hen. And, of
course, there was plenty of that famous and remarkable
product, laverbread. I am happy to say that it is still sold there.

This dark, treacly-looking food is made from a special
seaweed, *Porphyra umbilicalis*. Unkind visitors used to declare
that it was the world's only edible cow-pat, but we who were
brought up on it called it Welsh caviare and quoted with pride
the medical analysis that it was rich in iodine. Frankly no
laverbread fan worried about any medical advantage that
might accrue from eating it; he knew that it tasted delicious for
breakfast when cooked with crisp bacon. The laver, itself, is a
thin purplish, india-rubber looking type of seaweed, which is
collected off the rocks at low tide. For some reason it grows more
plentifully in winter than in summer. After collection it has to
be carefully and thoroughly washed, for it is found fairly high up
the rocky shore and sand can get mixed with it. There is no
question that the best laver-weed grows on limestone rocks.
Hence the supremacy of the Gower and South Pembrokeshire
variety.

But truth to tell, not much of the laverbread you now buy in
Swansea market comes from weed collected in Gower itself.
People are no longer willing to go to the trouble of collecting it
on a big scale and other sources of supply have been found as far
afield as Cumberland and Scotland. But two other products sold
in the market can guarantee their local origin—Welsh flannel
and Penclawdd cockles!

The second main avenue that runs westward from the centre
of Swansea is the new Kingsway, with its hotels, stores and
cinemas. It leads into the older St Helen's Road and so past the
buildings of the original Swansea hospital—all Victorian spiky
pinnacles—to the Civic Centre. I am afraid Swansea will never
be a place of pilgrimage for the amateurs of architecture,
although, surprisingly, it adopted a zoning system for industry
in mid-Victorian days. Mining or factory building was not
encouraged westward around the curve of Swansea Bay or on
the wooded slopes that led down to it from Town Hill. Instead

the long lines of residential terraces climbed the slopes and looked out over the sea. They may not have architectural distinction but they have an incomparable view, which now includes the white classical façade and tall tower of the Civic Centre.

The City Hall and Law Courts were completed in the late thirties on the edge of the sea and certainly make their effect. They are not exactly in the modern tradition. There is no suggestion of Gropius or the Bauhaus about them, but they are not without architectural merit and contain one attraction which was as unexpected by the architect, Sir Percy Thomas, as it was welcome to the city. Sir Frank Brangwyn had been commissioned to prepare a new decorative scheme for the House of Lords as a memorial to the peers who had fallen in the 1914–1918 war. Brangwyn worked on the panels for seven years but, to his fury, they were rejected by the peers—the colours may have been far too gay for their sober lordships. Luckily for Swansea, Sir Percy Thomas was an old friend of Brangwyn's and he was able to re-design the big, new assembly hall at the Civic Centre as a worthy setting for the panels. The paintings are defiantly 1910 in style with a touch of Art Nouveau thrown in for good measure. One unkind critic of the modern school described them as the "largest postage stamps in the world". How wrong he was! Brangwyn had a superb decorative sense and a tremendous delight in the use of vivid colour. The Brangwyn panels are coming triumphantly back into fashion and demand a visit. The whole hall now makes a splendid setting for Swansea's important annual Festival of Music.

From the Civic Centre the Mumbles Road runs around the curve of the bay towards Oystermouth. We will be making this journey in detail in the next chapter, but let us note that here, for once, Swansea has risen to its architectural opportunities. The shore is fringed with sand dunes. On the strip of level ground, that runs behind the dunes for the next two miles, lies a succession of pleasant open spaces and worthy buildings. The Promenade fronts the sea. On it stands Swansea's war memorial, a cenotaph on the same lines as that in Whitehall. Near at hand is the St Helen's ground of the Swansea Cricket and Football Club, where Glamorgan play on occasions during the summer. St. Helen's has more fame, however, as a historic centre of rugby. The club celebrated its hundredth anniversary in 1974 and is one of the great rugby clubs of Wales. All internationals are now played at the new National Stadium at Cardiff Arms Park, but between the wars a clash between England and Wales at St Helen's was a memorable tribal festival, with the whole of the male population crammed into the ground to sing their team to victory, to be followed—if Wales won—by a glorious Saturnalia through the centre of the town.

Beyond St. Helen's is the Recreation Ground, sacred to circuses, and then Singleton Park. Swansea was lucky in having the fine, rolling parkland of Singleton within the borough boundaries. Here the copper kings, the Vivians, had built their elegant Victorian Gothic 'abbey', which the town was able to acquire in the 1920s. It made an ideal setting for the University College, founded in 1920 as a constituent college of the University of Wales. When the big university expansion began in the 1950s, Swansea had space for it. Today a splendid campus confronts the Mumbles Road, with an array of modern buildings around it which can deal with over 4,000 students. The university has now been joined on the site by the new hospital. So now, from the Civic Centre to Singleton and beyond stretches a fine complex of civic and university buildings set amongst parklands and fronting the wide sweep of the bay. This western exit from Swansea is a staggering contrast to the eastern entrance to the city via Landore or St Thomas. No wonder visitors to Swansea sometimes feel that they are in two completely different cities which have no real contact with each other.

There is also another Swansea, a smaller, almost a private Swansea which an increasing number of visitors demand to see, especially if they be American. This is the Swansea of Dylan Thomas. I suppose that Dylan is the city's best known 'local boy'. The wild roaring young poet—the Rimbaud of Cwmdonkin Drive—has now become a highly respected national institution. There seems to be no end to the procession of earnest university students from the U.S.A. who arrive at Swansea to complete their thesis on "Some Aspects of the Prosody of Dylan Thomas". I often wonder what impression they take away with them once they have travelled up Walter Road, the third of the avenues that lead westward from central Swansea, and come to the Uplands. I suppose that this is technically suburbia, but as this is also Swansea, the Uplands is Suburbia set at an impossible angle. Every street of neat villas climbs up a steep hill as a matter of course, and Cwmdonkin Drive, where Dylan was born, is one of the steepest. "You're a Swansea Sherpa if you're born here," said Dylan to me, and I have met many a poetic pilgrim puffing his slow way upwards to gaze on the plaque which now marks the house.

Near the house is Cwmdonkin Park, where the young cherubic curly-haired Dylan I remember so well used to sit working on his early poems. His father was my English master at the Swansea Grammar School. The old building still stands on Mount Pleasant. Dylan early declared that he was going to be a poet and nothing else, and the old Grammar School was the perfect place to nurture his wayward genius. Discipline was—shall we say—civilized and relaxed. The headmaster was gloriously absent-minded but understanding. To boys of promise all was permitted. Dr Daniel Jones, the musician, tells the story of how he and Dylan were once tiptoeing past the headmaster's study, intent on dodging the French class. "Too much French is bad for a poet who writes in English," said Dylan, "Let's go down town." They had just reached the front door when the headmaster poked his head out of the study, "Ho, you boys, where are you going?" Dylan decided to put a bold face on it. "We're going to play billiards. Any objection?" "Oh, you wicked boys," sighed the headmaster, "I hope you get caught."

But old Swansea was the one place where a young poet would never get caught, never get buried in the common-place, and in the days of Dylan's youth it was a remarkable nursery of creative talent. Dr Daniel Jones, one of Dylan's closest friends, became one of Wales's leading musicians and still lives in the area at Newton. Fred Janes the painter was also there and, later, the poet Vernon Watkins, also a Swansea man, became Dylan's most trusted critic and poetic advisor. Vernon it was who wrote the poem which sums up, for so many Swansea folk, what they felt about their unblitzed town long before it became a city. The words still ring true today.

> Bright town, tossed by waves of time to a hill,
> Leaning Ark of the world, dense-windowed, perched
> High on the slopes of the morning
> Taking fire from the Kindling East:
>
> Look where merchants, traders and builders move
> Through your streets, while above your chandler's walls
> Herring-gulls wheel, and pigeons,
> Mocking men and the wheelwright's art.

Prouder cities rise through the haze of time,
Yet, unenvious, all men have is here.
Here is the loitering marvel
Feeding artists with all they know.

Vernon Watkins was a classical scholar and a dedicated poet, who had a promising career at Cambridge and entered Lloyd's Bank at Swansea almost as a convert enters a monastery. This was his safe refuge from the world, the base where he could meditate and then polish his pieces to his own meticulously high standards. The bank was understanding even when, on one memorable midnight, the police had hurriedly to check on Vernon's whereabouts with his solicitor. The constable on duty, on going his rounds, had found the front door of the bank wide open. Vernon had forgotten to lock it! As Dr Johnson once said about Goldsmith, "Was ever poet so trusted before?" And as most of Vernon's friends could have added, "only in Swansea!"

2

Around the Bay

The time has come to make our first journey into the Gower peninsula itself. We shall travel on the route by which most people get their first taste of the Gower scene—around the wide curve of Swansea Bay to the Mumbles. I have a deep affection for these five miles because I first travelled them in the famous old Mumbles train, claimed to be, with justice, the oldest passenger railway in the world. It had a long, fascinating and checkered career from 1804, when an Act of Parliament was passed authorizing the construction of a line from Swansea to Oystermouth "for the passage of Wagons and other Carriages", to 1960, when the last public train left the Rutland Street terminus and made a ceremonial journey along the line, to the cheers and the tears of everyone in Swansea.

In its very first few years the line set up a number of curious records. There was the strange attempt to use wind power, as reported in the Cambrian newspaper in 1807:

An experiment of a novel kind was made on the Oystermouth Tram-road yesterday, to ascertain the practicability of a carriage proceeding to the Mumbles without horse, by the aid of the wind alone. Some Jolly Sons of Neptune rigged a wagon with a long-sail, and the wind blowing strong and as fair as could be wished, set out from our quay, and after clearing the houses dropped anchor at the end of the tram-road in less than three quarters of an hour, having come a distance of about 4½ miles.

The trains in my day sometimes did not achieve this dizzy speed! A second record for the Mumbles Railway was claimed by Mr Kenneth Brown in an article in the *Railway Gazette*, under the title "The First Railway Journey in History". Apparently Miss Isabella Spence, in her *Summer Excursions through parts of Oxfordshire, Gloucestershire, Warwickshire, Staffordshire, Herefordshire, Derbyshire and South Wales*—what gloriously compelling titles authors permitted themselves in 1809!—

describes her journey to Oystermouth in what must have been the first passenger train in the world.

> I never spent an afternoon with more delight than the former one in exploring the romantic scenery of Oystermouth. I was conveyed there in a carriage of singular construction, built for the convenience of parties who go hence to Oystermouth to spend the day. This car contains twelve persons and is constructed chiefly of iron, its four wheels run on an iron railway by the aid of a horse, and is an easy and light vehicle.

Later travellers did not share the gallant Miss Spence's enthusiasm. Richard Ayton declared in 1813 that the carriage "rolls along over an iron railroad, at the rate of five miles an hour, and with the noise of twenty sledgehammers in full play. The passage is only four miles, but it is quite sufficient to make one reel from the car at the journey's end, in a state of dizziness and confusion of the senses that it is well if he recovers from in a week."

These were pioneer days. The old Mumbles train reached its real peak of glory in the period before the First World War. There was no motor-bus to challenge its service and the horses had long since disappeared. The Hughes tramway-type locomotives went into service in 1877 and later came the saddle-tank engines. But it was the weird and wonderful rolling stock that gave the railway its charm—open tram-cars with rows of 'toast-rack' seats on the roofs. As small boys we would rush to get on top of the carriage nearest to the engine, to have the forbidden glory of seeing the smoke pant out of the smoke-stack almost into our faces. At the Slip and Brynmill ragged youngsters used to turn cart-wheels and beg from the passengers with shouts of "Ha'penny a Penny, O". And the last train home on a Saturday night was a sight to remember, with hundreds clinging onto the cars like the trams in Calcutta. The railway was immensely popular and carried as many as 40,000 people on a Bank Holiday. Eighteen to twenty loaded cars were included in one train, so that you could easily find yourself one of 1800 passengers pouring off a single train at Mumbles Pier. Few trains in Great Britain have approached such record numbers.

The line was electrified in 1929 and went on prospering. In 1946 it carried the extraordinary figure of 4,237,000 passengers. But, alas, it could not survive the post-war car boom and the astronomical increase in repair costs. By 1960 all was over.

The lines were taken up. The section along the sea-front from Blackpill to Oystermouth became a pleasant footpath; the rest of it has faded into the roadway and the old Mumbles train has puffed away into the Past.

So, too, has the L.M.S. line that also ran along part of Swansea Bay to Blackpill and the Clyne Valley. Swansea now has a completely railway-free sea front. But the L.M.S. retaining wall is still there, so for the moment you can not see the sea as you drive for the first few miles along the Mumbles Road. Yet it is worth stopping for a moment—if you dare to do so on a crowded week-end, when the cars are bumper to bumper—and walk out onto the sands at, say, the entrance known as the Slip, near the Civic Centre. To your right you will see a large, elaborate footbridge, rather like the Sydney Harbour Bridge on a tiny scale, with wide stone steps leading down to the sands. It stands as a memorial to those long departed days, just after the First World War, when Swansea thought it had a serious traffic problem and decided to make an ultra-safe passage over the road and the two railway lines for the thousands who then used Swansea sands on every summer's day. Not so many patronize Swansea sands at the present time, when the motor-car can take people further afield into remote Gower.

The bay is extensive and at low tide a vast area of sand, some of it admittedly somewhat dark, even muddy, is uncovered. The tides in the Bristol Channel are regarded as second only to those in the Bay of Fundy in Canada, in their range between high and low. Swansea Docks register a rise and fall of forty feet. The long row of stakes are gone that used to be set out in V-shaped patterns to net fish on a big scale. But you can still see the patches of peat and tree-trunks near Blackpill—proof of the change in level of the sea since the last ice age. Southwards, the Devonshire coast is visible on a clear day. The Channel here is just over twenty-five miles wide and you can look across to the high ground of Exmoor and the two shapely tors that guard Ilfracombe. In the days when the Campbell Brothers ran their fleet of paddle steamers, including the *Glengower* and the *Lady Moira*, the trip to 'Combe was one of the great Swansea institutions, especially on Sundays when Glamorgan still suffered from Sunday closing! A single steamer service still goes across channel in the summer. When the Devon coast is clear, Swansea Bay can look like a huge, land-locked lake.

But as you resume your drive around the bay, past Singleton, the playing fields and the miniature golf course between the sand dunes and the main road, you ask yourself where exactly does Gower begin. We are talking of Peninsula Gower, of course. There is no doubt at all where the old legal Lordship of Gower, the old Welsh 'commote' of Gwyr began. The boundary ran through the middle of the strange marshland east of Kilvey Hill known as the Crumlyn Bog. Today it is surrounded by industry, from the Tir John power station to the Llandarcy oil refinery on the hills behind. But it is still a genuine piece of wild marshland, sacred to rare birds and plants. It was also the boundary of the old diocese of St. David's.

Peninsula Gower has no such clearly defined legal boundary. I would suggest that, for all practical purposes, it begins at Blackpill. Here is the point, about three miles from the centre of Swansea along the Mumbles Road, where the old railway embankment turns into Clyne Valley and you can see clearly out onto the bay. This was also the point which was recognized in the old days as the dividing line between Gower Wallicana, Welsh-speaking Gower, and Gower Anglicana or English-speaking Gower. We will be discussing this distinction later when we come to Oystermouth Castle and seize the chance to take a quick look at Gower history. But there is also an even more clearly marked dividing line, based upon the character of the rocks. At Blackpill you reach the edge of the coal-measures, and the Clyne brook itself marks the South Crop, as geologists call it, of the South Wales coalfield. This coalfield is basically like a saucer with the coal seams dipping down to the centre. The Clyne Valley is part of the southern rim of the saucer.

The coal-seams outcrop along the line of the Clyne brook and they were worked at a very early period by 'bell pits'. A pit was dug through the boulder clay into the seam and then 'belled out' at the bottom as far as it was safe to do so. About ten feet was the maximum before the shaly rock started to crumble. The miners then moved on a few yards and sank another bell-pit. The western side of Clyne Valley is riddled with these curious and ancient workings, although they are almost impossible to see since the trees have once again spread a dense cover over the hillside. More modern mining methods were applied in the nineteenth century and there were several coal-pits and drifts active in Clyne well into the twentieth century. But the seams of the South Crop are very contorted and set at a high angle. They became unprofitable as the costs rose as steeply as the seams.

Today all mining is over in Clyne and in spring the floor of the valley is an azure mist of bluebells beside the stream. You can walk along the deserted railway bed the whole length of the valley. All would be beautiful but for a caravan invasion at the beginning of the valley and a municipal rubbish dump placed, with unerring skill, in the most attractive part! By the way, the so-called 'Roman bridge' in the little open space at the valley entrance is anything but Roman—eighteenth century at the earliest!

The western side of the valley in its lower section still maintains its wooded splendour. Here is Clyne Castle, a Vivian residence, and in later days the home of Rear-Admiral Heneage-Vivian. He was everything a retired rear-admiral should be, with his pointed beard, his memories of service at sea and his brisk quarter-deck manner in dealing with local problems. His house is now a hall of residence for Swansea University College, and the grounds are a fine, public park sloping down from the Mayals to the Mumbles Road. The old admiral has left the town one legacy of beauty. He was a keen gardener, with a delight in rhododendrons, and in early June the glades that slope down towards the sea, past the nineteenth-century Gothic castle, are a blaze of rare colour. Lost in the middle of them is a curious stone pillar, entwined with a metal hand-rail. The old admiral built it to look out over his growing rhododendrons or perhaps, as local legend maintained, to admire the slim ankles of the young ladies who climbed it. Now the rhododendrons have long since overtopped the tower.

If you continue up the Mayals Avenue, which leads up from Blackpill parallel to the wall of the Clyne Castle estate, you come within half a mile to a different landscape. You shake yourself free from the ever-growing housing development that has clustered around Clyne in recent years, and suddenly enter open country—breezy common-land up on the 250-foot level. There is a golf course here. The larks sing overhead in early summer, the lapwings call, and from the highest point of Clyne Common you can take in a wide extent of the landscape of both English and Welsh Gower, with the whole wide sweep of Swansea Bay around to the Mumbles. It is the right place to pause and study a little geology, for Peninsula Gower is a notable attraction for the professional geologist. Its rocks ring all through the summer to the happy hammers of the students of Swansea University, and remarkable rocks they are, ranging through the full gamut of the Carboniferous series with the Devonian beds of the Old Red Sandstone thrown in for good measure. The order of the rocks has dictated a good deal of Gower's past history as well as the appearance of the present-day landscape. So it is worth while looking out from Clyne Common summit and taking a lesson in elementary geology before you penetrate deeper into Gower. Even a nodding acquaintance with the nature of the rocks will add immeasurably to your pleasure in the Gower scene.

At the risk of boring the knowledgeable may I just remind you of the sequence of our rocks as recognized by the geologists. The oldest series are the Pre-Cambrian which stretch back through unimaginable periods of time, from about 600 million years ago almost to the origin of the earth, which scientists now put at about 5000 million years back. I try my best, but I just cannot picture such vast and forbidding time cycles. 5000 million years seems to mean nothing! There are Pre-Cambrian rocks in nearby Pembrokeshire but none in Gower. Our rocks were formed very much later although they are still of respectable age compared with the Jurassic and Cretaceous rocks that cover most of Southern England. They came after the Cambrian, Ordovician and Silurian systems that form the lower section of the Palaeozoic Era—Palaeozoic indicates that the rocks were deposited during the period of 'ancient' life.

The lowest Gower rocks are the Old Red Sandstone, at the top of the Devonian system. They come to the surface in the hills of the peninsula, at Cefn Bryn, Rhossili Downs and Llanmadoc Hill. They are coarse, pebbly conglomerates overlying red sandstones and marls and were laid down in vast estuaries under tropical conditions some 360 million years ago. Next come the rocks that most people feel to be the very heart and hallmark of Gower, the Carboniferous Limestones. They are the lowest rocks of the Carboniferous system that succeeded the Devonian and were deposited when the winding estuaries of the Devonian gave way to warm, shallow seas surrounded by coral reefs. If you can have such a thing as a favourite rock, mine is the Carboniferous Limestone. I always think of it as a clean, glittering and dare I add, happy rock. Or is this because I associate it with the green, close-cropped cliff tops and the white plunge of the Gower coastline, which seemed to me the most carefree of all coastlines in my untroubled youth.

The next rock upwards in the Carboniferous system is the

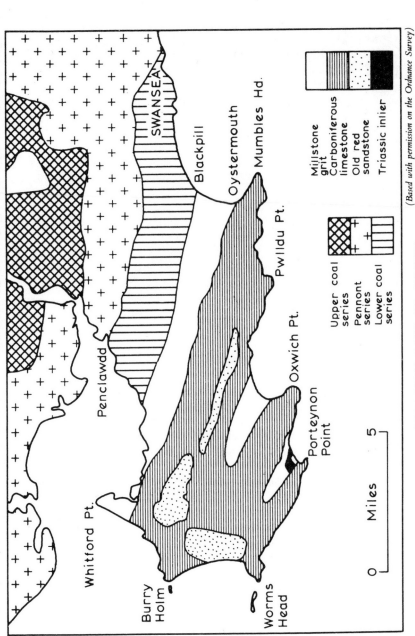

THE GEOLOGY OF GOWER

(Based with permission on the Ordnance Survey)

Millstone grit
Carboniferous limestone
Old red sandstone
Triassic inlier

Upper coal series
Pennant series
Lower coal series

Whitford Pt.
Burry Holm
Worms Head
Penclawdd
SWANSEA
Blackpill
Oystermouth
Mumbles Hd.
Pwlldu Pt.
Oxwich Pt.
Porteynon Point

0   Miles   5

Millstone Grit. Again this is mere fancy, but I have always regarded the Millstone Grit as rather a dull rock and I cannot work up much enthusiasm for it. It was deposited when the rivers came back into that clear limestone sea and polluted it with sand and mud. Perhaps the word grit gives a wrong impression in Gower for the sequence here is made up of muddy shales. But all the words connected with this dreary rock—grit, shale, mudstone—seem to be to sum up its character perfectly. Needless to say it is not a rock that encourages a fertile soil in Gower. The untilled open commons—from Clyne and Fairwood to Pengwern Common and Welsh Moor—all lie on this, to me, strangely unsympathetic rock of the Millstone Grit.

Curiously enough I cheer up again when I come to the coal measures. The northern edge of them follows the Millstone Grit in its north-west course across the peninsula. The old miners gave the romantic name of the Farewell Rock to the narrow layer that marked the juncture. Once you hit it, it was 'farewell' to any chance of finding a workable seam. We have met the coal measures already in the Clyne Valley and they run up along the northern flank of Fairwood Common, then on, roughly parallel to the Morlais stream, to plunge under the sea at the Loughor Estuary. All right, I will admit that coal brings tips and dirt, although nothing like as much as it did in the past. But it is also closely bound up with the very way we live in South Wales, with the tragedies as well as the triumphs. No one born near a coalfield can fail to be deeply influenced by it. The coal measures that outcrop so steeply across the neck of Gower belong to the lower coal measures and every schoolboy knows that they were formed in steamy swamps and mud-flats through which the sluggish rivers wound to a shallow sea. Then follow the middle and upper coal measures separated by thick beds of that Pennant sandstone which weathers into such an attractive russet colour on exposure to the weather and which forms Town Hill and Kilvey Hill in Swansea. But now we have gone away to the north of Peninsula Gower into the high uplands which you can see on a fine day from our vantage point on Clyne Common.

This long sequence of Devonian and Carboniferous beds was laid down horizontally over a period of a 100 million years. Then it was dramatically disturbed. At the end of the Carboniferous period an era of tremendous earth movements, known as the Armorican 'oregony' or mountain building, ushered in the Permian. The earth's surface was subjected to drastic pressures and changes. Gower was at the edge of the turmoil which was at its peak in Brittany, or Armorica; but the peninsula was buckled into huge folds running roughly from south-east to north-west. For example, the Limestone and Millstone Grit curved in a huge arc over the Old Red Sandstone of Cefn Bryn. In addition there was severe faulting, and while the rocks made a gigantic arch, or anticline, over Cefn Bryn, they formed an equally big downfall, or syncline, on the other side of it. Then came intensive weathering which removed much of the cracked rocks of the up-fold and levelled off the surface of Gower.

Geologists suspect that after this levelling process occurred, Gower was overlain by Triassic beds and then by the Chalk. But all traces of these beds have disappeared except for a tiny Triassic patch in the syncline of Port-Eynon. The levelling process was not yet finished with, however. In comparatively recent times, a mere 3 million years ago, the sea cut back steadily across the land, maybe removing a lot of the Triassic and Chalk deposits in the process, to form a level platform of marine denudation, now at the 600-foot level. You can see how even are the hilltops of Peninsula Gower—all around the 600-foot mark. Then twice again the sea level fell, or did the land rise? Again the sea cut marine platforms, the lowest and most prominent of which is the famous 200-foot platform, cut about a million years ago and then uplifted to its present height. You can see it finely displayed along South Gower. All the headlands, from Caswell to Port-Eynon and the Worm, are variants of the 200-foot platform. The hard conglomerates of the Old Red Sandstone resisted this last erosion and stand like islands above it at Cefn Bryn, Rhossili Downs and Llanmadoc Hill.

But was the sea cutting its platforms—and still at it, by the way—the final agent in shaping the Gower landscape? Not by any means. Another and an immensely powerful agent now comes onto the scene—ice! Gower in successive ice-ages was overrun by immense sheets of ice, sometimes moving across it from west to east as part of the gigantic glacier of the Irish Sea; at other times melting back, or advancing again when reinforced by the ice pouring down from the mountains to the north. The sea-levels constantly changed. Raised beaches were plastered around the coastline, together with that thick layer of 'till'—earth packed with rounded stones—down which you have to scramble when you visit so many Gower bays. And the post-glacial period led to formation of sand-dunes, drowned forests

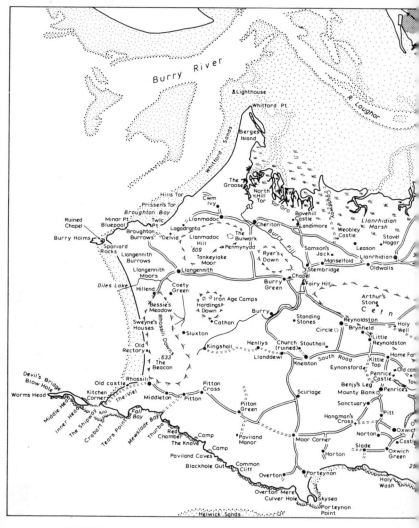

1. GOWER

(Based with permission on the Ordnance Survey)

and pebble beaches. We will be noting them all as we travel the length and breadth of the southern coast.

In the meantime I have left you on the top of Clyne Common. Or perhaps you have not yet been tempted by the delights of walking in Gower and have just drawn your car off to the side of the road and looked at the swelling ridge of the common from across the golf course! Wherever you are, I hope that you will now have a better understanding of the landscape that lies ahead. We therefore return down the Mayals to continue our journey around the edge of Swansea Bay. The road lies back a few yards from the old bed of the Mumbles Railway, which forms the actual border of the coast. Over a long stretch the space has been cleared, lawns made and trees planted. Swansea may yet have that promenade around the curve of the bay that the whole landscape seems to clamour for.

From Blackpill to West Cross we are still passing over the rocks of the Millstone Grit, and on the shore at low tide near the West Cross Hotel, you can distinguish the worn-down top of a small anticline. And if you care nothing for geology but are a keen fisherman, you can dig for lug-worms for bait out on the flats. This is the best place in the bay for them and on occasions the whole area is dotted with devoted diggers until it looks like a miniature diamond field in the early days of Kimberley. How the lug-worm survives under such constant attack is a mystery known only to Nature and fishermen.

But you are now approaching a place which once lived mainly on its fishing and felt itself, and indeed still thinks of itself, as totally separated from Swansea, although it has long since been swept within the borough boundaries. Oystermouth may now be hopelessly tied to Swansea by the crowded Mumbles Road, and the villas and houses stretch almost continually around the bay. In high summer it may be overrun by tourists, day-trippers, yachtsmen and the rest. No matter. Once you are there, you feel unmistakably that you are well into Gower and English Gower at that. The linguistic pundits may declare that the name of Oystermouth has nothing to do with the delicious bivalve for which the place used to be famous, but is a corruption of the Welsh "Ystum Llwynarth". Native-born Oystermouth folk do not care. They are solidly English with true Gower names like Ace, Grove and Beynon and a host of others. The old village has, of course, long been overwhelmed by new housing and the villas now stretch back over the high ground towards Langland and

Caswell or lap around Newton. But the old Oystermouth is still there if you look for it.

You can walk along the sea-front from the Dunns. The bus terminus now occupies the site of the old station. The promenade along the front has almost been annexed by the yachtsmen for Southend has become a major yachting centre. There is a fringe of hotels, restaurants, cafés and boarding-houses, and behind it climb the narrow streets, or 'slades', where once lived the fishermen and the limestone quarrymen. Today these little houses have become much sought after and change hands at prices that would have astonished their original occupants. Quarrying has ended but it has left its mark on the cliffs of Mumbles Head, which have weathered into great, overlapping slabs of white limestone.

Most of the headlands of South Gower were quarried in the same way all through the nineteenth century. Lime was vital to agriculture in those days, and a busy trade was carried on between limestone-rich Gower and North Devon and Cornwall, where it was conspicuously lacking. The small schooners would lie up as close to the cliffs as possible while being loaded, and the blocks of stone were dropped down the rock-faces on sledges to the shore. Besides the Mumbles, the headlands of Pwlldu, Oxwich, Port-Eynon and Rhossili all bear the marks of this trade, but the scars have long since faded and indeed have added to the bold face of the cliffs.

The oyster trade lasted longer. Mumbles oysters were still sold in little oyster-bars along the front up to the 1930s, and when dredging was at its height in the 1880s nearly 200 oyster-ketches operated out of Oystermouth. The beds lay down-Channel and out beyond Mumbles Head but the hauls were kept fresh in the 'perches' or enclosures close inshore. You can still see traces of the perches close to the pier at low tide. The Mumbles oyster had a great reputation for its refined and delicate taste and quantities were sent up to London by rail. One of the delights of my childhood was being taken by my uncle to digest 'a dozen of the best' before making the trip over the hill for a glorious day on the golden sands of Caswell. Uncle had a theory that if you ate oysters regularly you would never suffer from rheumatism. I have no idea if there is any basis for this fantasy; it was probably on a par with the theory that laverbread was so rich in iodine that it prolonged your life. We embraced both theses with uncritical enthusiasm. I can still remember the pleasure of standing beside the trestle table placed outside the oyster-bar and watching the proprietor opening the oysters with a deft twist of the knife, while the salt tang from the shells in their wooden buckets pervaded the whole promenade. We always patronized the Gladstone Oyster Bar, with its portrait of the great Liberal leader over the door, for we were all radicals in those days and it was a pious tribute to the Grand Old Man's memory to stand where he had once stood and swallow oysters as easily as we swallowed his speeches.

Gladstone was not the first to appreciate the Oystermouth 'natives'. The Romans knew of them and have left traces of their presence here in the remains of a large villa, excavated in 1860. Maybe it was not just love of oysters that brought the Romans to Oystermouth. They may well have worked the vein of iron-ore on the headland. Small pieces of the mosaic from the villa are preserved in the parish church of All Saints, which may have been built on the very site. The church has been extensively restored and rebuilt and the tower contains three bells of Spanish origin from the Cathedral of Santiago de Cuba and brought to Swansea by one of the famous copper barques, the 'Cape Horners'. The tower is thirteenth century and one of the finest examples of the embattled type, so characteristic of Gower churches. Every church tower in the peninsula had to serve a double purpose in the early days of the English settlement—a place of refuge and defence as well as a housing for the bells.

In the churchyard lies the grave of the Rev. Thomas Bowdler, the early nineteenth-century cleric who published expurgated editions of Shakespeare and other classics and thus added a new word to the English language. He settled in Oystermouth towards the end of his life for reasons of health and died in 1835. Poor Bowdler! He has had a bad press, but as the inscription on his grave implies, he was a genuinely good man who, after all, was only acting in the spirit of his times when he undertook to produce a Shakespeare which "would not bring a blush to the most innocent cheek of youth". I was secretly rather glad when the Rector refused permission for an elaborate ceremony of homage to Bowdler, to be held in the churchyard. It was to be organized by my friend Kingsley Amis, in his 'Lucky Jim' days as a lecturer in Swansea University. The climax would have been the laying of an enormous wreath on Bowdler's grave—of fig leaves!

From the churchyard you look over the roof-tops and wooded

gardens of Oystermouth towards that building of white limestone which seems to dominate the view—the castle. The first
castle on the site was built by William de Londres around 1100
during the Norman conquest of Gower, but was eventually
burnt by the Welsh. From then on the castle was linked with
that of Swansea and the Lord of Gower held them both. The
stone castle was built around the mid-thirteenth century but
was severely damaged in the revolt that followed the conquest of
Wales by Edward I. The keep and gatehouse were then enlarged
and in the early fourteenth century; the keep area was reconstructed to make a more comfortable residence. An elegant
chapel was added. Oystermouth then faded gracefully out of
history. Swansea Castle became the administrative centre of
the lordship and Oystermouth gradually decayed. It did not play
much of a part in the Civil War, in spite of the legend that
Cromwell picketed his horses in the field near it known as
Pickett's Mead. Cromwell was hastening westward towards the
siege of Pembroke at the time and had no intention of bothering
with a small fortification which was described as "an old
decayed castle . . . being at present of noe use, but of a very
pleasant situacion and near unto the sea-side".

But the "very pleasant situacion" of Oystermouth Castle
tempts me again to pause for a moment, and while looking out
over the bay from the battlements, embark on a dissertation on
the history of Gower. We sat on Clyne Common and talked of
Gower geology. Now is the time, before we go deeper into the
peninsula, to take a little history on board for the journey. Let
me admit straight away that there is no outstanding event or
great turning point in history to take on board. Gower was
always a side-show, an interlude in the great historical pageant.
It was off the mainline and tended to be bypassed by the kings
and conquerors as they marched westwards. With the exception
of Edward I who stayed for a brief moment at Oystermouth
Castle, and the mythical figure of King Arthur, no ruling
monarch penetrated into the remoteness of Gower until our own
day. But Gower's story is fascinating in spite of, and indeed
because of, its isolation.

"To begin at the beginning", as Dylan Thomas said in *Under
Milk Wood*. Man may have reached Britain as far back as
200,000 years ago during the early Ice Ages. Throughout this
long period of time the ice caps advanced and retreated, sometimes allowing warm conditions to return over great areas of the

country, Gower shared in these vicissitudes and man may have wandered into the area at very remote periods. The first certain indication of his presence, however, comes during the final period of the last glaciation, when the edge of the ice lay just north of the south coast of Gower, and hunters occupied the caves that looked out over a dry Bristol Channel. Great herds of game roamed over this tundra country. Their remains have been found in the numerous bone caves that lie along the south coast and at other points as well.

But the classic exhibit, that put Gower firmly on the pre-historic map, was the skeleton of a youth discovered at Goat's Hole at Paviland. The discovery has now been dated by the radio-carbon method at round about 18,000 B.C. These earliest inhabitants of Gower were hunters and must have lived a pre-carious existence shivering in their caves with the ice not far away. We will be hearing more about them when we visit Bacon and Mitchin Hole and the Paviland caves themselves.

But around 9000 B.C. the climate started to ameliorate. The woodlands crept slowly back over the tundra. The ice melted and the seas advanced. The great game herds disappeared, but hunters could still make a living along the Gower coast on fish, shellfish and water fowl, and left their traces in chipping sites on Burry Holms in West Gower. These hunters were primitive folk compared with the next wave of people to arrive. The so-called Neolithic revolution had taken place in the Middle East, when the security of agriculture was substituted for the uncertainty of hunting. The practice of the new techniques spread outwards from the Mediterranean. Somewhere around 3000 B.C. the first Neolithic people reached Gower. They may have come by sea as part of that great folk movement which crept up the Atlantic coast of Western Europe, moving from peninsula to peninsula—from Spain to Brittany and onwards to Cornwall and Wales.

These were the people who constructed the grest megalithic tombs which were Gower's first architectural monuments, and very impressive they are. Arthur's Stone on the top of Cefn Bryn is the showpiece, with a huge cap-stone that weighs twenty-five tons and a site that seems to dominate the winding Loughor Estuary far below. Equally well sited are the Sweyn's Houses high on Rhossili Downs or the Giant's Grave in the green valley of Parc le Breos. We can know little of how these builders of great tombs really lived around 3000 B.C. Maybe they hunted as

well as tilled their little patches of fertile soil, and they probably
had to do their building with the minimum of metal tools. Their
achievement is therefore all the more extraordinary.

After them came the Bronze Age civilization. The round
barrows and cairns of this period are numerous throughout
Gower. There are ten on Rhossili Downs, twelve on Llanmadoc
Hill and over seventy on Cefn Bryn. Most of them are worn,
almost flattened by the passage of time but there is a particularly fine mound of the Bronze Age near the main road at
Cilibion. In addition a fine hoard of swords dating from the tenth
to the eleventh century B.C. turned up at Pennard.

Inevitably bronze gave way to iron and with iron, around 500
B.C. came the warrior race of the Celts. Bronze could not stand
up to iron and the newcomers overran the country. This was
obviously an age of warfare and Gower is covered with Iron Age
earthworks great and small. At Cil Ifor in North Gower lies a
complex of huge ramparts and ditches encircling a hill, but
there are equally impressive fortifications at the Bulwark on
Llanmadoc Hill and on Hardings Down. On numerous headlands lie smaller forts and ring-works. It is unlikely that people
lived permanently in these forts. Rather did they drive their
cattle and carry their valuables into them when danger
approached. A fort like the Bulwark would be heavily palisaded,
and an enemy ill-equipped for a long siege would eventually be
compelled to retire.

But by A.D. 50 an enemy arrived on our shores supremely
equipped to deal not only with the fortifications of the Celts but
with any force they might put into the field. The Romans made
swift work of the tribes in Southern England but had a far
tougher time of it in South Wales. Here the Silures were the
ruling tribe. They probably held Gower as well as the country
from Gwent to Glamorgan, and they gave the Romans the fight
of their lives. But by A.D. 78 the Silures were subdued and the
Romans drove their great road westward from Neath over the
neck of Gower to Loughor. At both these places they established
forts. As we have seen, they must have come down into
Peninsula Gower, for the villa at Oystermouth has the distinction of possessing the most westerly mosaic floor in Europe.
There have been other small scattered finds as well. Gower must
therefore have been reasonably peaceful under Roman rule,
with none of the necessity for a strong military presence that we
find in other parts of Wales.

Then between A.D. 350 and A.D. 400 came disaster. The unbelievable happened and the Roman Empire collapsed. The Dark Ages were upon us. Gower lay too far to the west to receive the ravages of the Anglo-Saxons. It did not, however, avoid the miseries that followed the withdrawal of the legions. The Irish crossed the sea in their skin boats, crawling over the surface of the water like black beetles, in the vivid words of Gildas. We can be sure that Gower did not escape. The Irish eventually settled and ruled in Pembrokeshire but Gower might have been a sort of no-man's-land on the edge of Irish rule. By the seventh century, however, we find Gower back completely under Welsh control. And Christian as well. The Celtic saints had done their work and Gower has a whole series of settlements dedicated to them. Gower even produced a saint of its own in Saint Cenydd, whose monastery lay at Llangennith in West Gower.

The next invaders were the Norsemen. It is extremely unlikely that they made any intensive settlement in Gower, although Swansea—if the derivation of the name from "Swenn's Ey" (or island) is correct—might have been a small trading settlement. There are Norse-sounding names scattered along the coast, with Burry Holms and Worms Head as prominent examples, but modern historians tend to play down the Norse influence on Gower's history and point out that the names could equally well have been derived from Anglo-Saxon forms.

There is no doubt at all about the impact of the next invaders who entered Gower. The Norman advance into South Wales reached a climax around A.D. 1100. The Vale of Glamorgan was firmly in their hands by that date and it is probable that they had entered Gower as well. How did they come? Modern historians are now convinced that they came by sea from bases along the southern shores of the Bristol Channel. They built early 'motte and bailey' castles to hold their newly conquered lands from the Welsh. There is a concentration of such structures around the shores of Oxwich Bay, which seems to confirm the fact that the invasion was a sea-borne one. Once the footholds were firmly established, the settlers poured in from Devon and Somerset and Gower, like Pembrokeshire, rapidly became a 'Little England beyond Wales'. The settlement was obviously encouraged by Henry de Newburgh, the first Lord of Gower, and Peninsula Gower took the political form that has continued to this day; a land clearly divided into two. The newcomers took the well-drained, light, easily worked soil in the fertile

limestone country of West and South Gower, which became
Gower Anglicana. The Welsh remained in the more mountain-
ous uplands of Gower Wallicana, or 'The Welshery' as it was
called. In between them, on the unfertile belt of Millstone Grit,
lay a no-man's-land still marked by the line of open commons.
The contrast is still strongly marked between the two areas,
apart from the striking language barrier. The villages of Gower
Anglicana (the Englishry) are typically manorial, grouped
around the church with its strong defensive tower. The villages
of the Welshery are more scattered, and the church, as likely as
not, will stand apart and possess not a tower but a bell-cote. The
land in Gower Anglicana was held by feudal tenure, but the men
of Gower Wallicana paid tribute. Contrast Reynoldston,
grouped around the church and the village green, with the
scatter of houses that compose Three Crosses and you will sense
the difference at once.

Here we must dispose of a strongly held theory that bedevilled
the historians of Gower for a hundred years and still goes
rumbling on in some quarters. This is the belief that the men of
Gower Anglicana were not Devonians or Somerset men in
origin but were Flemings. We know that there was an important Flemish settlement in Pembrokeshire in the days of Henry
I. Why not in Gower? Many were the arguments that thundered
to and fro in the 1860s on this knotty point. The eminent
Victorian historian Freeman rushed to defend the Flemings in
Gower: "I do not think that we can allow our good friends the
Flemings to be turned out of Gower without some stronger
arguments than have been brought by the gentlemen on the
other side." But turned out they were, in spite of appeals to the
'Flemish chimneys' of some Gower farmhouses, learned
attempts to derive Gower dialect words from Flemish origins
and even suggestions that the old Gower game of 'Five Cards'
resembled a similar Flemish game in Pembrokeshire and that
Gower practised the ancient custom, also observed in Flanders,
of divination by the blades of sheep bones!

Today no one refers to the Flemings. The contacts of Gower
Anglicana have been and always were with Somerset and
Devon. Even the dialects are similar. Gower is, in fact, a 'Little
West Country across the Channel'.

The Welsh did not abandon the peninsula without a struggle.
Again and again they conducted major raids into the Englishry
in 1136, 1151, 1159 and 1215. The newcomers were compelled to

see their motte-and-bailey castles continually captured and burnt; but they still clung tenaciously to their holdings. We know from the earliest documents that, almost from the first days of the settlement, the Englishry was organized into twelve manors described as the "old knight's fees" in the famous Gower Charter, given by or extorted from William de Breos in 1306. During this early period the Lordship of Gower seems to have changed hands. The original holders, the Earls of Warwick, kept possession for roughly the first hundred years of the conquest, but in 1192, Henry, Earl of Warwick, was a minor and his lordship passed into the tender care of King John. The king promptly granted it to the equally ruthless and formidable William de Breos. This William was the founder of his family fortunes. He began his career with the notorious massacre of his neighbouring Welsh princes in his castle of Abergavenny, and then expanded his estates in Breconshire with no holds barred. He was a man of strange contradictions, a ruthless enemy who would stop at nothing to gain his ends and yet could never pass by a wayside shrine without stopping to pray, and who spoke to children in the street in order to hear them murmur "God Bless You" in answer to his greeting. The story goes that he got the Lordship of Gower by blackmailing John with the threat of leaving him in the lurch during the King's campaign in Normandy.

In the long run William fell out with John, fled abroad and died in poverty in 1212. The King, meanwhile, starved William's wife and let one of his sons die as well. Such things are to be expected when unprincipled men clash. Yet William has left a strong imprint on the imagination of Gower men.

However, his family held the lordship after him and the William de Breos of the day successfully defended it in the great lawsuit of 1306. Thereafter it passed through various hands ending up, in late Tudor times, in those of the Earls of Worcester. Gower by then had already become a bit of a backwater in history. All serious danger of it ever reverting to the Welsh passed when Edward I disposed of Llywelyn the Last in 1282. The chief castles had been rebuilt in stone by 1300 and some, like Oystermouth, had been beautified and reconstructed more as pleasant dwellings than fortified positions. The peninsula shared in the chaos of Glyndwr's rebellion in the early fifteenth century, but thereafter its story is a local rather than a national one.

There was plenty of family feuding in the sixteenth century, when the 'new men' of the Tudor period were building their vast estates. New names like Mansel and Lucas come to dominate the scene, with the Duke of Beaufort brooding over all. Gower's dramatic events dwindle into rioting, election squabbles and smuggling—and so on into the nineteenth century. Like the old castle of Oystermouth, Gower sat back pleasantly in the sun.

After that short scamper through Gower's history it is time to resume our Gower journey. We still have a short half mile to travel from the castle, to complete our circuit of Swansea Bay. We do it through the Cutting, driven through the limestone cliffs when the railway was extended to the headland in 1898. The railway was then at the height of its popularity and the directors felt that no respectable holiday line could be complete without a pier. The railway has gone but the pier is still there, shorn a little of its former glory. I remember the time when it still possessed its Winter Gardens, all palm courts and Sunday Celebrity Concerts! The cross-channel boats called on their way to Ilfracombe and the evening trip along the Gower coast, and the photo machines clicked in line along the side-walks. It was on the Mumbles Pier that I first paid a penny to find out "What The Butler Saw". As I remember it, not very much in those non-permissive days! The pier still retains some of its early twentieth-century delights and some of its curly cast-iron décor. In 1920 the Mumbles lifeboat was housed in a new building at the top of a steep slipway, connected to the pier by a gangway. This slipway gives the lifeboat a spectacular launch at low tide, as it takes the water in a shower of leaping spray.

The Mumbles lifeboat has had a long and heroic history. After a certain amount of false starts, a lifeboat station was finally established in the Mumbles in 1863. In 1867 a new lifeboat was installed, the *Wolverhampton*, so-called because it was bought with funds collected in that city. It gave seventeen years of splendid service until, on a wild night of January 1883, it met with a disaster that startled the whole nation and was still remembered when I was a boy at Swansea. The barque *Admiral Prinz Adelbert*, of Danzig, crashed into the outlying rocks of Mumbles Head. The lifeboat made a tremendous effort to reach her, after rowing through the Inner Sound in the teeth of the gale. But the lifeboat was itself flung against the wreck. Four of its crew were drowned, including Coxswain Jenkins and two of his sons. Two men in the lifeboat were saved by the courage of the Sisters Ace, the daughters of the lighthouse keeper, who went down into the swirling surf and threw their shawls to the drowning men and thus dragged them into safety on the shore.

The Victorian critic and ballad writer, Clement Scott, immediately rushed into print with a splendid tear-jerker that made the round of the halls and became a favourite recitation at all popular concerts at Swansea. We children, at one time or other, sat spellbound as the verses rolled out. They began with the brisk announcement:

Bring, novelists, your notebook! Bring, dramatists, your pen!
And I'll tell you a simple story of what women do for men . . .

They continued with a rather curious description of the coxswain's motives for putting out to sea in a gale:

When in the work did the coxswain shrink? A brave old salt was he,
Proud to the bone of four strong lads as ever had tackled the sea,
Welshmen all to the lung and loins, who, about that coast 'twas said,
Had saved some hundred lives a-piece—at a shilling or so a head.

However the final verse did full justice to the Sisters Ace courage in plunging into the foam and flinging their knotted shawls to the drowning men.

Wait for the next wave, darling, only a minute more,
And I'll have him safe in my arms, dear, and we'll drag him safe to the shore.
Up to their arms in water, fighting it breast to breast,
They caught and saved a brother alive! God Bless Us, we know the rest—
Well, many a heart beat stronger, and many a tear was shed,
And many a glass was tossed right off to the Women of Mumbles Head!

Stirring stuff! But there was no doubt that the Mumbles continued to produce lifeboat heroes. The lifeboat met disaster again in 1903, when she capsized in a great wave at the mouth of Aberavon harbour and the coxswain and five men were drowned. Still there was no lack of volunteers to come forward to replace them. The third disaster occurred in 1947, when the *Santampa* went ashore on the Sker rocks near Porthcawl. In a furious gale the *Santampa* broke up with the loss of her whole crew of thirty-nine. The lifeboat was again caught in a hurricane and flung onto the rock. All the eight men who manned her were drowned. The Mumbles lifeboat has one of the finest records in Britain of heroism and service.

From the pier, you look across at the two white limestone islands of Mumbles Head itself. No satisfactory explanation has been given of this curious name. A recent attempt to derive it from the Romano-British word *mammulae*, or breasts, has not met with much acceptance. Maybe Mumbles comes from the sound of the sea rumbling in the big cavern of Bob's Cave on the outer head. Who knows? One thing is certain, however; the Mumbles form one of the most notable headlands of the Welsh coastline.

The outer islet was crowned with an elegant white tower in 1794. The first light was made by a fire on the top of the tower, but oil lanterns were introduced early in the nineteenth century. Later on defences were added; and today a picturesque clutter of buildings is grouped around the tower. In the 1870s they were the scene of the remarkable experiments in over-water telegraphy of Dillwyn Llywelyn and Professor Wheatstone. The lighthouse is now automatic. The Mixon shoals stretch to the westward from Mumbles Head and are marked by a bell buoy.

The high ridge behind the headland is a notable viewpoint on a fine day when the full tide floods Swansea Bay. No one has caught the charm of this scene better than that most gentle and lyrical of diarists, the Rev. Francis Kilvert. Kilvert was a curate in the Radnorshire border village of Clyro, and his diary is now recognized as one of the best in the language. He paid frequent visits to Gower and, on an April day in 1874, sat on the Mumbles headland and described what he saw:

The lurid copper smoke hung in a dense cloud over Swansea, and the great fleet of oyster boats under the cliff was heaving in the greenest sea I ever saw. We had luncheon up on the cliffs overlooking the white lighthouse tower of the most seaward of the Mumbles. A shepherd was halloing and driving the sheep of the pasture furiously down a steep slope into the sea, and a school of boys came running down the steep, green slope, one of them playing "Rosalie the Pararie Flower" on an accordion as he ran. A steam tug shot out of Swansea harbour to meet a heavily laden schooner under full press of canvas in the bay, and towed her into the port, and the great fleet of oyster boats which had been out dredging was coming in around the lighthouse point with every shade of white and amber sails gay in the afternoon sun as they ran each other into their moorings under the shelter of the great harbour cliff. As we went along the narrow cliff path among the gorse towards Langland and Caswell Bay, a flock of strange and beautiful black and white birds flew along the rock-faces below us towards the lighthouse piping mournfully. They were I suppose a small kind of gull but they seemed to me like the spirits of the shipwrecked folk seeking and mourning for their bodies. Among the sighing of the gorse came upon the lift of the wind a faint and solemn tolling of a deep bell from sea-ward. It was the tolling of the buoy bell moored off the Mumbles, a solemn awful sound, for the bell seemed to be tolling for the souls of those who had gone down at sea, and warning the living of their graves.

A little mournful perhaps, at the end but the Mixon does sound rather lost and fateful on a dark, wintry day—although I claim that the coastline beyond the Mumbles is anything but mournful. Here begins that magnificent line of limestone cliffs and sandy bays that runs for sixteen miles to the west and is the glory of Gower. The first two bays lie immediately to the west of the Mumbles headland. They are small and separated by a rugged little tor called Tutt Hill, and crowned with a coastguard look-out. Bracelet Bay is circled with a bank of car parks and has a restaurant under the slopes of Tutt. Limeslade looks to the westward and has a slight rash of bungalows in the little valley that leads back from it. 'Slades' are common along the Gower coast. In addition to Limeslade we will come across Deepslade, Heatherslade, Rotherslade and Mewslade. The word comes from the Old English *slaed*, which in place-names denotes a low valley, a dell or dingle or an open space between banks or woods.

Do not look for lonely seclusion at Bracelet or Limeslade on any warm summer evening. They are too near Swansea and the cars pour through the cutting onto the car parks. But at Limeslade the coast road comes to a dead end, although a side road curves back to Oystermouth through the bungalows. Gower has been profoundly lucky in one way—no one has promoted a road around the coast in the style of that around the Great Orme in North Wales or the Antrim coast road. Roads reach the coast at various points, but you can only see it at its best if you are prepared to walk. A path leads all the way round; happily still a narrow walker's path for most of the distance; and it begins at Limeslade.

From Limeslade to Caswell the path has been widened a little by the Swansea Corporation, for Caswell was the boundary of the old borough. But the widening has not really affected the quality of the walk. It is still the unspoilt cliff-side that Kilvert saw, bright with sea-pinks and gorse and with the gulls crying above the white rocks. You walk around Rams Tor, and a mile after leaving Limeslade reach Langland Bay, with its little preliminary cove of Rotherslade.

Langland, together with the next bay of Caswell, is still very much under the influence of Swansea. There are hotels here and a line of municipal bathing huts goes around the edge of the bay. It is not so bad as it sounds. There are plenty of trees in the gardens that slope down to the sea. Snaple Head, which guards the western arm of the bay, is not built over, and looking at it I am tempted to breathe an unexpected prayer, "Thank Heavens for Golfers!", since the high land behind the head forms part of the Langland Bay golf course and is thus saved from 'development'. In the centre of the bay is a Gothic construction which was once the seaside home of one of the great Merthyr iron masters in the mid-nineteenth century. It was built in a style which Ruskin approved and Sir John Betjeman delights in, with a church-like tower and pointed arches. It is now part hotel and part miners' rest home.

The Osborne Hotel stands on the little spur in the centre of the bay that separates Langland from the small cove of Rotherslade. In the early 1890s, the hotel had a surprising visitor in the person of the famous French Impressionist painter, Alfred Sisley. In the London 1974 exhibition of Impressionist canvases in private hands, I was delighted to see that Alfred Sisley had painted in South Wales. How romantic the Welsh landscape sounds under French titles such as "Le Rade de Cardiff, crepescule", or "Les Falaises de Penarth!" Sisley had come to Cardiff, however, for a somewhat unromantic reason. The records in the French consulate of that city reveal that he had journeyed to Wales to legitimize his two illegitimate children. From Cardiff he went for a short stay at the Osborne. He set up his easel a few yards from the hotel and painted a series of canvases of the Storrs Rock, in the middle of Rotherslade. This was the rock from which we used to demonstrate our diving skill at high tide. Sisley endowed it with a warm glow that makes it seem to be a lost piece of the Mediterranean coastline.

It is strange that more painters were not attracted to Gower. Lucien Pissarro, the son of Camille Pissarro, came in 1933 and painted a view of Cefn Bryn from Pennard which is now in the Glyn Vivian Art Gallery at Swansea. Ceri Richards, the greatest colourist that Wales has produced in modern times, was born in Dunvant in 1903. Dunvant is on the edge of

Peninsula Gower and Ceri knew his Gower well, but he never made it a central theme in his painting. Fred Janes, as a Swansea man, was bound to turn to Gower, and he seems to me to have got closest of all to penetrating in paint into the mysterious, luminous quality of the limestone rock.

There were earlier water-colourists at work locally in the 1880s, men like Chapman and Harries, whose work now has a period charm. And, of course, the indefatigable eighteenth-century engravers, the brothers Samuel and Nathaniel Buck, included the Gower castles in their *Buck's Antiquities: or Venerable Remains*. The great men of the Golden Age of British landscape painting, Turner, Girtin, Constable, never came to Gower although many of them made extensive tours of other parts of Wales. I would give a lot to have Turner's impression of Worms Head in a gale. As it is, I must be content with the delightful print of it in 1812 by William Daniell, who also produced a charming evocation of Mumbles Head in the same period.

From Langland the cliff path goes round Snaple Point into Caswell Bay. The name comes from the Caswell stream that flows down to the sea here, and means 'cress stream'. It has thus the same origin as the Carswells of Berkshire and Gloucestershire, Caswell in Dorset and Cresswell in Pembrokeshire. The road drops steeply down into Caswell from the village of Newton, past the house on the top of the hill which carries a plaque proclaiming that Frances Ridley Havergal (1836–1879) once lived there. Who now, I wonder, reads her collection of hymns and poems, her *Ministry of Song* or *Under the Surface*? Yet some of her hymns are still sung, and she became a well-remembered figure in the short time she stayed at Newton. The *Memoir*, written by her sister, brings back a picture of one aspect of life in the village in Victorian days that now seems as remote as the other side of the moon.

> The cottagers around us soon won my sister's interest and regard and she invited them to a Bible reading in our house. (I may say that she never began any work of this kind without the Vicar's consent.) My dear sister Frances had promised to meet some men and boys on the village bank on May 21st. Although the day was very damp she went, taking her Bible and her temperance book with her. As she passed thro' the village of Newton, quite a procession gathered round her, her regiment of boys eagerly listening. Her donkey-boy Fred Rosser remembers that Miss Frances told him, "I had better leave the

Swansea Bay and the Mumbles from Town Hill

The curve of Swansea Bay from Southend

Oystermouth Castle

Mumbles Pier

The limestone islets of the Mumbles

Caswell Sands

Pwlldu Bay

Mitchin Hole
Bone Cave

The coast
westwards from
High Tor

Three Cliffs Bay

Pennard Castle

devil's side and get on the safe side; that Jesus Christ's was the winning side; that He loved us and was calling us and wouldn't I choose Him for my Captain?"

Arriving at home, Frances ran in for her book, and on the saddle Fred signed the pledge.

The hordes of donkey-boys have long since gone, that used to wait for the arrival of the Mumbles train at Oystermouth to transport the trippers over the hill through Newton and down to Caswell. Today the cars and buses bring the thousands that crowd Caswell on summer week-ends. There are villas, and a hotel in one corner of the bay, but once the tide goes down the crowds seem to scatter over the wide expanse of yellow sands and Caswell becomes a true Gower bay, backed by its steep limestone slopes covered with gorse and bracken.

The Gower path goes up the western corner of the bay with some difficulty. The old windmill that used to crown the point near Redcliff, and work the water-supply pump, has finally disappeared. As you walk on the narrow ledge just underneath its side, look down. The headland is about 200 feet high and a great slab of limestone drops fiercely down to the sands and rock-pools below. I have reason to look down that 100-foot slab with some anxiety. Over fifty years ago I was in Oxford and had just been enchanted by the art of rock-climbing and mountaineering. I had begun to try myself out on the great cliffs of North Wales, following in the footsteps of such masters as Jack Longland and Menlove Edwards. This was in the days long before Joe Brown, when even a climb in gym-shoes was regarded as unorthodox, and all the artificial aids used so freely by climbers today ranked as unmentionable offences against public decency. As one stalwart climber of the old school pontificated: "the hand that could drive a piton into English rock could shoot a fox".

But I felt that I should keep in training when I was back in Swansea on vacation, so I bicycled down the dusty roads of Gower to try my skill and courage on the nearest rock-face. I climbed nervously at Mewslade Bay. I made a chancy route up the west face of the Great Tor; but the Caswell Slab was the real challenge. One morning when no one was about, I set off up the edge of the slab. There was a cave on the left and I balanced carefully on small holds along a crack above it. I got a foot into a sort of small sentry-box about three-quarters of the way up and found I was stuck. The slab seemed suddenly to have become

impossibly smooth. I will never forget the ten minutes I spent
balancing there until I plucked up courage, launched myself
across the ten feet of spoke-shaved limestone and—with a flood
of relief—grasped the edge, and so up onto the safety of the cliff
path. I showed the slab a few weeks later to some climbing
friends. They shook their heads. Every climber in those days
knew that limestone had a bad reputation. It was "friable", said
the experts. The Caswell Slab would never be classified as a
serious climbing route. Better to say nothing about it.

How times have changed! In the 1950s modern climbers
sought out the Gower rocks and found them delightful. New
routes of a high standard were opened up on every cliff face of
importance. Mewslade became a favourite climbing centre and
hardly a Gower crag has been left unexplored. Jeremy Taylor's
climbing guide to the Gower Peninsula, issued in 1970, declares
that there are now about 600 climbs available here. I turned
nervously to the Caswell section to see modern opinion on my
daring adventure of forty-five years ago. Alas, standards have
risen. "Great Slab," says the guide book briskly, "a good exposed
climb, 90ft", and continues, "follow a crack line exiting at a
slanting grass ledge at the top; awkward." I'll say it was!
Modern experts may scamper up it and then pass on to such
delectable frolics as 'Deborah's Overhang' in Paviland—"200
feet about twelve 10mm and a few 8mm rawl bolts should be
taken". Or 'Power Trap' at Mewslade—"an excellent line, steep
and exposed". As for me—well, the Great Slab at Caswell will
always be the climax of my Gower climbing career.

As the path goes over the top of it, I feel that you enter a new
section of this South Gower coastline. No road comes near the
cliff edge for the next delightful three miles. This is walker's
country, from Brandy Cove, up the secret valley of Bishopston,
to the highest headland in Gower at Pwlldu Head.

3

Cliffs and Caves

A short mile separates Caswell Bay from Pwlldu, but it is a delightful walk by the cliff path. The first tiny inlet is Brandy Cove. Its original name was Hareslade, but it became Brandy Cove in the Napoleonic Wars for obvious reasons. From here onwards the Gower coast is full of smuggling stories, and the kings of the Gower smuggling rings, the Arthurs, father and son, lived a mere mile back from Brandy Cove and Pwlldu. More of them later. For the moment you can enjoy Brandy Cove best at low tide, when the little golden strip of sand is exposed among the white limestone rocks and the wooded glade behind is dappled green in the sun. It is possible that the Romans worked iron-ore deposits here. The coast path continues around the steep slope that looks down on the tooth-shaped rocks known as the Seven Slades. And so you come to Pwlldu.

Pwlldu means the Black Pool in Welsh and it is strange to find a Welsh name surviving in this very English part of Gower. The Black Pool is there all right, formed by the Bishopston stream as it is dammed back by the finest pebble beach in Gower. The stream seeps out onto the sands through this huge mound of shining stones that stretches right across the bay. The stones clatter strangely as you struggle across them. The impressive bulk of Pwlldu Head, the highest headland in Gower, shuts in the western side of the bay and makes Pwlldu a place apart. You have to walk to reach it, although cars can come down to the cliff-top above Seven Slades from the narrow lane from Pyle Corner on the eastern side, and a steep track tumbles down from Hunts Bay to the west. Pwlldu Head is over 300 feet (ninety-seven metres) high and its eastern flanks are scarred in part with long parallel trenches down which the limestone blocks were slid on wooden sledges in the old quarrying days. Pwlldu Head, like all of the prominent Gower headlands, was worked for limestone all through the nineteenth century. The quarries—called 'flotquars' in Gower—were a vital part of the peninsula's economy. The Ring Rock, jutting prominently on the foreshore, was an obvious mooring spot for the sailing craft from Devon and Cornwall who lay up to load in the shelter of the headland. Part of the headland has a sinister name attached to it on the Ordnance Survey. Graves End commemorates an equally sinister event. In 1760 the Admiralty tender *Caesar* was wrecked here and sixty-eight men were drowned. Maybe they were pressed men who had been battened down under hatches. Their bodies littered the sand and were all buried in a mass grave near the scene of the wreck.

Two surprisingly large houses for so isolated a spot lie tucked behind the impressive pebble beach. One was once the Beaufort Inn, which no doubt was the heir to the old ale-house which catered for the quarry men. I remember patronizing it gratefully in the days when we were walking through Gower between the wars. It is now a private house. Near it begins the delightful path that runs up the secluded Bishopston Valley. The valley twists and turns inland between densely wooded slopes that become craggy in places. At times you struggle through thick growths of tangled woodland, stepping over the fallen boughs that block the path. You come out suddenly into lost meadows with a trout stream running clear beside you. This stream springs surprises, as you can expect in limestone country. It rises on Fairwood Common in the Millstone Grit belt, but sinks underground in dry weather at Barland Quarry, where it hits the limestone. For a mile beyond Bishopston Church it remains hidden, although you can detect its presence in strange sinks and impressive hollows. One such is the Guthole, where you can hear the stream running far out of sight below. A walk down this hidden valley is a delight in late spring and early summer when the valley floor and the woods above are full of bluebells, wild garlic, celandines and violets.

The original little hamlet of Bishopston is wedged in the bottom of the valley near the junction with the limestone. The church is dedicated to St Teilo and the Welsh name of the village is Llandeilo Ferwallt. St Teilo was a contemporary of St Illtud in the sixth century, when Wales was being Christianized by the travels of the Celtic saints, and Teilo may well have founded a church in this then remote spot. Bishopston Church has great charm, with its small nave and chancel and its typically castellated tower. In the early days of the conquest they built the tower more for defence than for the bells. Beyond Barland

Quarry the Bishopston stream wanders northward through fields and small copses to its source on Fairwood Common. The Ordnance Survey marks a motte-and-bailey fortification on Barland Common. The O.S. may be sometimes wobbly when it comes to Welsh place-names but it is infallible when it comes to objects on the ground. All I can say is that, when I looked for the motte-and-bailey, I got lost among new country houses, old gorse clumps and middle-aged bushes. You may have better luck. In any case, on week days you will not get out of the range of the sound of Barland Quarry, grinding deep into the limestone.

The new Kittle Road sweeps down into the valley, up past the quarry and on into the modern village of Kittle. The old Kittle Hill zigzagged steeply behind Bishopston Church. It was a famous test piece in the early twenties, when the motor-cycles raced through the water-splash and petered-out half way up the zigzag.

There has been considerable building development in this area. Houses are creeping out along the roads in all directions—in Bishopston, in the little hamlet of Murton on the edge of Clyne Common, and at Kittle at the top of the hill. Curiously enough they do not destroy completely your feeling of being in the country. As you drive towards Southgate you come to a sharp turn in the road. Pennard Church stands on the corner.

This church is somewhat larger than the general run of Gower churches, and its embattled tower is corbelled out, an unusual feature in the peninsula. It used to be thought that the church was basically sixteenth century, built to replace the old Pennard church which had been overwhelmed by the sands. But clearly the design of the structure dates from an earlier period. It was probably a chantry in the fourteenth century and became the parish church when the advance of the sands made the old church untenable. Within, Pennard has a barrel roof and a fine Jacobean pulpit. The old barrel-organ which was once the great curiosity of the church is now in the National Museum of Wales. There is a memorial tablet to the poet, Vernon Watkins, on the north wall of the nave.

A few hundred yards beyond Pennard Church, along the road to Southgate, you pass two farm buildings, Great Highway and Little Highway. They have been extensively modernized but they were once famous—or should we say notorious—in the annals of Gower. Here lived the kings of the Gower smugglers, the Arthurs. Arthur *père*, came from Devon and built up the business in the late eighteenth century so successfully that he was able to retire across the Bristol Channel and live "rich and happy ever after". His son also prospered exceedingly during the wars with France, until his organization was seriously affected in a memorable raid carried out by the Excisemen in 1804. The vivid official report on the raid shows how the whole of the Gower countryside was implicated in the smuggling business. A huge crowd collected and the 420 casks seized by the officers of the law were repeatedly stolen, stove in or tapped. The unhappy officials, heavily outnumbered, were compelled to let the crowd have some of the casks to keep them quiet. 404 casks reached Swansea, "several of them not full"; even then a mob of country people collected around the Customs House, sipping up the brandy with quills brought for the purpose. It took a unit from a corps of the Volunteers to disperse the mob.

The smuggler was a popular hero. In Oxwich, in March 1794, the vicar noted that "poor Thomas Mathews" had died as the result of drinking too much smuggled gin, and that nearly 200 people had crowded into the church to pay their last respects to this early martyr to the principle of free trade. The temptation to smuggle was irresistible. Customs duties were high. When you could buy tea in Holland for 7d. a pound and sell it in Britain for 5s. and when excellent brandy could be obtained in France for £1 per four-gallon cask, the profits of successful runs could be enormous. The Arthurs covered the whole coast down to Oxwich and a big operation could involve anything up to a hundred men. The men were hired for each run at a rate far exceeding the average wage of an agricultural labourer in eighteenth-century Gower. Horses were 'borrowed' from the farmers, who were in no position to refuse. The casks could be landed already equipped with rope loops to fit over the shoulders, and a sturdy man could manage two kegs. The horses, naturally, carried more. A boat could run into Brandy Cove on a still night or up on to Oxwich Sands, and the whole cargo could be dispersed miles inland in a matter of hours.

You can picture the shadowy procession moving through the Gower lanes at night, the lights being flashed to guide the boat in, the quick, expert unloading with hardly a word spoken, and the scouts out among the undergrowth along the main road watching for any sign of an approaching Excise patrol. To this day one of the tracks that leads down from Great Highway into the lower Bishopston Valley is known as Smuggler's Lane.

For a long period the smugglers had things very much their own way. The whole of Gower was on their side and the forces of the Law were thin on the ground. There were once eight Customs men stationed at Port-Eynon, with a boat on wheels at their disposal, and they could call on the help of the Sea Fencibles, the volunteer force enlisted for coastal defence during the Napoleonic Wars. But the gallant Sea Fencibles were hardly keen on arresting their fellow Gower men. Almost in despair, the Customs authorities at Swansea in 1795 reported officially that at least 5000 kegs of brandy had been landed on the coast between the Burry Inlet and the Mumbles over a period of six months.

Stories and legends have gathered around the Gower smugglers and who can now disentangle fact from fiction? William Arthur became the centre of what might be called Gower's Smuggling Saga. According to the story, a Customs official on a chance prowl discovered a keg of brandy at Arthur's farm at Great Highway. He sent a messenger to bring up help and transport, and for safety took the keg into the farm kitchen and sat on it. He reckoned without the ingenuity of the bold Arthur who quietly went down into the cellar immediately below the kitchen, took an auger and bored upwards through the wooden floor into the keg. The keg was emptied and the contents whisked away. When reinforcements arrived the Customs officer lifted the keg only to find that it was curiously light. The evidence had "evaporated".

Then there is the story of Mollie Stote, the wife of the most successful smuggler in Rhossili. He lived in Middleton and one day, when he was away, the Excise officials came riding by. The day was hot. They had a suspicion that the Stotes were deep in the smuggling game so they called on Mrs Stote. She knew that the proceeds of a successful run were hidden in the barn. She immediately complied with their request for a glass of water each, but she took care not to give them water but neat gin. After the first gulp, the officials demanded a refill of this remarkably attractive water. It was not long before they were, in the words of the old Gower dialect, 'albeleigher',—in other words, rolling in the aisles. In the meantime the casks of brandy were safely removed.

The records show, however, that Mrs Stote's husband was in

constant difficulties with the law. He was accused of releasing all the horses caught in a smuggling operation from the parish pound in Middleton. No doubt the long-suffering farmers were glad to have them back. There was also the cunning stratagem employed by the Rhossili men, who built a strange cellar whose ruins can be traced today. It was excavated in the bed of one of the streams that comes down steeply off Rhossili Downs behind the old Rectory. The water poured over it and the most zealous Exciseman would not have suspected its existence.

I remember old Mr Grove taking me into Port-Eynon Church. I must have been ten at the time and he seemed a white-bearded patriarch of endless age to me, although he was barely sixty. "Tell thee, boy, this place ha' been all redone." He pointed to the altar and said "Gran' father, he worshipped at th'old place. Oh, he were a real Crow [native of Port-Eynon], boy, a proper inklemaker [inquisitive person]. Ay, boy, and he were in the Big Run, zz snow [you know]. An the Exciseman cam and he said, 'The Lord 'ull help. Into the Church, boys.' An the Lord were kind and Parson understood. They put arl the kegs inside t'altar. Those herring-gutted Excisemen, boy, didn't knaw a thing. I say, t'was the true Spirit of the Lord, even if it were brandy."

Maybe many of the Gower stories were also told about smuggling from Sussex to Cornwall. The hero was always the smuggler, the Exciseman always the dupe. But slowly the Excisemen got control and brought off some notable successes. In 1805 Customs officer George Beynon and his men caught a big gang in the middle of a major run on Rhossili Sands. A furious fight followed, but eventually the gang fled leaving the sands littered with abandoned kegs and equipment. By 1822 the Bristol Channel was permanently blocked by naval patrols and by 1830 the modern coastguard service was established. The great days of Gower smuggling were over.

From Pennard Church the motorist drives in a few minutes to Southgate and the delights of Three Cliffs Bay. I would prefer to complete the walk along the coast to the same spot. So we return from our foray inland to leave Great Highway by the smuggler's route, and walk back through the leafy charms of the Bishopston Valley to Pwlldu.

Here the walker has a choice. He can cut up the steep path that leads out of the bay to the west, and so onto the narrow road that leads past Hunts Farm and over the clifflands to Southgate.

Or he can make the circuit of Pwlldu Head. Naturally as a keen walker I recommend the latter course. The car can take you to a great many places in Gower that are worth seeing, but the real pleasures of the peninsula are revealed to the man or woman who is prepared to tramp the secret paths. And the path around Pwlldu is certainly secret as well as rugged. You do not meet many people on it even in high summer. It takes you under the cliffs of the bold headland.

You look to the east and see the long succession of yellow-sanded bays and white cliffs that leads round to the Mumbles. Then the cliffs fall back and you come to the wider circle of Hunts Bay. There is practically no sand. When the tide goes out it leaves a wide expanse of rock pools. Tradition maintains that Hunts Farm, which looks down on this shallow indentation of the coast—for you can hardly call it a bay in the strict sense—was given to his huntsman by William de Breos, when he was Lord of Gower. Why not? The transaction may have taken place 800 years ago but Gower memories are tenacious. In any case, I feel that geology not history is the attraction of Hunts Bay, for it is one of the best places in Gower to see the sequence of raised beaches and glacial deposits that are such a feature of the Gower coastline.

Visitors to the bays often find themselves climbing down onto the sands on paths that cut through a face of thick clay and rubble. Sometimes deposits of what looks like roughly made concrete lie plastered on rock faces or in cave mouths. All these are the product of the great Ice Ages that ebbed and flowed across Gower. The first glaciation started around a million years ago, and the last finally ended some ten thousand years ago. Geologists recognize four major advances of the ice, with warmer interglacial periods. We can see the traces of the last two glacial advances in Gower. The sea levels rose and fell as the ice melted. In Hunts Bay you can trace some of the platforms cut by the sea at various levels. On them rest the remains of the early beaches, which in turn were covered by tilth and more recent deposits formed by the breaking down of the rock in tundra conditions. The lowest concrete deposit is recognized by geologists as the 'patella' beach, from the quantity of limpet-like shells it contains. It was traced on the Gower coast by Professor Neville George, the distinguished geologist, who wrote the invaluable handbook on South Wales in the British Regional Geology series, issued by the Institute of Geological Research. I always remember the account he gave me of his 'patella' investigations, with as much enthusiasm and excitement as if he had discovered an immensely rich diamond-bearing deposit. But then, Professor George lived in Gower and loved it.

Just beyond Hunts Bay we enter classic ground. The coast steepens again. There are craggy outcrops on the 200-foot contour and below them scree, gorse and bracken go plunging down to the rocks that fringe the sea. The path winds above these lower rocks and brings you to one of the most fascinating parts of the coastline. We are now in the country of the Gower bone caves and two of the most famous of them, Bacon Hole and Mitchin Hole, are near at hand.

The Gower coast is naturally rich in caves. They form easily in the limestone and can be of great extent. Along the cliff line of the south coast many of them lie at a height of twenty or thirty feet above the present sea level at high tide. But as we discovered at Hunts Bay, the long period covered by the various Ice Ages saw great retreats and advances of the sea. In some of the interglacial periods the Bristol Channel was a vast plain on which great herds of animals roamed at will. And the remains of these animals have been found in the caves.

People have been digging in the Gower caves for nearly 200 years, but the men of the nineteenth century had the cream of the discoveries. The delightful Dean Buckland made his sensational find of a skeleton of prehistoric Man at Paviland as far back as 1823. From 1850 onwards the indefatigable Colonel Wood of Stouthall dug up the majority of the thirty-odd bone caves of Gower. Such enthusiasts lacked modern techniques. How much more we would have learnt if they would have been able to apply the complicated disciplines employed by excavators today. But as we look at the cases of bones and artefacts carefully laid out in the Royal Institution in Swansea, we can forgive those early explorers their indiscriminate rummaging in the rubble of the caves, and share their astonishment as they uncovered the remains of animals which they never dreamt had ever existed in Britain. Here in Gower once lived the mammoth, the woolly rhinoceros, the giant ox, the straight-tusked elephant, the cave-bear, the lion and the hyena and many more equally unexpected animals. The finds turned all the old ideas of pre-history upside-down.

Not all of the animals lived in the caves. The remains of the mammoths and the rhinoceroses, for example, must have been dragged there by the wolves or hyenas. There were traces of the presence of man as well, above all in Paviland. But Gower has not yet yielded any human remains earlier than the Upper Palaeolithic, roughly 20,000 years ago. There are no skeletons of Neanderthal Man or any of the predecessors of *Homo sapiens*, although the great plains of the Bristol Channel must have teamed with game. Maybe the absence of flint for easy tool-making might have had something to do with it. But there is no question that early man did eventually come to the peninsula and live in many of the caves.

Both Bacon and Mitchin Holes possess a strange, eerie quality as you creep down into them from the cliff top. Bacon Hole is the easier of the two to find and enter. A path comes down from above and you can get across without too much trouble into the wide cave mouth. Within, the floor of the cave slopes backwards into the gloom. An iron grille once guarded the innermost recess where it was thought that prehistoric paintings had been discovered. Back in 1912, ten horizontal bands of dark red colour were noticed on one wall of this recess, and the wild hope arose that Gower might show the only example in Britain of the sort of cave art which is the glory of the caves in France and Spain. No less an expert than the Abbé Breuil was called in, and he gave a qualified assent that these red marks could well have been made by early man. But over the years it seems that the markings have slowly changed their shape and may thus be due to minerals seeping from the rocks. I was sorry to hear it. Bacon Hole seemed exactly the right mysterious place for prehistoric man to have painted his magic signs in its dark depths.

Mitchin Hole lies further west and is more difficult to find. The easiest way to get to it is to walk down from the car park on the cliff top at Southgate, through the bracken-covered 'slade' of Foxhole, until you hit the path at the bottom. Follow this eastwards until you are directly under the prominent High Tor, then look carefully down along the sea-washed rocks at the foot of the tor. A scramble takes you into the narrow cleft out of which the cave proper opens.

A remarkable piece of raised beach clings to the rock surface at the entrance. The floor of the cave slopes up very steeply, and is slippery in places. It is also uneven, as can be expected in a place where excavation has been going on for over a century and is still in progress. Inevitably, Colonel Wood arrived first in the 1850s and found the remains of two types of fauna. One was temperate and interglacial and included bones of the narrow-nosed rhinoceros and the straight-tusked elephant; the other colder and therefore more favourable to the mammoth and the woolly rhinoceros. Other distinguished archaeologists have also worked here, and in 1973 important investigations were conducted by a team of geologists to settle the question of the correlation of the deposits at Mitchin Hole with deposits elsewhere. Mitchin Hole and the other Gower caves still have a lot to give to modern trained investigators. It is all the more important, therefore, that the casual visitor does not go scuffling about in the earth of the caves in the off-chance of finding souvenirs. It is very unlikely that he will.

What he will find, however, as he struggles up the steep slope at the back of Mitchin Hole and looks out through the narrow cleft of the entrance, is a strange feeling of being carried back thousands of years into the remote, mysterious past. In the eerie half light it is possible to picture the skin-clad families crouching around the fires, awaiting the return of the hunters from the cold, hostile world outside, and the ceremonies carried on in the depth of the cave in the hope of warding off the endless dangers that beset our early forefathers. On a chill autumn day, with the mists blowing up the Channel, those Palaeolithic hunters still seem present and close to one at Bacon Hole and Mitchin Hole!

You come out into the clear Gower sunshine again and make for the top of the cliff. Suddenly you are back in the modern world. The little hamlet of Southgate has expanded over the last twenty years. There is a car park on the cliff top and a hotel, and low bungalows extend in the fields on either side. But, again, all is not lost. There is no high building here. Everything lies well back from the cliff edge and great tracts of the cliffs are in the hands of the National Trust. You walk westward along the cliff top through the gorse and the heather. In one of the bungalows to your right lived Vernon Watkins and surely a poet has a right to live in such a delectable spot. For you are now approaching one of the great Gower views, the classic 'show-piece' of Three Cliffs Bay.

As you walk towards Three Cliffs you look down first on Pobbles Bay—a little inlet with a small storm-beach. The view westward is splendid. Before you is one of the biggest indentations of the Gower coast, Oxwich Bay. In the distance, closing the view, is the long Oxwich headland with the characteristic Gower feature of a level upland around 200 feet ending in white limestone cliffs. Then comes the lovely curve of Oxwich Bay backed by sand-dunes and the deep woods that still surround Penrice Castle. The glittering crags of the Great Tor guard Three Cliffs Bay to the west. Close at hand are the Three Cliffs themselves—a perfect composition of three linked and pointed cliffs penetrated by a wide arch. The eye travels round towards the north. Pennard Castle crowns a crag on the high sand-dunes and away in the distance Cefn Bryn shows as a cone of old Red Sandstone, perfectly placed in the centre of the landscape. When the tide is in, the whole of the bay within the Three Cliffs becomes a still mirror. I like it even better when the tide is out. Then the stream of the Pennard Pill winds over the golden sands in curving patterns, and you can walk along the edge of the waves from the Great Tor to the cliffs around Heatherslade.

All is beauty. One warning however. Three Cliffs Bay is notoriously treacherous for bathers. The very formation of the cliffs that makes it so attractive also sets hidden currents swirling. Three Cliffs, and Broughton Bay in the north-west of the peninsula, are the two most dangerous bathing bays in Gower. Take care.

From the Three Cliffs themselves a wilderness of dunes stretches back to the crag on which stands Pennard Castle. Pennard is a bit of a fraud. It looks splendid from a distance but it is a mere shell when you get close to it. No Gower castle has a finer site and none has less history known about it. It was probably built towards the end of the thirteenth century, during the period of the consolidation of the conquest. A curious square annexe was built out onto the edge of the cliff when the rest of the building was already complete. Near at hand, buried in the sand-dunes, are the remains of what was originally the parish church. The dunes give the clue to the fate of Pennard. Not very long after it was built, the sand started to encroach. We know from the records of Kenfig, further east on the coast of Glamorgan near Porthcawl, that a succession of furious gales in the fourteenth century set the sands moving over a big area. The encroachment lasted over a hundred years and did not finally stabilize itself until well into Tudor times. The same thing must have happened at Pennard. The whole of the cliff and the high ground behind it has been buried under the dunes. They are now mostly grass-covered and give sporting hazards to the players on the excellent Pennard Golf Course, but they must have represented tragedy to the peasants of this part of Gower in the Middle Ages.

Naturally legends accumulated around the castle over-whelmed by the sands. At Pennard, so the story goes, once lived a great warrior. A prince of North Wales sought his aid in an unjust quarrel with his neighbours. The Lord of Pennard did not trouble himself about the justice of the cause. He demanded the hand of the prince's daughter as the price of his aid. His demand was granted, and the allies attacked and overthrew the prince's enemies. After the campaign, the Lord of Pennard held a great wedding feast. There was harping, wine and dancing and the castle resounded with the sound of revelry by night. But at the height of the merriment, a dark cloud came driving up the Channel. Then another and another, until the whole air was filled with flying sand. All night the hurricane continued, and when dawn broke castle, church and village were all buried in a golden winding-sheet. No one escaped. And from Ireland a whole mountain of sand had suddenly and mysteriously dis-appeared during the night!

The sands may have ruined the castle but there is one remarkable little Gower treasure they left untouched at Pennard. On the crag below the castle wall grows a rare plant, so rare that it grows nowhere else in the British Isles except Gower. It is an Alpine, belonging to the *Cruciferae* (the wall-flower family), and rejoices in the splendid Latin name of *Draba Aizoides Montana*—alias the Yellow Alpine Whitlow Grass. Its root goes deep into the crevices of the rock so, luckily, it is very difficult to remove. Its bright yellow flowers appear in March and it seems to flourish best on the limestone. All the authori-tative books declare that it is only found at Pennard. This is not strictly correct. It occurs in other places along the coast towards Worms Head, but there is no virtue at all in naming them. Collectors have strange passions. They would rather eliminate a plant, or a bird for that matter, than lose it from their private cabinet. So I had better not tell you the location of other Gower rarities like the Isle of Man Cabbage once reported from some-where near Three Cliffs, or the Welsh Gentian which may, alas, have disappeared from Oxwich. I often wish that I knew more about botany, for I would like to have seen all these rare plants with their impressive Latin names which make Gower a botanist's paradise—the small rest-harrow (*Helianthemum chamaeoistus*), the spring cinquefoil (*Potentilla tabernae montani*), goldilocks (*Astor linosyris*), the gold samphire (*Inula crithmoides*), or the sea asparagus (*Asparagus officinalis*). Experts have shown me some of them. Not all of them look impressive to the uninitiated eye. But here they grow on the Gower cliffs, and there is still a mystery about how many of them ever came there.

One of the first people to take an interest in the plants of Gower (and its geology and antiquities as well) was the celebrated Edward Lluyd, a Welshman who became Keeper of the Ashmolean Museum at Oxford in 1691 and gained an European reputation as a pioneer in a whole range of scientific research. To ensure accuracy for his numerous publications he not only travelled the ground himself but established a network of reliable correspondents. In Gower, Lluyd first relied upon the Swansea-born cleric, the Ven. John Williams (1649–1701) who became Archdeacon of Cardigan. He then turned to Isaac Hamon of Bishopston. Hamon produced a remarkable survey of Gower which is preserved in Lluyd's papers, now in the Bodleian Library at Oxford. There are two or three key documents which everyone concerned with the story of Gower in the past continually quotes. First comes the famous survey undertaken in 1650 at the command of the Lord Protector, Oliver Cromwell. Then comes the account by Dineley of the tour of the Duke of Beaufort in 1684, and the list of the legal rights of the Duke compiled in the eighteenth century by his steward, the powerful and domineering Gabriel Powell. The most human of these documents is Hamon's. He gives fascinating details of the old dialect words and their pronunciation, the extent of English Gower and accounts of all the parishes, or "pishes" as he contracts the word in his manuscript—with delightful effect. His roll-call of the flowers of Pennard, Bishopston and Oystermouth has a mysterious rhythm all of its own.

"Of field herbs (especially in the said 3 pishes) Agrimony, wild carret, mulleyn, Dandelyon, Pelamountain, mallows, Burdock, Tutsan, Eybright, Bettony, Elecampane, Foxfingers, yellow and blue Kay-roses, Rames or Ramsey, Centry, Yarrow, Adders tongue, vervain, St. John's wort, Cancker wort, Devilles bit, Ragwort, mugwort, Breakstone-pasley, Larks bill, plantane, Pimpnell, Fumitory, Burnet, Botchworth."

I wonder what Pelamountain was, or mulleyn? The only one of the list that I can recognize as still growing at Pennard is my friend the "dandelyon".

The Pennard Pill runs inland past woodlands rich in simple flowers that I have no difficulty in identifying and enjoying—daffodils, snowdrops, bluebells—and through the flowery woods you can reach Parkmill. Parkmill is one of the key junctions of Gower, a place that everyone comes to sooner or later, for it is here that one of the two main roads from Swansea into Gower first comes down to the coast. The south road runs from Killay over the breezy Fairwood Common, where now the municipal airport has succeeded the R.A.F. wartime aerodrome. From the Common the road runs down the deep, wooded dingle that leads to Parkmill and passes Kilvrough Manor and its high, curving boundary wall. Kilvrough is now a holiday and training centre for young people, run by the Oxfordshire Educational Committee and originally purchased by the South Africa Aid to Britain Fund. It was once one of the great houses of Gower, ranking with estates like Penrice, Parc le Breos and Stouthall. The original manor house was built by Rowland Dawkins in 1585 but the present house is late eighteenth century and a good example of the period. There are now only six acres of ground around it, which include a round tower, a typical 'folly' beloved of rich and cultivated eighteenth-century landlords. Gower can show quite a few of them, especially around Stouthall further west.

I never pass Kilvrough without remembering the only time a military unit exclusively recruited from Gower went into action. This was the Swansea and Fairwood Corps of Yeomen Cavalry, recruited as a volunteer force during the Napoleonic Wars. It consisted of 160 men, raised from the gentry and farmers of Swansea and Peninsula Gower. There was need of such a body at the time, for back in 1797 Gower had been swept by the rumour that the French had landed in force on the Gower coast. The story was not so far fetched as it sounds, for earlier in the year a body of 1,500 French soldiers had been put ashore near Fishguard in the celebrated "Last Invasion of Britain!" After three exciting days of manoeuvring the French commander, General Tate, had surrendered to the Pembrokeshire volunteer forces led, with great dash, by the Earl of Cawdor. To Gower also there came a morning of hectic mounting of horses and despatch riders dashing in all directions. But the invasion scare did not last long and the gallant yeomanry had to wait for over thirty years before their next chance of action. This, unfortunately, was against their own countrymen. In 1831 the Reform Bill agitation was at its height and the big industrial centre of Merthyr was in serious insurrection. Thomas Guest, an iron master and a magistrate, came hurrying down to Swansea with orders from the Lord Lieutenant to Major Penrice, then the squire of Kilvrough and the commander of the Yeomanry. Penrice was an old Peninsula War veteran and had settled in Kilvrough on his retirement from the army. He was roused from his bed and went into action with Wellingtonian speed. About twenty to thirty men were immediately assembled from Gower and off they went as an advance guard. But as they approached Merthyr they were suddenly surrounded by thousands of rioters armed with muskets, pistols, scythes and pikes. Major Penrice looked around for Guest, who had to read the Riot Act before Penrice could open fire. That gentleman had tactfully and quietly melted from the scene. The major and his men were disarmed and retreated disconsolately to the strong-point of the "Lamb and Flag" pub at Aberpergwm. True, when reinforcements arrived, the Yeomanry advanced again and gave yeoman service at Dowlais. Very unfairly Major Penrice and his men fell under a slight cloud in high governing circles. The vanishing Mr Guest had been the sole cause of their unfortunate accident, but the Government thanked the major for his services—and then dissolved the Corps! Such is the way of Authority when it senses an awkward situation.

Major Penrice, however, will always be beloved by me for it was he, I think, who built that invaluable hostelry, the Gower Inn. Parkmill was the natural meeting-place for farmers from South Gower coming to and from Swansea market, and the Gower Inn rapidly became one of the great institutions of Gower. Back in mid-Victorian days it was the only respectable hostelry at which a visitor could stay. Court leets, sales, political meetings, official dinners, everything took place there. In my boyhood it held a very special place, for this was the first long stop of the Vanguard bus as we came riding out on it for our holidays at Port-Eynon. The journey was always a romantic adventure, for we would ride perched among the parcels on the roof-top. After the long crawl up Killay Hill we came out onto Fairwood Common where we felt that Gower really began. Here were the curlews crying and the ponies tossing their wild manes as they cantered away from the noise and fumes of the bus. Carefully we rounded the Devil's Elbow—the summit of danger on the South Road—then on into the green tunnel through the dense woodlands that then filled the valley from Kilvrough to the mill at Parkmill. The whole of the little village seemed buried in trees.

We were far too young to be allowed to go into the bar of the Gower Inn, but we wandered around the horses and traps and heard the rich Gower dialect on the lips of the farmers. In those days the Gower dialect was still alive. Certainly all the older people spoke it. When I once asked the name of the little stream that flowed beside the inn, "Why, boy, 'tis the Killy Willy!" came the reply. Killy-willy is an expressive word also used in Somerset for anything that goes wandering all over the place, and everyone was a boy to a Gowerian no matter what his age. There was also a lilt in the speech that may have come from the proximity of Welsh-speaking neighbours, although the accent and vocabulary were more akin to Devon. But none of the old Gower folk that I remember spoke with the slow, calculated sentences of a Devon countryman. The tone of the speech was far more lively.

My old friend, Horatio Tucker of Overton, made a special study of the dialect and listed most of the words in use. As you might expect, he found that a great number of them were paralleled in the West Country, but there were also others which had more in common with the Scottish, North of England and even with the Wexford dialects. Mr Tucker suggested that these particular words were widely distributed in medieval Britain but died out in the south although they survived on the outer fringes of the English-speaking world. Well, Gower was certainly 'on the fringe'. Mr Tucker's glossary shows such intriguing words as "bumbagus", used in Oxwich for a bittern, and "bubbuck" for a scarecrow. The "mucka" was the rick-yard—and a very expressive term for it in old Gower! "Kerning" was ripening or turning sour, and "leery" was empty. I particularly liked "nestletrip" for the smallest pig in the litter. If you had tea in a "dobbin" you were drinking it in a very large mug, although you could hardly be having a "frawst" or dainty meal. And the fire would probably be sending up "blonkers" or sparks.

You will not hear any of these words being used in the Gower Inn of today. No-one now drops in there to ask for "nummet"—a midday meal. The place has been enlarged and reconstructed and furnished with big car parks to cope with the ever increasing holiday trade. Little Parkmill has indeed changed with the times.

I wonder what Kit Morgan would have made of it. Now if you

ask who was Kit Morgan (or C.D.M. as all Gower called him), I can tell you that he was my predecessor, the first man to write a real guide book to the peninsula, and he was born here in Parkmill in 1834. He was Parkmill's grocer-cum-postman in his younger days and published his *Wanderings in Gower* in 1862. People had visited Gower before him and some of them had written about their experiences. But they had arrived rather as gentlemanly tourists, entertained at friendly vicarages or country mansions and then expressing their cultivated approval or disapproval of the Gower scene. But C.D.M. knew every inch of his Gower from the inside. His book is a walker's and a sportsman's book. He pours out lavishly the stories, gossip and legends of the Land of Gower. Well, maybe some of it was not quite accurate. Historians have raised their eyebrows at his account of the smuggling exploits of the Arthurs or his strange speculations around the Red Lady of Paviland. I do not think it matters. He was the first to get down in print the real feel of the place, and anyone who tries to write a guide book knows how difficult that is, myself included.

C.D.M.'s style is, to say the least, idiosyncratic! A few sentences selected from the very first paragraph show you what you can expect.

There is a sweet little spot round which the wild waves of the ocean unceasingly roll—sometimes rearing their snowy crests, huge as mountains, against the iron rocks that stand like guardians defying their fury. Grand indeed is the scene when the white clouds of silvery foam are flung wildly into the air—strange weird sounds are heard as cavern after cavern re-echoes with the wild and deafening chant— when the storm fiends flap their pinions in the gale. . . . Here we find sweet and lovely nooks where fairies love to gambol beneath Cynthia's pale and mellow rays. . . . This little spot, gentle reader, is Gower, the land of the setting sun.

The gentle reader soon realizes that C.D.M.'s book is a connoisseur's piece. We may chuckle but we enjoy it all the same. C.D.M. published a second edition in which he toned down some of the more flamboyant passages and added a lot of practical information. I stick to the first edition. Perhaps the Gower Society might see its way clear to issuing the *Wanderings* as a reprint, for it rarely appears nowadays in second-hand bookshops and every copy tends to be quickly snapped up.

C.D.M. held his court in his grocery-cum-post office at Parkmill to the Gower intelligentsia of the time, and his friends hailed him in poetic tribute as "Genius of Gowerland". I would like to read his reactions, in his best invective, to some of the changes in Gower and Parkmill since his day. Some things he might still recognize; the two little valleys that unite at Parkmill, for example. The streams from the Ilston Valley and the Green Cwm join to form the Pennard Pill, which flows under Pennard Castle to enter the sea at Three Cliffs. They both retain the charm they must have possessed in C.D.M.'s day.

The Ilston Valley really begins behind the Gower Inn and the Killy Willy trout stream runs clear under the deeply wooded sides of the *cwm*. 'Cwm' by the way, is the Welsh word for a valley and is the same as the 'combe' of Devonshire. It is strange how Gower woodlands seem to shelter in the deep valleys. The winds in West Gower certainly have a free hand in winter to roam over the landscape. The path through the Ilston Cwm is a delight of the same order as the Bishopston one. All these little lost Gower valleys are deep cut, with craggy sides buried in trees. After about a quarter of a mile's walk you come to one of the most tree-bowered parts of the valley. Here are the ruins of Trinity Chapel. Before the scanty walls stands a stone memorial pulpit, and on it a Bible also carved in stone. The memorial records the work of John Myles who was once Rector of Ilston.

He was a Hereford man, educated at Brasenose College, Oxford, and lost his living under Charles I for refusing to read the Book of Sports from the pulpit, as commanded by the law of James I. This edict allowed what now seems to us a kindly and modern tolerance in the matter of Sunday recreation. James may have been the Wisest Fool in Christendom but he declared that it was his pleasure that "after the end of Divine Service, our good people be not letted, disturbed or discouraged from any lawful recreation, such as Dancing, either man or woman, Archery for men, leaping, vaulting or any such harmless recreation, or from having Maypoles, Whitsun Ales or Morris dances, and the setting up of Maypoles and other Sports therewith used".

Myles belonged to a new and more intellectual, Puritan generation. On the site of the old medieval chapel of Trinity Well he founded what is regarded as the first Baptist chapel in Wales. It flourished strongly under the Cromwellian regime but, with the Restoration of Charles II, Myles' position became untenable. He felt compelled to leave the country. He led his followers to North America and founded a Baptist chapel at

Swansea, Massachusetts, one of the numerous Swanseas that
are scattered overseas. The memorial was unveiled in 1928 with
a crowded pilgrimage to the quiet peace of Ilston, a choir in
Puritan dress and a resounding speech by that master of Welsh
eloquence, David Lloyd George.

From Trinity Well the track leads on through the narrow
valley to the little village of Ilston. Ilston Church is one of the
most tucked-away and least known in Gower. The stream runs
along the churchyard wall, and the church seems almost to fill
the narrow valley. It is dedicated to St Illtud, one of the greatest
of the early Celtic saints of the sixth century. The monastery
founded by his followers at Llantwit Major in the Vale of
Glamorgan was a centre of learning in the darkest period of
Welsh history. Illtud—also spelt Illtud in Gower—must have
played a personal part in the conversion of the peninsula to the
Christian faith for the church at Oxwich is also dedicated to
him. The Ilston church fabric dates from the thirteenth century,
but like so many Gower churches it was restored with a heavy
hand in the nineteenth. The chancel arch and east window are
splendidly out of line. The tower is massive, with the characteristic Gower saddle-back roof and battlements. The interior of
the tower's lower storey has given rise to intriguing speculations. The masonry in some places seems rough and irregular.
Could it be the remains of the old Celtic cell on which the
Normans built their conquering tower? Set up in the main part
of the church—on a stand made and presented by "Jack the
Mill", the talented son of "Will the Mill" of Parkmill—is the
remarkable Pre-Reformation bell, a magnificent example of
late medieval casting. Its green patina is subtle, and almost
shines against the white walls of the church. A bad crack in the
crown might have been caused by a mistake in hanging the bell,
or by the iron of the 'cast-in' staples in the bell metal. It bears an
inscription *"Scante Thoma ora pro nobis"*—St Thomas pray for
us. This St Thomas is, of course, St Thomas-à-Becket, who
remained one of Britain's most popular saints down to the
Reformation. The bell was cast by the Bristol family of iron-
founders, the Jeffries, and dates from somewhere around A.D.
1520.

The church possesses two other bells, both larger than the St
Thomas bell. Curiously enough, they were cast in Oystermouth
by a family named Davis. They have now been re-hung in the
tower. An enormous yew shades half the churchyard and is

reputed to be at least 600 years old. Tucked away behind the tower is a memorial slab to Joseph Price, an eighteenth-century squire of the local 'big house' of Gellihir, which leaves one in no doubt about his qualifications for immediate admittance to Heaven.

Quod mori potu

All that was mortel of Joseph Pryce, Esq late of Gellyhir in this Parish whose amicable qualities endear'd him to all his friends: Religious without hypocrisy humble without meanness charitable without ostentation humane benevolent hospitable and affectionate Husband and indulgent Father. A sincere friend impartial Magistrate. His life exemplary his Death happy; unfeigned Piety accompanied him thro every scene to the last moment of life; supporting him with assurance of hope, the source of Peace and Earnest of Blissful Immortality

The old rectory lies on the edge of the hill above the church. Here the Rev Francis Kilvert, the diarist, often came to stay with his friend Westhorp, who was Rector of Ilston in the 1870s. His diary is full of the pleasures of his long walks from Ilston down to the coast, and of the elaborate picnics that seem to have been the principal occupation of the country clergy in those halcyon days. And what walkers they were! The Vicar of Sketty and his sister, Miss Brown, thought nothing of strolling over from Sketty, just outside Swansea and five miles across Fairwood Common, to drop in for dinner. Says Kilvert of the Vicar:

"He has for some unknown reason taken the name of Bonley, because he dislikes the name of Brown. I think while I was about it I would have taken a better name than Bonley which does not seem to me a bit better than Brown. We sat up till 1 o'clock disputing about the Athanasian Creed. . . ."

Ilston, hidden in the green seclusion of its out-of-the-world *cwm*, seems the right place for such recondite and esoteric disputations. The stream flows into Ilston past a small, disused quarry which is an important geological site. A hoard of Roman coins was found here in 1933, when the quarry was still being worked. The find confirms one's feeling that the Roman occupation of the peninsula penetrated to the furthest parts and that the Romans exploited all its minerals very thoroughly. Geologically the quarry shows a formation which is rare indeed in Wales. Here the crinoidal limestone alternates with clay, and two of the clay beds are associated with lenses or seams of thin coal. The quarry has therefore been declared a Naturalist's Trust Reserve, one of the many now certified in Gower.

The Ilston stream rises in Fairwood Common and thus almost flows across the whole of the peninsula from north to south. In following it we have come a long way from Parkmill. We must retrace our steps. But before we go, let us note that a road into out-of-the-way Ilston runs across part of Fairwood Common near the point where the north road dips down towards Cartersford. There are not so many north-south links in Gower, so it is also worth noting that another narrow road runs up a steep hill out of Parkmill past the little hamlet and big farm of Lunnon, to link again with the North Road near Pengwern Common. Lunnon is a very English-sounding name but nomenclature is never simple in Gower. The word turns out to be an Anglicization of the Welsh *"llwyn onn"*—the ash grove.

The second valley that comes down into Parkmill is the Green Cwm. At the entrance is the mill that gives Parkmill its name. The old, white-washed building is still there. The Green Cwm stream runs before it, and the road goes through a water-splash beside it. More important still, the old mill-wheel is still working, turned by the clear water of the stream; and they still grind flour on the massive wooden-framed machinery and work the sawmill by water as well. My old friend Mr William Davies— Will the Mill to everyone in Gower—would be glad of that. The mill was his life, as it was for his father before him. He was a real Gower stalwart. I remember him telling me, with a chuckle, of the famous occasion in 1917 when a cargo of wine barrels was washed ashore at Three Cliffs Bay. It was a Sunday morning, but that did not prevent the whole of Parkmill being on the spot in double quick time. "There were hundreds there," said Mr Davies, "and a lot of them woke up on the hill next morning." Then he chuckled again. "To tell you the truth, I had nine gallons myself and couldn't think where on earth to put them. Then I had a brilliant idea. I put them under the mill wheel and kept it turning happily. Luckily the Excise never came near it!" Now Will's son, Jack the Mill, keeps the old wheel turning, filling the house with the cool music of tumbling water.

The Green Cwm valley, which leads in past the mill, ranks high among the hidden valleys of Gower, and like the Bishopston and Ilston valleys, it is strictly walker's country. Again it is deeply wooded. Much of the area is now in the hands of the Forestry Commission but the authorities have respected the Gower Scene. They have kept the deciduous woodlands of ash, oak and elm, which are the proper trees for the landscape, and have not buried the *cwm* under the usual depressing blanket of conifers.

For the greater part of the valley the stream runs underground, as you expect it to in limestone country. As in the Bishopston valley, there are surprises ahead. Higher up the *cwm* holds one of the most remarkable of the Gower cave systems. It also possesses one of the peninsula's finest archaeological treasures. Not far from the point where the stream reappears is the Giant's Grave. This remarkable megalithic tomb was first excavated by Lord Avebury in 1869. In the galleries and transepts he found the remains of some two dozen people as well as some animal bones and pottery fragments, since identified as Windmill Hill ware. The site is now in the care of the Department of the Environment. About two hundred yards further north, in a rock face almost hidden by trees, is Cathole, one of the best known of the Gower bone caves and the only big one inland from the sea. Excavations here in 1955 uncovered a quantity of flint blades used by hunters who inhabited the cave towards the end of the last Ice Age, around 12,000 B.C. Strange to find two such remarkable witnesses to our remote past so close together. The Middle Ages are also represented here in the name of the big estate of which the Green Cwm forms part, Parc le Breos.

The Parc le Breos estate was sold in 1950, a year which saw the break up of some of the other great Gower estates, including Penrice and Clyne. Their owners had dominated the life of Gower for many centuries. But the name commemorates the great Le Breos family who were placed in power over Gower by King John, and who supplied more than their fair share of violent and colourful characters during the hundred odd years when they were Lords of Gower. There is even a somewhat doubtful tradition that William de Breos, a grandson of the first William, is buried near at hand in a field called Cae Gwilim Ddu, Black Williams field. This particular William lived up to the family tradition by coming to a sticky end. He had been captured in battle by Llywelyn the Great, the Prince of Gwynedd and North Wales. He had profited by his captivity to conduct an intrigue with Llywelyn's wife, Joan. Llywelyn heard of it after he had liberated de Breos. He invited him back, then seized him and hung the philanderer on a gallows-tree, at Aber in North Wales. The whole of Wales and the Marches applauded the judgement for the de Breos family was not much loved in any part of Wales. So Black William's body might well have been hurriedly whisked away from North Wales and buried on his property in Gower. The Big House of Parc le Breos was used by Polish airmen during the Second World War. I will always remember it for the visits of the talented, formidable and eccentric Miss Dillwyn. She died in 1935 but all through my youth she enjoyed being a local celebrity. She was a novelist, but she also reviewed books for the *Spectator*. In 1884 she was given *Treasure Island* to review and it was her notice that first launched Robert Louis Stevenson on the road to fame. But it was not her literary activities that made her a famous figure in Swansea and Gower. She was an early example of Women's Lib. She wore a man's hat and coat and a thick tweed skirt fitted with pockets into which she used to thrust her hands in a most unfeminine style. The final touch, that sent a *frisson* of delighted horror through South Wales, was her habit of smoking cigars in public. She made a splendidly defiant defence of her cigar smoking.

"I like a smoke, and I can see no objection to it. Let others do what they like, it suits me, and when I do it, I do it openly. I would never consent to smoking in secret."

Besides the cigar-smoking Miss Dillwyn, Parc le Breos is also associated in my mind with another strong-minded character who won fame in a far different field. This was Christopher Rice Mansel Talbot of Penrice Castle. He was a great huntsman, amongst other things, and the Parc le Breos estate contained many of his favourite coverts. The grassy track on the top of Cefn Bryn, along which he would lead his hounds home to Penrice after a hard day's hunting at Parc le Breos, is still marked on the large-scale Ordnance maps as Talbot's Road. I could not help thinking of the gallant Mr Talbot when I walked up the Green Cwm last autumn. The leaves were still vivid red on the trees and the air was crisp with a hint of frost. Then, echoing through the *cwm*, came the sound of a hunting horn. Hounds were at work on the edge of the woodlands and the fox was breaking away to the freedom of Cefn Bryn. Gower no longer has a local pack, but packs from Carmarthenshire come in for a day's hunting. There were flashes of red coats among the trees, and the baying of hounds. Squire Talbot would have been pleased.

The *cwm* winds its way among the steep woodlands and the valley bottom remains as dry as a bone until you reach Llethrid. A little cottage, hidden amongst the trees on the left near the exit gate from the valley, housed one of Gower's most remarkable men. Mr William Harry of "Llithrid" was well into his eighties but he was still active, still at his business of supplying power-saws—and his blades are reputed the sharpest in Gower. He published a fascinating book on sixty-six years with traction engines in Gower, going back to the period when the steam-engines chugged away on the farms at harvest time. His house is a link with the past. The story goes that the old Squire of Kilvrough was riding here one day when he saw some shadowy figures skulking in the woods on the skyline. "Poachers," he murmured. "Can't have them on my property!" Will happened to be passing by. "Will," the squire called out. "Would you live here and keep an eye on this ground if I built you a cottage and gave you the house and garden freehold? "Done," said Will over sixty years ago. And he lived there ever since.

At Llethrid the north road cuts across the valley. It is also the point where the Limestone meets the Millstone Grit, and the stream is still running above ground. Its headwaters are on Welsh Moor, and the sea in the Loughor Estuary is only a mile away. Curious how both the Green Cwm stream and the Killy Willy at Ilston Cwm flow almost right across the peninsula from north to south. But at Llethrid you can see the point at which the waters seep underground to create one of the finest cave systems yet discovered in Gower. The great Llethrid cave is actually entered from a cleft in the rocks hidden in the woods and protected by an iron grille, which is just as well for the cave contains dangers as well as glories.

The Gower caves are of two kinds. We have been looking at the bone caves, which are mainly on the coast and comparatively easy of access. They look fine when they are well placed, as at Paviland and Bacon Hole; but their main appeal is archaeological. Very few of them lead deep into the earth or open out into vast halls linked by narrow passages. Llethrid is different. It is a 'caver's cave', on a par with those discovered in the Mendips or around Craig-y-Nos. You should be properly equipped to try it. I have been taken caving by experts and I know how strenuous and skilful a business it is. We tackled what the experts call a "wet cave", and that is putting it mildly! We had on special suits of the skin-diving variety, miners' helmets, lights, ropes and rope-ladders. You have to wriggle, crawl and splash your way through streams in a mysterious gloom. And you always tend to forget that you begin by going down and then have to climb back at the end of the day. It is like rock-climbing upside-down in the dark!

But the rewards are great. Until you see them, it is hard to imagine what strange, disturbing beauties and adventurous excitements lie under your feet as you walk up the peaceful Green Cwm to Llethrid Farm.

The Llethrid Swallet was first explored by members of the South Wales Caving Club, but its full glories were revealed when Mr Clague Taylor and his sisters succeeded in re-opening the entrance after it had been blocked by floods in 1953. They were able to penetrate down into the Great Hall, one of the biggest underground chambers yet discovered in Wales and a 200-foot high cavern of cathedral proportions and astonishing beauty. It contains a wealth of stalactites, great calcite columns and hanging curtains of the 'bacon-rind' type. Llethrid Swallet can also show some remarkable curiosities such as the calcite 'mushrooms' and mud stalagmites which are extremely rare in the caves of Britain. In 1961 the Nature Conservancy declared it to be a site of special scientific interest.

There are other fine 'sporting' caves in Gower. Within a mile of Llethrid Swallet is Tooth Cavern, which is the most complex cave system in the peninsula and also contains fine formations. Again the authorities have wisely gated the entrance. Other caves well-known to the experts are Bovehill Pot near Landimore—although this should perhaps be classified as a true 'pot' in the Yorkshire sense, for you can descend it vertically in a series of platforms—and Stembridge cave, not very far away from Bovehill. Intensive exploration continues, for there are any amount of swallow-holes along the lower slopes of Cefn Bryn, where the limestone joins the Old Red Sandstone. Gower is well and truly on the Caving Map of Britain. Only, once again, take care. Consult the experts before you explore the glories of Gower's underground.

Pennard, Ilston and the Green Cwm mark another stage in the landscape of Gower. A mile and a half to the west rises the graceful cone of fern-clad hillside that forms the eastern end of the long ridge of Cefn Bryn, the 'backbone' of Gower. Parkmill is crowded in summer, and almost, at times, earns the title of the ice-cream capital of the peninsula. But after offering a tantalizing but impressive peep through the trees at Pennard Castle on its cliff surrounded by high dunes, the south road climbs up through the woods onto the open country at the foot of Cefn Bryn. The deep trenches of the Pennard valleys seem to me to be the dykes that stop the spread of suburbia. Beyond we will meet danger from caravan parks but not—so far—from housing development. Ahead lie the delights of Oxwich Bay, with the back-drop of Cefn Bryn. We are now well and truly into Gower Anglicana.

4

Cefn Bryn and Oxwich Bay

To me Cefn Bryn and Oxwich Bay always seem to go together. Oxwich, with its fine headland and curving sand-dunes, is one of the most attractive of the Gower bays, but it would lose half its charm if the wooded slopes and the long bracken-clad ridge of Cefn Bryn did not form its ever varied background. The south road runs between the coastline of the Bay and the high walks of the Bryn. The little hamlet of Penmaen lies high up on the eastern flank of the ridge, with a wide view back over the way we have come.

It is a tiny but charming place, for the moorland seems very close even if the south road in high summer is one, long traffic jam. A few houses are grouped around a small green. The church, dedicated to St. John the Baptist, stands close by, with the churchyard wall forming one of the boundaries of the green. The church dedications in Gower are a curious contrast. It was the practice of the conquering Normans, in great areas of the Marches of Wales, to remove the names of the Celtic saints from the churches and rededicate them to some more fashionable saints approved by Rome. This certainly happened in some places in Gower. The little church here in Penmaen is dedicated to St John, Pennard to St Mary, Penrice to St Andrew and Reynoldston to St George. But the learned Illtud was left undisturbed at Ilston and Oxwich, and Gower's own saint still presides over Llangennith. Some extremely obscure Celtic saints have hung on to their churches. I am not certain what St Rhidian did to deserve his sanctity or why the holy Cattwg is still commemorated at Port-Eynon. But they were not turned out by the new lords of Gower, which makes one feel that, despite their obvious hostility at the time of the conquest, Gower Anglicana and Gower Wallicana eventually succeeded in reaching a tolerant way of life together.

How else can you account for the tombstone on the church which unashamedly flaunts a typically Welsh pedigree in the middle of English Gower. "Here resteth the Body of David the sonne of David the sonne of Richard the sonne of Nicholas the sonne of Rys the son of Leison the sonne of Rys the sonne of Morgan Ychan the sonne of Morgan the sonne of Cradocke the sonne of Iustin ap Gwrgan Sometime Lord of Glamorgan interred the 21st day of August in the yeare of our blessed redemption 1623. In this bit of earth likewise reposeth the body of Iane his wife deceased the 23 of Febr 1631 whome God consorts in sacred rites and love death cannot separate the marrow from the dove. . . ."

The family concerned, the Davids, were connected with the Bennets of Penrice, and they were proud to trace their lineage back to Jestyn ap Gwrgan, the last Welsh ruler of Glamorgan. They recorded it in stone at Penmaen in the old Welsh style, with that multitude of 'ap's—the son of—which were the despair of English lawyers after Henry VIII's Acts of Union had united Wales finally with England. It all takes us back to a distant past when memory was as important as writing, and a man had to master every detail of his descent to prove his place in society.

The church itself has been heavily restored and contains a variety of interesting memorial tablets, although none to beat the splendid commemoration of David the sonne of David . . . and so on, *ad infinitum*!

A little further along the road on the edge of Cefn Bryn is the finely built Old People's Home of Glan-y-Mor. In my young days it used to be known as the Union, and it is certainly the most prominent building on the sky-line. Behind it, Talbot's Road makes its grassy way up to the ridge of Cefn Bryn. For the moment we will resist the temptation of that glorious ridge-walk—one of the great Gower expeditions. We must first do the delightful walk that begins down the lane leading from the small car-park on the main road, some 400 yards beyond Penmaen Church. This takes us out onto the Penmaen Burrows; a small but lovely wilderness of sand-dunes and bracken-covered hillocks which corresponds to the similar wilderness around Pennard Castle, which is clearly in view across Three Cliffs Bay. It was formed around the same time, in the fourteenth and fifteenth centuries, when a long series of great gales drove the sands from Oxwich Bay high up over the cliff-lands. Again a church was slowly overwhelmed and abandoned and the ruins are still there among the dunes. It used to be claimed that a whole village was also buried here called Steadworlango, and much learned and ingenious speculation used to be expended discussing the derivation of this curious name. Was it Norman, Norse, Welsh? Alas, historians now doubt if Steadworlango ever existed and no one will ever disturb the sands to find out.

Nearby is a far more ancient relic, the megalithic tomb of Pen-y-crug. This was a passage grave with a date going back to somewhere around 3000 B.C. The chamber was covered by a massive capstone which is estimated to weigh seven tons. It was first excavated in 1893, when human and animal remains were found together with a few pieces of pottery. The far bigger megalithic monument of the Giant's Grave in the Green Cwm at Parc le Breos is only a mile away as the crow flies, and the greatest of all the Gower cromlechs, Arthur's Stone, is within a three-mile radius on top of Cefn Bryn. It is tempting to think that there was some powerful attraction to the Neolithic settlers of long ago in these lands around Oxwich Bay. Perhaps, just as happened thousands of years later in the Anglo-Norman conquest, the newcomers by sea found that this was the most convenient spot at which to come ashore.

The Anglo-Normans have also left a memorial to themselves on Penmaen Burrows, right on the cliff edge that looks directly down into Three Cliffs Bay. Here stands a massive circular stone bank, overgrown with bracken and fronted by a deep ditch. Mr Leslie Alcock conducted extensive excavations here in 1961 and revealed traces of a timber entrance tower which had been burnt down by a fierce fire. Clearly the structure was earlier than the stone-built castle of Pennard. It probably dated from the first period of the Anglo-Norman invasion of Gower. Its design was somewhat unusual, since the Anglo-Norman advance in Wales was usually consolidated by the throwing up of a motte-and-bailey castle—basically a quickly built mound, surrounded by a ditch and crowned by a wooden tower. A 'bailey' or enclosure would be added. The Penmaen Castle is much more of a ring, and is matched by a similar type of structure at Penrice. It does however give one the feel of the early days of the conquest, when the invaders had to keep, at all costs, their contacts with their supply lines by sea, and when they could still be surprised and killed in fierce Welsh raids. Now in summer, the gulls cry above it and the sea crawls in lazily over the golden sands below.

We follow the cliff edge westwards and come to the Great Tor. This divides Three Cliffs Bay from the main sweep of Oxwich

Bay, although at low spring tides the two are joined and a magnificent circle of sand stretches right round from Pobbles to Oxwich Church. The Great Tor is not the highest of the Gower cliffs—it is just under 200 feet—but it is certainly one of the most impressive. It goes soaring up from the sands in a series of bold slabs. Ravens nest high up towards the summit. A slippery and narrowing path leads out onto the highest rock from the landward side, past a 'camel's hump'. It is possible to traverse across northwards to reach Leather's Hole, one of the most inaccessible of the Gower bone caves. I take my hat off to the nineteenth-century pioneers who made the sliding traverse on grass and loose rock to get at the cave and then to bring back the remains of mammoth, woolly rhinoceros, wolf and hyena with which it was filled. The cave itself consists of a passage going deep into the rock. It is possible to crawl or wriggle—depending on your size—down a short tunnel which opens up into a more roomy cavern right in the limestone heart of the tor. This is an eerie place, a true hyena den, for no mammoth or rhinoceros could ever have got in here. The bones were dragged in by the hyenas. A quaint entry in Isaac Hamon's manuscript survey of Gower, states "in this pish near the sea standeth a very high steep Rock like a tower, in it is a large cave called Glather hole, in wch cave, in formr time (as reported) was the working & lodging place of Robers clippe Coyners". They must have been desperate men indeed to live through a sixteenth-century winter in Leather's Hole!

I emphasize that the path is slippery and could be dangerous to the inexperienced, but perhaps, in this guide-book, methinks that I protest too much. Who are the inexperienced these days? Anyone who has been trained in mountain walking or has a steady head will find many of the places about which I croak warnings in this guide-book easy enough. But there have, after all, been accidents on Great Tor and in places like Paviland and the cliffs at Rhossili. Not every tourist has skill or even common sense. I remember one old hand at this business of guide-books telling me: "All guide-books should be written for a middle-aged family consisting of a placid pipe-smoking father, an anxious mother and two adventurous boys!" Well, I would like to include the still active grandfather keen on history as well as the highly intelligent aunt who paints and knows her botany and geology. But the ideal guide-book family has never existed. I propose to continue my warnings and let

Giant's Grave, Green Cwm

Penrice Old Castle

The Mansion of Penrice

Oxwich Church

Penrice Church

Arthur's Stone on Cefn Bryn

Reynoldston on Cefn Bryn

Llanddewi Church

Culver Hole, Port-Eynon

Memorial to the lifeboat men, Port-Eynon

the active visitor chuckle if he likes. It is better to be safe than sorry.

But it is quite safe to drift down the sand-blown slopes to the west of the Great Tor and come out onto the wide expanse of Oxwich Bay itself. The rocks of Little Tor are on your right, with a maze of rock-climbing routes up them. Then the steeper ground goes back from the water-line. The dunes begin, backed by the steep tree-clad slopes of Nicholaston Woods. I confess that I prefer this part of the bay when the tide is out. The sands seem to stretch away in an inviting curve towards the wooded headland of Oxwich Point. I can remember when an invasion of cockles occurred in the 1920s on this very section of beach, and the excitement of us youngsters when we thought that we had a new Penclawdd all ready for development! We scrabbled in the wet sand at low tide and filled buckets full of cockles. It did not last. Too many people arrived with too many buckets. The Oxwich 'cockle-rush' was over within a couple of years. They were never given a chance to establish themselves.

Roughly half-way around the curve of the beach the stream from the Oxwich marshes, the Nicholaston Pill, comes out over the sands and makes a convenient turning point for our walk. We turn back inland over the low sand-dunes, to a strange landscape of encroaching sand, lost green levels amongst the dunes, and woodlands clothing limestone slopes where ivy-covered crags show through the waving leaves. Directly under Nicholaston Woods lies a shallow sheet of water, turning into a reed swamp, and small salt marshes that are a vivid green in winter and yellow with iris in early summer. Patches of willow scrub and low alder trees are dotted here and there. The dune 'slacks' behind the front rampart of still forming dunes, are rich in rare plants. Over 100 different species have been recorded, many of them extremely uncommon. The area is unique in Wales and has only two or three counterparts in the whole of Britain.

As you climb up along the sandy tracks towards the shelf of farmlands behind the woods, you can look for the ruins of the old Nicholaston Church. Here once again you have an old medieval church buried by the great medieval sandstorms. You will have difficulty in finding it under the tangled trees of Crawley Woods. As a local farmer told me: "We had a devil of a cloud-burst some years ago—the water poured down off Cefn Bryn and smothered

those ruins—You'll have a job to find them. And it never was
'Crawley Woods' until the buses came."

To the public, however, Crawley Woods has come to stay. No
visitor now uses the name Nicholaston Woods for this attractive
part of the Oxwich landscape. But Nicholaston is still there—a
scatter of houses back from the main road which you would be
hard put to recognize as a formal village. The church at
Nicholaston is right on the South Road; and it is a rich example
of what the Victorians could do to an old Gower church when
they were really given their head. The old church, as shown in a
drawing in the Rev J. D. Davies's *History of West Gower*, was a
typical Gower construction, and, next to Llanmadoc, the
smallest in the peninsula. It had clearly gone into decay. As
Professor Freeman pontificated, "the rudeness of these churches
is wonderful". There was no "rudeness" left after the 'reconstruction' was completed in 1894, with the money and encour-
agement of Miss Olive Talbot of the Penrice family as a
memorial to her father C. R. M. Talbot. The Rev J. D. Davies was
loud in his praise of the results.

> This church may be said to be the most elaborately treated ecclesias-
> tical building in Wales, if not in the West of England. The Sanctuary
> is paved with polished Devon marbles. The steps leading to the Altar
> are of black, red and white marble respectively. In the cornice, angels
> are represented playing on various instruments. The angel figure in
> the north-east corner is a likeness of the architect's daughter, she is
> represented striking the chord on her harp, and is about to join in the
> chorus, the other figures being represented in the act of playing.

But the great joy of the reconstruction is the hanging pulpit,
decorated with alabaster figures of some of the giants of the
Oxford Movement including Keble and Pusey. The reredos is a
wonderful religious firework in stone, all pink alabaster, with
red and green Irish marble shafts. There was a time when such
exuberance in ecclesiastical architecture would have met with
my stern disapproval. Today, after a diet of streamlined concrete slabs, which is all the modern church architect can supply,
I am not so sure. Nicholaston Church now seems a confident,
rich Victorian jewel-box. We shall not look on its like again. As a
matter of fact, it is rather difficult to look on it at all today, for, at
the time of writing, Nicholaston Church has to be kept locked—
a sad comment on the vandalism and total disrespect for their
heritage that infects some visitors to Gower today.

After Nicholaston Church the main south road runs for nearly a mile towards the west, with glimpses of Oxwich Bay on your left and Cefn Bryn your faithful companion on your right, until you suddenly come to a turn in the road and rub your eyes. There before you are the towers of a castle that is certainly not marked on the map and is totally ignored by the records of Gower history. Rightly so, for it is not a castle at all. It is an eighteenth-century folly, built by the squire of Penrice, Thomas Mansel Talbot. It incurred the censure of the Rev Henry Skrine in his tour of South Wales in 1798. He did not think much, anyhow, of Mr Talbot's decision to build the present fine eighteenth-century mansion of Penrice under the shadow of the old castle ruins, and was even more scornful of "the design which has introduced the principal approach through the fictitious fragments of a modern ruin, within sight of an ancient castle whose ivied walls, overhanging the beach, seem to frown defiance at this newly created rival". I have a feeling that the reverend tourist may not have been invited to dinner at the castle and therefore took a jaundiced view of the whole affair. He had already found Gower "in general a rocky and uninteresting district" and could not understand why Mr Talbot had chosen to desert his other house in Glamorgan, "the noble seat of Margam in the midst of a populous and plentiful county to form a fairy palace in a dreary and desolate wild far from the resorts of men and near the extremity of a bleak peninsula".

Today it is extremely easy to understand why Mr Talbot preferred Penrice to Margam. Poor Margam, once so romantically beautiful, is threatened by motorways and the ever-expanding giant steel-works of Port Talbot. But the great park around Penrice Castle, the deep woodlands that encircle it, and the strange marshlands at its foot are still intact and form a landscape composition that is hard to beat in the whole of South Wales. If you add glimpses of the prow of Oxwich Head and the rich brown background of Cefn Bryn, the whole area lying at the back of the dunes of Oxwich Bay takes on an Arcadian quality, a place that seems a piece of totally untouched nature. This is an illusion. Most of what we see and admire in Oxwich was the deliberate creation of Thomas Mansel Talbot and his successors, and in spite of the partial break-up of the Penrice estate in 1950, the park and the great house still remain.

It has a long history going back to the first days of the Norman conquest of Gower. Penrice—a corruption of the Welsh

'Penrhys'—was one of the original 'fees' into which the conquered portions of the peninsula were divided. We know that it
was in the possession of Sir Robert de Penrice in the twelfth
century and the family held it for generations as Lords of
Penrice, Oxwich and Port-Eynon. The first Penrices may well
have been responsible for the early 'ring'-type bailey whose
overgrown banks, called the Mounty Brook, can be seen behind
Penrice village. The same family must have been lords of
Penrice when the time came, in the middle of the thirteenth
century, to replace these early 'castles' with something far more
permanent. All over South Wales the old-fashioned 'motte-and-
baileys' were giving place to stone. The Lords of Penrice
followed the fashion and moved out from the old Mounty Brook
to a far more defensible site about three-quarters of a mile away.

They chose a fine position on the craggy hill which rises
behind the modern mansion of Penrice. The earliest portion to
be constructed was the round keep, which was built around
1240. The great gatehouse and the curtain walls belong to the
last quarter of the thirteenth century. The main hall and the
residence of the castle owner were grouped around the keep.
Penrice had become the largest and most impressive castle in
Western Gower.

By the time the castle was completed, times had changed.
Gower had fallen firmly into the hands of the conquerors and the
new defences were never seriously put to the test. Apart from
the Glyndwr rising in the early fifteenth century, when the
rebels made a ruinous foray in the peninsula and damaged most
of the castles, Penrice went quietly out of history, and equally
quietly out of the hands of the original Penrice family.

With the death of Sir John de Penrice the estate, which now
included Oxwich, passed to his daughter and heir, Isabel de
Penrice. She married Sir Hugh Mansel and so the Mansels
became the Lords of Penrice. The Mansels were already a family
of some repute, but at first their holding in Gower was comparatively small—just the knight's fee of Nicholaston. They
soon put that right. I always think of them as the Hapsburgs of
Gower, pursuing the same tactics as the famous imperial
family, of whom it was said "*Alia belli gerant tu, Felix Austria,
nube*"—"Others wage war, you, happy Austria, marry". The
happy Mansels married with equal effect and added half Gower
to their estate. Sir Rice Mansel obtained great office under
Henry VIII, and found the old castle out-of-date and

inconvenient. Sometime around 1500 a *columbarium* had been added in a tower against the curtain wall. These big pigeon-houses were important in the days when there was no method of keeping many cattle through the winter and allowed for some variation in diet. The *columbarium* at Penrice is one of the finest examples still extant.

But Sir Rice was rising in the world. The Mansels had backed the Lancastrians in the bloody Wars of the Roses. Philip Mansel had fought for Henry VI and lost his life in the cause. When the Lancastrians finally triumphed in the person of Henry VII, the Mansels were on the winning side again. Sir Rice Mansel (1487–1557) was one of the Tudor 'new men'. He was a successful soldier and was in an excellent position to benefit out of Henry VIII's sale of monastic lands after the Dissolution. He bought Margam Abbey and at a stroke became one of the great land-owners of Glamorgan. For the next 350 years, the two great estates of Margam and Penrice remained in the Mansel family's hands. Sir Rice soon abandoned the old Penrice Castle and built himself a fine new castle at Oxwich, on the wooded hillside overlooking the little village and with a glorious view of the bay. The new Oxwich Castle was a big, fortified manor-house in the style of the day.

So the Mansels flourished until the eighteenth century. Then through the marriage of the Rev Thomas Talbot, of Laycock Abbey in Wiltshire, to Mary, daughter of Thomas, the first Lord Mansel, and through an entail to the will, the great estates of the Mansels passed to the Talbots. From now on the family were the Mansel Talbots.

It was Thomas Mansel Talbot who revived the old glories of Penrice. He built the classical-style house on its fine site under the lee of the old ivy-clad castle. He filled it with pictures both Dutch and Italian, some of which were shipped directly from Italy to the Mumbles. The nucleus of the collection is still at Penrice, which is now in the possession of Mr C. Methuen-Campbell. It contains paintings by Terborch, Salvator Rosa, Bruegel and Van de Velde. As the well-known expert, the late Mr Rollo Charles noted: "When Thomas Mansel Talbot shipped his treasures to Gower in the later part of the eighteenth century, there can have been few other houses in Wales—none perhaps except Wynnstay—where such things could be seen!"

Thomas Mansel Talbot did not stop at collecting pictures. He decided to turn the whole landscape around him into a work of art. Inevitably the name of 'Capability' Brown has been attached to the 'improvements' at Penrice, but with slender evidence. The park, however, is very much in the free, English style so much admired in the period. The course of the stream was dammed to make a series of small, ornamental lakes. Groves were planted and woodlands created to make romantic vistas. The work was continued under his son Christopher Rice Mansel Talbot, who was also a connoisseur besides being a huntsman, yachtsman and a distinguished politician.

Today great estates of this sort are hard to keep up. Changes are inevitable. The ornamental lakes in the park have relapsed into wildness in sections, but this seems to suit them as much as their original formal beauty. The winding road that turns down off the south road at the Towers and follows the wall of the Great Park, brings you out onto the road through the lakes and marshes. This is the way most people come to Oxwich, driving through the waving reeds in high summer. A strangely beautiful place! There is nothing like it in Gower. I have a peculiar affection for it, for it was here that I caught my first fish. We had been given a pass by the estate and cycled down over the dusty and lonely road—how strange that sounds today—to spend a long afternoon amongst the rustling reeds. I remember the quiet of the marshes, and the thrill of seeing a majestic heron flying slowly past us over the mirrored water as if he owned the place. As well he might, for there is still a large heronry at Penrice, one of the two left in Glamorgan. The warblers chirped in the reeds, and then suddenly I actually had a fish on the line. A big roach—big, anyhow, as roaches go! We immediately cycled home in triumph and demanded that the fish be cooked for supper. Mother did her best and loaded it with every spice she could. No one can claim that the roach is a gastronomic treasure. But I had caught it at Oxwich myself and was determined to eat every bit of that muddy, bony horror. "How did you enjoy it?" mother inquired. "Excellent," I lied gallantly. I can still taste that roach every time I drive through the avenue of swaying reeds. I am glad to think that I will never fish at Oxwich again, for the marshes are now a Nature Reserve.

The marsh road ends at Oxwich itself. Here, in summer, all solitude also ends. Oxwich is one of the most popular of the Gower bays. Big car-parks have been laid out behind the dunes, which fill up early on hot summer week-ends. Caravan sites lie in the fields or in the woods behind Oxwich Castle. Oxwich in summertime is a tourist's 'honey-pot'. I hope that you can visit it in the off-season for Oxwich still has delights to offer besides the pleasure of the wide beach and its sands. Park your car and walk first through the little hamlet and out onto the path that leads through the woods beside the sea to the church. St Illtud's Church must be one of the most charmingly sited of all Gower churches, buried in trees with the steep wooded hillside above and the sea below. The chancel is tiny and this led some authorities to suggest that it could be the original Celtic cell. The tower, as usual in Gower, is a battlemented, military affair which dates from the thirteenth century, as does the nave. The decorations in the chancel were paid for by Dame Lilian Baylis, the powerful and legendary director of the Old Vic. She spent most of her holidays on a nearby farm and came to love the little church of St Illtud. The primitive font was brought to Oxwich by none other than St Illtud himself. At least, that is what the legends say, and standing alone in the quiet of the church under the old-fashioned oil-lamps and with the murmur of the sea outside, who would disbelieve them!

There is mystery, too, attached to the stone effigies of a knight and his lady which lie in the richly arched recess on the north side of the chancel. The naughty children of Oxwich used to be told that, if they did not behave, they would be put into the "Doolamurs' Hole". This gave the clue to the identity of the couple buried there. The "Doolamurs" must have been the De La Mares, of the family who held Oxwich from the original conquest until their lands passed by marriage into the Penrice estate, and then—inevitably by marriage again—into the ever-open hands of the Mansels. The effigies date from the late fourteenth century. Legend again has it that the knight and his lady were drowned in the bay.

But then, strange stories do tend to cling to this church, so curiously placed in the deep woods above the waves. When autumn comes and the wind sighs amongst the falling leaves, you remember the story set down by the Rev. J. D. Davies, who was born in the Rectory.

My oldest brother, now deceased, when a lad of about thirteen or fourteen years of age, had been out one evening with my father fishing in the bay. It was late when they landed, and by the time they had finished mooring the boat, it was nearly twelve o'clock. They had just gained the top of the beach, which here abuts the narrow path leading to the church, when my brother happened to look

behind him, saw what he described to me, to be a white horse walking
on his hind legs and proceeding leisurely along the path to the church
gate; having called my father's attention to this strange spectacle, he
turned round for about a minute, and watched the creature, or whatever it was, until it reached the gate, or rather the stone stile by its
side, which the animal crossed, apparently without the slightest
difficulty, still going on its hind legs. The uncanny thing then disappeared. The only remark my father made was, "come along". They
were soon inside the rectory, which was only a few yards off. The
strange adventure was never afterwards spoken of by my father, nor
alluded to in any way. I have often been on the point of questioning
him about it, but some vague feeling of undefined alarm always
prevented me!

Could this be the Gower version of the Celtic 'Kelpie'—the
sinister white horse that comes out of the sea? The rector was
wise to say nothing but "come along", for Oxwich rectors were
used to seeing curious sights about which they were well
advised to keep silent, especially in the smuggling days. The
journals of Rector Collins (1771–1814) are full of entries such as:
"March 13, 1794. Thursday. Smuggler chased into the bay by
the *Speedwell*, cutter, and taken. Sixteen men landed and saved
some casks, etc., etc.—several of the parishioners got very
drunk on gin."

Or later, in 1803: "Oct. 20. An armed vessel came into the bay,
said to be a privateer from Liverpool. People alarmed." Then the
entry for the next day. "Fine day. Late in evening Press Gang
came to Oxwich. Secured a lighterman, prizemaster, clerk,
surgeon and boy belonging to the privateer, who were on shore
all night, and privateer on hearing it, set sail towards the west."
Poor chaps! They were, no doubt, being made happy with some
of Oxwich's famous smuggled gin when the dreaded press gang
arrived. It must have been an unfortunate accident, for one
thing is certain—no one in Oxwich, from the Rector to his
humblest parishioner, would ever have given a 'tip-off' to the
authorities.

Rector Collins was unlucky in his rectory. It was undermined
by the sea but Mr Mansel Talbot came to his rescue and built the
present rectory, which still stands, in all conscience, near
enough to the waves. This building at least met with the
approval of the censorious Rev Henry Skrine, who wrote of the
new rectory: "Mr Talbot has erected a neat, roomy building for
the accommodation of the incumbent of Oxwich, which is

delightfully situated on the shore near the sea, so as to command an awful prospect of its extensive surface, calculated to incite, in the reverent pastor of the flock, and the rising olive branches around his table, daily sensations of wonder and filial obedience towards the Creator of the Great Deep."

I wonder what the Rev Henry would say if he saw the Rectory today, and what pious reflections he might assign to the "olive branches" who occupy it now. For today the old Rectory is given over to power-boat enthusiasts and a channel of plastic buoys is marked out over the beach. Now, it is no good pretending that you can sympathize with every form of human sporting activity. The speed-boat scene has always seemed a little strange to me. No doubt people get pleasure out of roaring about on dead calm water, but somehow I get worried when the speed-boat enthusiasts use the sea as an extension of the M4, especially in Gower. Ah well, no doubt the sinister white horse, the Kelpie of Oxwich, will eventually appear amongst the speed-boats to set things right!

Luckily the woodlands that run out to Oxwich Point from behind the church, together with the salt-marsh and the pools under Penrice Castle, have become a National Nature Reserve. A visit to the pools area requires a permit but the walks through the woods out to Oxwich Point provide open access to the point itself. This is still an unfrequented place and well worth a visit. There is a well-run information centre for the Reserve on the car-park behind the beach.

The single street, or rather lane, of the village runs back from the sea past the little school, the Post Office and the General Store. There is no pub in Oxwich. I have a feeling that the spirit of John Wesley may have something to do with this for he came frequently to Oxwich on his preaching tours. Perhaps I do him an injustice, for there was no pub here even in his day. He noted in his journal for 31st July 1769: "After I had stayed a while in the street (for there was no public house) a poor woman gave me house room. Having had nothing since breakfast, I was very willing to eat and drink, but she simply told me that she had nothing in the house but a dram of gin!" I wonder where the gin came from!

Wesley, in his heart of hearts, found Gower more sympathetic than the rest of Wales. He stayed at a cottage, now called the 'Nook', which is marked with a notice of his presence. He made another entry in his journal, "Here all the people talk English

and are, in general, the most plain, loving people in Wales."
Saints have their little vanities like lesser men. Maybe Wesley
was relieved to find himself, after long and difficult journeys, at
last among people who genuinely understood what he was
saying. It is only fair to add that when Hywel Harris and other
Welsh-speaking giants of early Welsh Methodism entered
Gower Anglicana, they were regarded with the same slight
bewilderment as Wesley was in Gower Wallicana.

Close to the school a road turns up westward through the
woods towards Oxwich Green. It bears the curious name of
Gander Street. The old antiquarians hailed the word street as a
sure proof that a Roman road of some sort ran this way. The road
passes the romantic ruins of Oxwich Castle, the splendid fortified manor-house that Sir Rice Mansel built for himself when
the first Penrice Castle had become old-fashioned. In its turn,
Oxwich Castle has fallen into decay. A farmhouse roosts amid
the ruins and the cows wander around the site of the Great Hall
and tractors occupy the wreck of the servants' quarters. But you
can still see traces of its former glories. Oxwich, like Penrice,
had a *columbarium*, although it is not so well preserved. Its
finest feature is the beautifully carved coat of arms that Sir Rice
Mansel set up over the doorway. You look at it, and remember
the tragic story of the death of Anne Mansel. She was killed
underneath it in the celebrated riot of 23rd December 1557.

The story is familiar to all Gower lovers for it is extensively
documented in the records once kept at Penrice Castle and now
in the National Library of Wales. It is worthwhile retelling, for
it gives a vivid glimpse into the life of Gower in Tudor days. The
peninsula was still a rough-and-ready place, where a great man
could accomplish much by personal power.

A wreck had occurred of a French ship in Oxwich Bay. The
Mansel family, particularly the branch that lived at Henllys
near Llanddewi in West Gower, were always first on the spot
when a vessel came ashore. The loot was quickly transferred to
Oxwich Castle. Back in Swansea, the news reached Sir George
Herbert, who was a leading citizen of the town and had certain
rights over wrecks along the coast. He rode hurriedly down to
Oxwich with a body of armed men and attempted to wrestle the
spoils out of the hands of the Mansels. Old Sir Rice was away but
his son, Edward, put up a spirited resistance. Sir George
Herbert had already marched through the village, broken into
several houses where booty had been stored and had put the

proceeds for safe keeping in the church. Now he tried to storm the castle. Poor Anne Mansel, who was an elderly lady at the time, came out to reason with the attackers, but one of the followers of Sir George Herbert, Watkyn John ap Watkyn, flung a stone which killed poor Anne on the spot. Immediately the cry of "Murder!" was raised by the defenders and Sir George Herbert, shaken by the incident, called off his retainers immediately.

The riot was in the old medieval tradition but the sequel was more in the true spirit of Tudor government. The long arm of the Law reached out after Sir George. He was haled before the Star Chamber, heavily fined and made to return the goods. The great lords might feel that they could still live in remote Gower as they did during the Wars of the Roses, but the Tudor "Big Brother" was always watching them.

From Gander Street the road comes out, past too many caravan parks, onto the little patch of Oxwich Green and then slides down to the dead end of Eastern Slade. This little hidden valley has some holiday houses tucked away unobtrusively, and goes down to a small cove which has sand exposed when the tide is low. Slade is a secluded place. From here you look back to the high prow of Oxwich Point. This is 249 feet (95 metres) high and is the second highest headland in Gower. Only Pwlldu is higher. A great viewpoint and a walker's reward alone. The car road ends at Slade, although from here you can walk through the lanes to Horton. But already you have spilled over from the Oxwich preserves into the world of Port-Eynon. You have now to drive back, past Oxwich Green and the castle, down the hill again into Oxwich village.

Little Oxwich used to be a gem. Every cottage was thatched and in them lived the old quarrymen who carved the lucrative limestone from the headland. I think that there are only one of two thatched cottages now left. The village comes under heavy pressure in the summer, but the visitors seem mainly to concentrate on the sands. They do not seem to come back inland, on the narrow and delightful road that leads up to the little hamlet of Penrice. As you drive you look down on the whole wide sweep of Oxwich Bay, the marshes and the long line of coves and headlands running away to the east. And how finely the cliffs of the Great Tor shine over the sands!

You pass old farmhouses like that of Pitt, with enormously thick walls, rounded chimneys and a record going back to the sixteenth century. I think it was from Pitt or from a similar farmhouse in the locality that came the first Gower chest I ever saw. These were the solid oak chests that were made in preparation for the happy marriage of daughters of the well-to-do farmers. They were also known as courting chests. They were usually made of Welsh oak, a tough material which was not easy to carve. In fact some experts have maintained that the curious decoration of roses, tulips and birds which are characteristic of the Gower chests might have been carved years after the chests had been originally made. We know that travelling wood-carvers used to go through the Welsh countryside offering to smarten up your furniture. But somehow, the carvings seem more eighteenth-century in feeling. One expert detected a touch of the Low Countries about them.

The late Dr Iorwerth Jones, a great lover of Gower with an extensive knowledge of its past, came forward with an even more fascinating interpretation. He suggested that the symbols such as the 'rose' and the 'bird' represented 'the king over the water'. South Wales certainly had a society of Jacobite sympathizers, the Sea Sergeants, who met at regular intervals to toast the Stuart Pretenders, and we know that the Sea Sergeants had members amongst the squirearchy of Gower. But when Bonnie Prince Charlie actually landed in 1745, none of the Sea Sergeants of Gower went off to join him. They seem to have contented themselves with drinking his health from the society's beautifully engraved glasses—and perhaps carving more Jacobite emblems on their Gower chests! It would be interesting to see what Arthur Negus would have to say if a Gower chest came before him in "Going for a Song".

Another interesting old farm lies on the road to Horton that turns off just before the village of Penrice. This has the intriguing name of Sanctuary, called locally the Sentry. Records that go back to the year 1400 show that it was then occupied by a David Crompe, but it seems clear that the Sanctuary belonged to the Order of St John. It was one of the many Sanctuaries in South Wales which were administered from the main house of the order at Slebech in South Pembrokeshire. The order possessed numerous estates in Gower and the Sanctuary could well have been the place where the records were kept and where the visiting priors put up on their tours of inspection.

There is no doubt at all about the origin of the name of the next junction on the road. Hangman's Cross commemorates the place where poor unfortunates were hanged for sheep-stealing.

It has an equally grim alternate name—Cold Comfort. For the moment we turn back to enter the warm, comforting little hamlet of Penrice.

Of all places in Gower, Penrice most retains the atmosphere of old Gower a hundred years ago. It is small—only a few houses grouped around the village green and an ancient church backed by tall elms. There are enchanting glimpses of Oxwich Bay far below. The early Norman fortification of the Mounty Brook, or Mounty Bank as most people call it now, lies at the back of the houses, covered with bracken and brambles. The base of the old cross is still on the green. The village pound is also there. Nothing now seems to stir in Penrice, and it is hard to think that the Penrice Fair was one of the great rowdy glories of the old Gower calendar. Charles II, no less, confirmed its charter and the Merry Monarch would have approved of the universal merrymaking that went on—even to the rows of inebriated gentlemen laid out like corpses to recover in the churchyard as the dancing went on outside the King's Head. All is now deep peace. There is no inn or fair at Penrice, and the rooks come drifting across from the great trees in the nearby park and caw in raucous chorus around the church.

St Andrew's Church is large for Gower and has escaped the usual drastic reconstruction that passes for restoration in so many Gower churches. The surprisingly big porch is a curious feature. It seems to have been added to the church at a much later date than the nave and chancel. The inner door of the porch is very strange. It seems to stand almost free from the jambs of the archway within a massive oak frame propped up by masonry inside. The porch might have been used as the village school or general meeting place. Inside the church is a memorial tablet to Lady Blythswood who died aged ninety and was the 'chatelaine' of Penrice from the 'twenties to the 'forties. She was a notable defender of the Gower scene. I have a picture of her when she must have been over seventy, striding along with a party of us who were concerned about the route of the new power poles on Cefn Bryn. One word from Lady Blythswood and they were immediately driven off the skyline. We who enjoy Gower today owe a great debt to her.

From Penrice the road north plunges steeply down into a secret valley. Here, surrounded by great trees, is the western gate of Penrice Park. You can catch a glimpse of the mansion itself through the gates. In the old days Penrice mill worked in this green dingle, and the lane that leads up from it, along the wall of the park to the south road, still rejoices in the name of Penny Hitch. A man used to stand at the corner to hire out an extra horse to farmers struggling with a heavy load up from the mill. When you see the steepness of the hill up which the poor horse had to pull his load, a penny does not seem any too big a fee.

I always like to pause in this out-of-the-world spot. It is so green, so secluded, so buried among the trees then, when I stand beside the little stream seeping through the rich ferns, I have no difficulty at all in believing the celebrated fairy story centred on the farmhouse of Eynonsford and related with such charm by the old Gower historian, the Rev J. D. Davies. What a delightful historian he is, by the way; always ready to break off from some learned discussion on the complicated pedigree of the Mansels or the true nature of the 1383 grant by John de Penres of a burgage in Swansea to John and Margaret Horton, to record some curiosity such as the great rock slip in Oxwich in 1855 or how to make Bonny Clobby, the special pudding eaten at the Rhossili Mapsant. Eynonsford lies up the little heavily-wooded valley from the point where we are now resting, and near a wood with the mysterious name of Benjy's Leg. You can also easily get to it off the main road. But the more pleasant way lies through the lost path through the woods then up from the 'ford of Eynon' over the stream.

Here the fairies of Gower, the 'Verry Volks', made a spectacular appearance. Many of the old Gower farmhouses were of the Long House type. The cattle stalls and the stables were under the same roof as the family accommodation, and very often the farmer could sleep in his cupboard bed and look down into the stalls and see if all was well with his fine beasts. Very unhygienic, no doubt, but very convenient on cold, rainy nights. Well, on this memorable night, the good farmer of Eynonsford was dreaming in his snug cupboard bed when it seemed, in his dream, that he heard the sound of sweet music and the patter of dancing feet and gay laughter. He opened his eyes and saw a sight that made him dumb with surprise. The cattle stalls were filled with tiny people, all enjoying themselves up to the hilt, laughing and singing and above all climbing up onto a fat ox, the farmer's pride, that was quietly chewing the cud in his stall. The little Verry Volks hopped all over him, slid down his back and spun around on the top of his horns to the sound of a fiddle.

Occasionally the men would show their agility by kicking off each other's caps amid great laughter. Then the farmer saw, to his alarm, that great preparations were now being made. The Verry Volks were going to slaughter his ox and eat it! Wisely, however, he kept quiet.

Sure enough the Verry Volks slaughtered the ox in a highly professional style and then sat down and ate it up. There seemed to be thousands of them everywhere, and each tiny Verry Volk seemed to have a gigantic appetite. The farmer resigned himself to seeing the last of his noble ox, but he was in for another surprise. No sooner was the feast over than the Verry Volks set to work and collected every bit of the skin and the bones; all except one small bone in one of the legs of the ox. When the Verry Volks failed to find it, they were almost in despair. They sat down, lamented, tore their hair in vexation, cried out in their grief and even swore—a thing the Verry Volks were never expected to do in Gower! The farmer afterwards reported that, though the confusion and excitement were beyond belief, "yet the noise was not louder than the ripples of the sea on the sea-shore on a fine summer's day".

There was no help for it; the tiny bone could not be found. But swiftly the Verry Volks refitted the skeleton together, drew the skin over it and then disappeared. The farmer looked again and rubbed his eyes. There was his fat ox quietly munching in his stall as if nothing had happened. Only, next morning, the farmer noticed one curious thing. His ox was slightly lame—in the very leg from which the Verry Volks had lost the small bone!

After that, you will walk up Penny Hitch on a dark evening, not daring to look back over your shoulder. The lane meets the south road near the Penrice Estate Home Farm. The entrance gate opposite, that leads into the park, is familiar to all Gower people, for the great annual event of the Gower calendar takes place in the wide meadow beyond—the Gower Show. The time is usually August before the harvest is safely in, and all Gower is there. If you want to find out how varied Gower agriculture can be, this is the place to see it on parade. And how great have been the changes in the sixty years that I have been coming to Gower! I remember the time, before the First World War, when motor transport had not yet spread through the farming world. Cattle and sheep were still driven on the hoof to market at Swansea, and the flocks from the farms furthest west would take two days at least on the journey, and they spent the night here, around the Home Farm at Penrice. Then, with the growth of the lorry business around 1930, some of the farmers in the well-drained parts of south Gower realized that, as the peninsula was comparatively frost-free, they had an excellent chance in the early potato market. Gower soon became a rival to south Pembrokeshire in this business. Today Gower farming is amazingly varied, from potatoes to cereals. Even the commons have come into their own with the increasing demand for Welsh ponies. And you will see them all in the parade ring.

The Home Farm at Penrice thus has always had a special place in Gower agriculture. You will notice the well spread buildings, and the elegant red-bricked granary perched on its stone stilts—an early nineteenth-century architectural delight. Close to the Home Farm, on the other side of the road as you go west, is Kettle—or Kittle—Top. This is a huge, rounded grassy mound, so regularly constructed that you feel it must be a giant tumulus and wonder why no one has excavated it. When I was a small boy we always used to keep a special look-out for it from our bus on the way to Port-Eynon. Old Mr Grove had told us that there was treasure hidden in it, and that a door would open in it for the man who discovered the secret password of the Verry Volks. Eynonsford is, after all, very near! There was also the story that, in the days of the long bow, an archer stood on Kettle Top and loosed off an arrow which killed a man standing on the walls of Penrice Castle. Pulling the long bow with a vengeance! The truth, as always, is more prosaic. Geologists point out that this fine, swelling, magical-looking mound was formed by glacial action. It is simply a natural accumulation of glacial sand.

All through this chapter we have been aware of the long ridge of Cefn Bryn in the background. The time has now come to ascend it. Half a mile along the South Road from Penrice Home Farm we turn off to the right through little Reynoldston. Almost immediately we come to a change of landscape. On one side of the road are the fields and scattered houses, some of them new, for Reynoldston is after all within easy motoring reach of Swansea. On the other side of the road the sheep graze and the curlews call amongst the bracken. The long whale-back ridge of Cefn Bryn rises before us. We turn the car just before entering Reynoldston proper and climb the long slope that leads up to the brow of the ridge. They used to call this the Red Road in my early cycling days, for before the tarmac was laid on, we could see the Old Red Sandstone rock underneath. Cefn Bryn is, as it were,

Near Paviland

The carved limestone of Mewslade Bay

Rhossili and Worms Head

Limestone fossils in a stone wall, Rhossili

Llangennith Church

Burry Holms from across the Burrows, Llangennith

The Old Lighthouse, Whitford Point

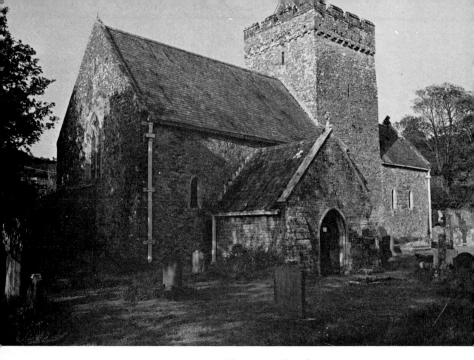

Cheriton Church

Weobley Castle

The Old Mill, Llanrhidian

The loneliness of Llanrhidian Marsh

the crest of the great Old Red Sandstone rock-wave that swells up from underneath the limestone. The limestone therefore lies like a white surf all around the strong red rock in this high centre of Gower.

As soon as you reach the brow of the ridge, stop. Perhaps I need not advise you to stop, for you will do it automatically. You feel compelled to get out of the car and take in one of the great views of Gower. I must also add that there will be a great many people doing the same thing on summer days and cars line the road or are parked on the turf. But there is five miles of ridge here and it is a matter of minutes to lose the crowd. Then you can take in the full splendour of the surrounding landscape. Gower stands back, as it were, from the main mountain mass of South Wales. To the north the hills rise ever higher over the lower ground of the coalfield, in wave after wave until they reach the high ridge of the Carmarthenshire Vans (2,600 feet) on the horizon. It is also possible to pick out the strange, flat-topped summits of the Brecknock Beacons (nearly 3,000 feet), if you know where to look for them behind the rounded hills of mid-Glamorgan. You can also see the houses of Swansea's suburbs in the same direction! Close at hand, to the north, is the Burry Estuary, with its vast sand-banks over which the Loughor River makes elegant curves when the tide is out. Llanelli is visible on the far bank, its old forest of chimneys from the tin-plate works now very much thinned.

Looking westward, the cone of the summit of the Preseli Hills in Pembrokeshire peeps up forty miles away, while the bold outlines of Gower's own hills, Rhossili Downs and Llanmadoc Hill, are close at hand. To the south the coast stretches from Oxwich Point away to Pwlldu and the Mumbles. On clear days, the long line of the Devonshire coast is in full view, with the high ground of Exmoor prominent and the graceful tors behind Ilfracombe.

As dusk falls the lighthouses start to flash far away along the Bristol Channel. It is fascinating to pick them up by the frequency of their flashing. Farthest away to the east is Nash Point on the Glamorgan coast (occulting every thirty seconds). Closer to hand, out in mid-channel is the Scarweather lightship (one flash every five seconds). Along the Devon coast are Contisbury Foreland (six flashes every fifteen seconds), then the Bull beyond Ilfracombe (three flashes every ten seconds) and Hartland Point (six flashes every fifteen seconds). On very clear evenings the bulk of Lundy Island stands out to the south-west with the two lighthouses of Lundy North and Lundy South. They are a good thirty-five miles away. Round to the west and much nearer is the Helwick lightship (one flash every ten seconds) and over the shoulder of Rhossili Downs comes the flash of the St. Govan's lightship of the Pembrokeshire coast. The light circuit of the Channel is complete. All these details are included in that most remarkable of publications, the Admiralty's *West Coast Pilot*. A glance through it will show you how tough the coast of Gower can sometimes be for sailing men.

The ridge of Cefn Bryn is highest at its eastern end above Penmaen where it reaches 609 feet (186 metres), but it runs fairly level all the way for over four miles. There is a grassed-over reservoir tank near the highest point, and the Holy Well on the northern flank has now been enclosed to add to Gower's water supply. This is a splendid ridge-walk, with the wild ponies always somewhere in sight and all Gower at your feet. Mr Talbot certainly chose a right royal way to bring his hounds a-hunting to Penrice. The open common is at its widest at the centre of the ridge where it slopes down northwards to Cilibion and the Broad Pool. This northern slope can also be the wettest if you are thinking of walking off the ridge.

Not far from the point where the 'Red Road' crosses Cefn Bryn is one of the showpieces of Gower, Arthur's Stone. This famous cromlech lies a short stroll away from the summit of the Red Road, and is finely sited looking down onto the Burry Estuary. The old neolithic builders knew how to choose a place fit for a royal burial. The capstone is enormous. It has an estimated weight of twenty-five tons and was originally even bigger, since a large part of the western side has fallen away. This central burial chamber was probably covered by a vast barrow. So notable a cromlech was bound to gather legends about itself. King Arthur, they say, was one day walking in Carmarthenshire when he felt a pebble in his shoe. He flung it away and it fell on Cefn Bryn. St David, too, has his share in the story of Arthur's Stone. He was worried by the religious awe in which it was held, so he drew a sword and clove it in twain. Well might the good saint be worried, for Arthur's Stone (Maen Ceti in Welsh) is reputed to have magical powers. All the old Gower folk knew that, on Midsummer Eve, it would creep down to the shores of the Burry Estuary to drink. Its fame spread far and wide, and apparently the Breton troops in Henry VII's army, after landing at Milford Haven en route to Bosworth Field, marched eighty miles out of their way just to pay their respects to it.

On the south-western slope of Cefn Bryn lies the scattered village of Reynoldston. It is the highest-placed village in Gower, visible from afar with the white walls of its houses. There is a village green, where the geese gabble and wander past you with that contemptuous manner possessed by geese the world over. The King Arthur Hotel looks out to Cefn Bryn—what other name could a hotel dare to have here in Arthur's country! The church by the green is dedicated to St George. Needless to say, it has been thoroughly restored. Reynoldston is a pleasant, airy place, and when I was young we were always taught to regard it as the capital of Gower. There are very few north-south routes across the peninsula and two of the main ones end up here. So, as the Gower Society's handbook puts it in a nutshell, "if you want a doctor, a policeman, an ambulance, a fire-engine, a butcher, a baker or a bag of fertilizer, this is where you can find one". You will also find the Welsh ponies standing in the middle of the road and the sheep nibbling on the green, or in your front garden if you are not careful. I was once told by a resident of Reynoldston that he was convinced that the Cefn Bryn sheep were not sheep at all but antelopes in woolly pull-overs.

The ancient house of Brynfield is probably the oldest house in Reynoldston. It has been remodelled and almost rebuilt, but it is noteworthy because it was one of the oldest homes of the famous Gower family of the Lucases. The Lucases originally came from Essex but they were well established in Gower by the end of the Middle Ages. Legends gathered thick about them. The earlier Lucases were bold, quarrelsome, adventurous men and as marrying as the Mansels. We shall meet the wild Lucases of Port-Eynon later. Brynfield was their starting point, and the Lucas clan spread extensively through West Gower. Their most conspicuous monument is the mansion of Stouthall, built by John Lucas around 1790. The usual date of 1754 given for its construction does not appear to be correct.

John Lucas seems to have been by far the most cultivated and artistic member of his line. The main branch of the family had already expanded from Brynfield to Stout Walls, a sturdily built Tudor-type fortified mansion. John Lucas decided that he needed an elegant residence on which he could lavish "all those soft beauties which taste could dictate". He pulled down the old

Stout Walls. In their place rose the present mansion of Stouthall. It may look a little four-square when you see it through the beech trees as you drive along the South Road, but it has some delightful features inside. The decoration was Adam in style and feeling. The hall rose through two floors and was surrounded by a gallery. The library was a splendid, elliptical room, nobly decorated. I remember it as a great mystery, for it had a secret doorway hidden in a bookcase which allowed John Lucas to slip into his library unnoticed, when undesirable guests were announced in the nearby drawing-room. But all Lucas houses inevitably have mysteries. There was talk of strange, blood-stained floorboards in the north-west bedroom, and of an underground passage from Brynfield to Stouthall, so big that a man could ride through it on horseback.

In the grounds you come across strange 'follies'—"Mr Lucas's whims", as the old Rector of Reynoldston called them. There is a fake druidical circle that you see on the side of the road down from Reynoldston. John Lucas obviously thought that no gentleman's park in Wales was complete without one. He also buried a favourite horse under a mound, which he surmounted with a carved, sepulchral stone he had discovered somewhere else in Gower, and which may date back to the tenth century. Today Stouthall has been repainted after looking rather neglected for many years. It will be used by the children of the London borough of Merton as a County Educational Centre. I hope they will all be told the stories that made Stouthall so thrillingly mysterious when we were young.

The little village of Knelston is the next one along the road from Stouthall. The ruins of the old church lie behind the farm. It was dedicated to St. Taurin, and the advowson and tithes of Knelston had been presented to the monastery of St Taurin in Normandy by Roger Beaumont, Earl of Warwick, when he was Lord of Gower back in the twelfth century. By the time of Charles I the little church was beginning to fall into ruin. Today it is almost buried in a tangle of ivy and thick briars. A few fields beyond is a huge standing stone or menhir. There are two others further north near Burry Farm. The Knelston Stone is a giant block of Old Red Sandstone from Cefn Bryn. There it stands, alone in this quiet place, hauled upright maybe over 3000 years ago. Who can tell for what mysterious purpose? Are these three ancient stones linked together in some way? Could there even have been an avenue of the Avebury type?

In any case, this has always seemed to me to be a strange, tucked-away part of Gower. Cefn Bryn comes to an end and sinks towards the valley of the little Burry stream. Beyond lie the high downs of Rhossili and Llanmadoc. But here we are, as it were, in the centre of a saucer-like depression with its centre at Llanddewi, a quarter of a mile beyond Knelston. Llanddewi was once a place of importance. It might have been the birthplace of Bishop Henry de Gower, who was a man of power and influence in the Middle Ages in South Wales. And near at hand are several old manor-houses and small castles now fallen from their high estate, but which once played prominent parts in Gower history. Llanddewi Church is dedicated to St David. It has been restored—what Gower church has not?—but it has a curiously remote feel about it, maybe because it stands back from the road and you enter it from a wide farmyard. The old farm buildings show traces of their Tudor windows. The church is hardly symmetrical and the gnomon of the sundial on the porch is placed obliquely to compensate for the curious line of the church, as if the early builders had had difficulty in finding the true east. The tower has battlements and a saddle-back roof.

From Llanddewi a long, secret lane leads westward towards the high Rhossili Downs. This is a remote, unfrequented part of Gower, deep country where you must leave your car and walk to enter it. The farms you pass on the way seem incredibly old and solid. Old Henllys—the old court—has the huge Gower-type chimney and a collection of ruined cellars once used by the Henllys branch of the Mansels for their smuggling enterprises. The inevitable Lucases were established still deeper into this lost land at Kingshall. Beyond is the loneliness of Rhossili Downs.

Just south of Llanddewi, and close to the south road is another of these old family seats now changed into a farmhouse, but retaining the grandiloquent name of Scurlage Castle. Again you can see traces of the ancient walls amongst the farm buildings. What a turbulent life they all led in this little corner of Gower, these Scurlages, Lucases and Mansels, feuding, inter-marrying, running contraband ashore on dark nights, varied by an enjoyable riot or two in handy churchyards. The authorities at Swansea throughout Tudor and Stuart times, were constantly worried by the goings-on in West Gower. But Llanddewi and its ring of 'castles' was a long way from Swansea over execrable roads. The little kings of West Gower, for a long time, did very much as they pleased.

How far off it all seems today, as you drive along the busy south road, and go carefully around the right-angle bend near Llanddewi. That bend was also a landmark on the old bus journey to Port-Eynon and Rhossili. If you were perched on the roof of the old Vanguard bus you were given a warning shout from the driver's seat, "hang on up there, boy". And the old bus, piled high with everything under the sun, swayed perilously around, changed gears with a glorious, grinding sound and then set its bonnet on a southward course. Once you passed Scurlage you felt you were really in the far, wild west of Gower. Ahead was Port-Eynon and its bay, the great line of cliffs to Rhossili, Worms Head—and a new chapter in this book!

5

Westward to the Worm

With Port-Eynon we come back to the sea and its splendour, for, after Oxwich, Port-Eynon Bay is the second largest indentation on the Gower coast. We have already taken a quick glance at it when we came over Oxwich headland to Slade. Now we look closer at this fine sandy bay, backed by its line of dunes and ending in Port-Eynon Point, with the low bank of Skysea almost melting into the sea. Port-Eynon village lies on the western end of the bay with its sister village of Horton on the eastern side; the two of them separated by the sand-dunes of the Burrows.

Horton tumbles down steeply to the sea. It has grown in recent years. They have even got a hotel there now, several in fact, and an ever-increasing mass of tents and caravans in the summer. Fifty years or more ago, things were different. Horton had a slightly superior air over Port-Eynon where visitors were concerned. Port-Eynon could be reached by the early 'chara-bancs' and Saturday trippers were actually seen on the sands. Horton did not encourage such goings-on, and the hill that dropped down into it was too steep for those early buses. In any case, Mr Joseph Chamberlain had set the seal of respectability on it by bringing his family, including the future Prime Minister, Neville Chamberlain, to Horton for a summer holiday.

The Port-Eynon of those far off days seemed to me more friendly, entirely because this was the place where we spent *our* holidays. We 'visited' Horton, we were 'at home' in Port-Eynon. Even under its modern covering of new bungalows, caravan sites and car-parks I can still recognize the old Port-Eynon I first grew to love, where every cottage was thatched and the gardens were surrounded by white-limed walls; where we went in procession to draw water from the well behind the churchyard and where we climbed the hill to watch the smith at work in the smithy at the side of the road, hammering red-hot horseshoes on his ringing anvil.

Port-Eynon takes its name from a Welsh prince of the eleventh century who was supposed to have built a castle on this spot. The little village is clustered around the church, like so many of the settlements in Gower that owe their rise to the Norman conquest. It is, however, still dedicated to St Cattwg. Again we lament a drastic Victorian restoration, but at least the 600-year-old, greenstone font is Norman, presented by the Abbot of Llantwit Major. In the nineteenth century the life of Port-Eynon came to centre more and more around the Point. Here are the little cottages of Crowders Quay, the old Lifeboat House and the romantic ruins of the notorious Salt House.

Port-Eynon, a hundred years ago, lived on oyster-fishing and limestone quarrying—there are plenty of traces of this last activity overgrown by brambles on the headland. The limestone trade was carried on with the Devonians and you can still pick up the bluish-green stones on the foreshore which were brought as ballast in the Devon trading ketches. The oyster fishery was also important. In the middle of the nineteenth century there were forty oyster skiffs sailing out of Port-Eynon. The price of the oysters had risen from 1d. for two dozen in 1800 to 1d. for a single oyster in 1870. They were whipped off to Bristol by steam packet from Swansea. The best fishing area lay south of the Helwick buoy and was known as 'Bantam'. The Port-Eynon oysters were regarded, in a survey made in 1674, as the best in Britain. The perches, where the oysters were kept after dredging and before sale, still make a regular pattern on the foreshore. The season lasted from September to early March and in the summer the men worked in the quarries. But by 1870 the great days were over. The beds seem to have been thinned by over-fishing. The last recorded haul took place in 1879, after which many of the boats moved eastwards to the Mumbles.

But the strong tradition of seamanship remained and assisted the establishment of a lifeboat in 1884, movingly named *A Daughter's Offering*. The wild coast that runs westwards from Port-Eynon has always been a shipping graveyard, especially in the days of sail, and in 1883 the terrible wreck of the steamer *Agnes Jack* off Port-Eynon Head shocked everybody. The rockets failed to reach the twenty-one survivors clinging to the rigging, and when the mast collapsed they were all flung into the boiling surf, and drowned in a matter of minutes before the eyes of the helpless watchers on shore. This led to the building of the Lifeboat Station and the beginning of the distinguished career of the Port-Eynon lifeboat. In 1906 a new thirty-five-foot self-righting lifeboat, the *Janet*, was sent to the station. This was the boat I remember so well as a small boy, when it was brought out for practice-launching every summer. It was moved down over the beach by a team of four stalwart horses supplied by the near-by farmers, and we used to watch with awe as Billy Gibbs, the coxswain, and his men all armoured in oilskins, were dragged into deep water with the great horses breast high in the waves. Then the oars were got out and the heavy boat was rowed towards the Point. How tough you had to be, in those days, before you became a member of a lifeboat's crew!

Alas, there came a sad day in January, 1916, when the Glasgow steamer *Dunvegan* went ashore on Oxwich Point in a howling gale. The Port-Eynon lifeboat rowed to the rescue, but found that the rocket apparatus could not reach the ship-wrecked men. The lifeboat turned for home as darkness came down. The great wind drove it eastward and in the tremendous seas off Pwlldu Head the boat capsized twice. Most of the men managed eventually to get back into the boat but three of the men were never seen again—the coxswain Billy Gibbs, the Second Coxswain William Eynon and Lifeboatman George Harry. Billy was sorely missed. He was a bachelor who used to play the concertina for us; a gay, friendly man. The white marble statue of a lifeboatman stands in the churchyard in memory of the lost men. It almost seems to dominate the village.

The Lifeboat House is now a Youth Hostel. Somehow I think that Billy Gibbs, with his kindness to children, would have liked that. Beyond the row of cottages on the point, you come to the ruins of the Salt House, which won such notoriety in the sixteenth and seventeenth centuries. Most of the scanty walls you now see belong to some nineteenth-century cottages which were built on the site, but below is the wreckage of the deep cellars which are a vital part of the Salt House story. The first Salt House was built in the reign of Henry VIII by David Lucas of Stout Walls for his son, John. This John Lucas was a wild, violent youth, described in those curious legal family documents known as the 'Lucas Annotations' as a young man "of fine and bold front, and very comely in the eye and brave as a lion", but lawless "and of fierce and ungovernable violence". He married Joan, daughter of John Grove, Gentleman, of Paviland, but this did not stop him for a moment from embarking upon a splendid career of piracy and general mayhem, in which he was ably assisted by his younger friends from the Llanddewi area; Mansels from Henllys, Scurlages from Scurlage Castle and George ap Eynon of Brynfield. This little piece of Western Gower was certainly no quiet country corner! It seemed to breed a very wild race of men. John Lucas was obviously a man with a magnetic personality—a naturally born leader.

At Port-Eynon, according to the ancient account, he made "a great stronghold of ye Salte House, with its battlements and walls thereof all round, reaching even unto the clift and the rocks ... and storing said stronghold with arms, and also rebuilted and repaired another stronghold called Kulvert Hall near thereunto, in the rocks, and rendered both inaccessible, save for passage thereunto through the clift". Inevitably there were stories of a secret passage underground, "whereof no man was tolde the mouthe thereof", between the Salt House and 'Kulverd Hall'. John Lucas went on his happy, roistering way with enormous success for years, safe in his Salt House, "so called because the outer battlements thereof were washed by ye salte water at ye flow of ye waves". His illegal activities, when he "succoured ye privates and ye French smugglers and rifled ye wrecked ships and forced mariners to serve him", may have infuriated the distant authorities in Swansea and London, but Lucas gaily maintained that, like Gilbert's Pirate King in *The Pirates of Penzance*, he was in the business for the best possible motives, "engaging his handes in much violation of all laws, but always for our Lord the King". And like a Gower Robin Hood he attracted the country folk to his side "by dividing to them the spoiles and maintaining the poor in the country rounde".

And he passed on his piracy business to his son, Phillip. Those great cellars of the Salt House were kept full of illicit liquor and smuggled goods for generation after generation. The Lucases held Port-Eynon in their firm grip and the villagers looked up to them with a sort of fearful admiration. There was a faint deviation into legality at the end of the seventeenth century, when the John Locas of the time discovered that he could produce paint material by grinding down some of the iron-stained shales that form a small inlier of Millstone Grit among the limestones of Port-Eynon. He prospered exceedingly, "possessed much wealth in moneys, and did buy skiffes at Swansey and Bristol to bear ye painte mineral away, to number of five, from near Ye Salte House which was his forefathers, across the seas to Apeldor and to coasts upon the high seas to Britain Very and Ogmoore and Nash and Kardiffe and even to Bristol".

But there was plenty of the Lucas fire in him. Once, when a Lucas ship was cast ashore at Nash in Glamorgan, the Lord of the Manor was rash enough to assert his rights to the paint mineral in the wreck. He reckoned without the Lucas speed of action. John Lucas immediately put to sea, swept the unhappy Lord of the Manor aside and possessed himself, not only of cash in compensation for his paint mineral, but of Margaret Seys as his bride as well.

The end of the Salt House and of the Lucases of Port-Eynon was in keeping with the wild, reckless, romantic lives they led. In 1703 John Lucas lay dying, so they say, when the memorable storm of that year raged through Britain. It struck Gower with tremendous force, lashing the coastline with huge seas. The waves crashed in on the Salt House. John Lucas's skiffs were flung on shore, the cellars were flooded and lightning struck the Salt House. The Lucases' stronghold and their fortunes perished in a manner worthy of Edgar Allan Poe. And now only the salt-encrusted, bramble-covered ruins remain.

But what of their other stronghold, 'Kulverd Hall'? To solve this mystery, one of the most intriguing in Gower, we climb up behind the old Salt House, past the old quarries where the scars are all mellowed by time, onto the open, breezy plateau of Port-Eynon Head. Near the site of the old Lookout; and right on the edge of the cliff, is the memorial stone to Dr Gwent Jones and Stephen Lee. I always pause here and take off my hat, for these were the two founder-members of the Gower Society. I remember how many of the things we now treasure in Gower were saved by their efforts and those of the society they inspired. They were the perfect counterparts; Stephen Lee precise, full of knowledge of the law and history, formidable in battle against the 'spoilers', and Dr Gwent, Welsh, equally knowledgeable and full of heart-warming enthusiasm. I remember, in the early days of BBC broadcasting in Wales, inviting Gwent to describe in Welsh the Ireland v. Wales Rugby International. He arrived hotfoot at the studios with only a few minutes to spare and I flung him remorselessly onto the air. Without rehearsal! He began, but in his haste he made a pardonable verbal slip. In spite of my frantic signals he kept on referring to Ireland, not as *Iwerddon*—the Welsh word for Ireland—but as the *Iddewon*, the Jews! It was a memorable report. For the first time in sporting history Israel beat Wales by nine points to nil. Gwent, in his kindness, bore me no ill will.

Near the monument you walk over the top of the cliff, or so it seems, for a narrow path plunges down a steep, limestone slope towards the sea and then turns suddenly into a deep cleft in the rocks. You look up and gasp with surprise. The whole of the cleft, which reaches almost to the top of the cliff, has been filled with a wall of masonry, pierced by two rectangular windows at the bottom and two circular windows at the top. This is the celebrated Culver Hole and there is nothing like it on the whole coast of Britain, as far as I know. An eerie place, when the sea drives in through the cleft and the wind sighs through the bleak windows; even eerier when you struggle carefully down the slippery path and worm your way up into the Hole itself. The semi-darkness is filled with the rich aroma of rotting seaweed and the wall at the bottom of the cave is ten feet thick. A flight of steps climbs the great wall, but there are no signs of any floors having been constructed. Instead a honeycomb of rectangular holes fills the inner wall and the thick sides of the rectangular windows.

What was Culver Hole? A smuggler's lair? But by the nineteenth century smuggling demanded secrecy as the very essence of the business. We have seen that the inhabitants of old Port-Eynon knew every trick of the trade. The last place they would have chosen for a storehouse of smuggled goods would have been a structure like Culver Hole, which may be concealed on the landward side but could be seen miles out to sea from any smart Revenue cutter. Could the wild Lucases have used it? We remember the reference in the Lucas Annotations to 'Kulverd Hall', which is obviously Culver Hole. Spelling, in those days, was distorted by local pronunciation. But would the Lucases have needed it for piracy? They already had the Salt House nicely fortified and were as bold as brass about their activities. They needed no secret stronghold.

Perhaps the curious, square holes in the walls may give us a clue to it. They are certainly like those in the *columbarium* at Penrice. Culver is an old English word for pigeon. Could Culver Hole have been a giant pigeon-loft for the Salt House? The Lucases certainly had the power and resources to build it, and pigeons were a welcome addition of fresh meat to the diet, in the days when you had no means of keeping lots of cattle through the winter. By the end of the eighteenth century there were no more pigeon houses built. "The mangold wurzel killed them", the old people used to say in Gower. But before that happened, Culver Hole would have been a worthwhile proposition as a pigeon-loft. Who can be certain? The family records of the Port-Eynon Lucases was swept away, like their Salt House, in the great storm. Again, the place—or something like it—was mentioned in a thirteenth-century document. Could it have been the *columbarium* of that early Port-Eynon castle? Culver Hole remains to puzzle and astonish us.

From Culver Hole a path leads back around Port-Eynon Head at a low level towards the Salt House. It passes over the top of a great, open cave which is difficult to enter except at low water. This is a bone cave in which were found the bones of mammoth, woolly rhinoceros and red deer. As you turn the corner back to Port-Eynon you will be looking out over a curious part of the coastline.

Stretching out from the Salt House is a little spit of low land called Sedgers Bank, on which the last Lucas was supposed to have been buried. Further out towards the sea's edge lies the group of lichen-covered rocks called Skysea. Both Sedgers Bank and Skysea remain uncovered at high tide, although the spume and froth of the sea buries Skysea in a gale. When the tide is low the whole shore changes character. A great wilderness of rock-pools is exposed, holding mysterious deep hollows and seaweed swaying softly in the clear waters. It is the same all around the south-western coast of Gower. The sea has cut back a level shelf into the land which is exposed at low tide. This shelf is surprisingly wide in places—on Port-Eynon Point, for example, in Overton Mere and around Worms Head. I cannot think of any other section of the Welsh coast with quite the same type of feature. These rock-pools of Gower have always been an enchantment to me since the days when Mr Grove first took me crabbing at Port-Eynon.

Now crabbing in Gower is at once a sport and an art. The 'huvvers and scarras', as the old Gower folk called the wide levels exposed at low tide, are the perfect hiding place for crabs and lobsters. The lobsters retreat into holes in the deeper pools. To persuade them to leave their hiding places the Gower crabber employs a hook at the end of a pole. I had my first hook made for me by the blacksmith at Port-Eynon, and long and learned were the discussions about the best shape for a crabbing hook. Mine turned out to be what the experts call a 'penny-bender', for a penny coin could exactly fit inside the curving point of the hook. With it I went proudly off to follow in Mr Grove's footsteps.

Those old crabbers did not waste their time looking under every ledge or into every pool. Mr Grove would always stop at a certain point beyond Skysea and say, with confidence, "There'll be a big 'un here after that low tide, boy." He would stand in the pool, find the deep hole under the swaying seaweed and push the pole in as far as it would go. Then he would advise me, "Now watch, boy. Never shuve or thrash 'un about. Just give 'un a hint with the hook and he'll come." Then, after a delicate move to get the hook behind the deep-hidden lobster, Mr Grove would just touch it—no crude pulling that could break off claws and limbs—and out would float the lobster, antennae waving, claws open and coloured a lovely, suffused blue with touches of red and white, one of the most beautiful sights I know on a seashore. Sometimes the lobster would hold the hook firmly in his claws and come gently out. "Grab 'un by the back of the neck and then he can't touch you." Into the sack he would go and away we would march towards Overton Mere and, as often as not, we would see a figure ahead of us working pools on the edge of the tide. "Charlie Phillips from Horton," said Mr Grove. "He's getting to be a good 'un."

For the old crabbers respected skill and kept bright the names of the great men and women of the past, like Billy Hopkins of Port-Eynon, who had the reputation of going crabbing by moonlight, and Kitty "Crabs" of Oxwich. Charlie Phillips lived on to become one of the great crabbers, still going strong in his seventies when he took me out on the Rhossili Crabart. They knew every hole almost by name, some of them with strange histories. One hole out beyond Skysea Mr Grove would never touch, although it looked deep and good. "No good came of meddling there," he said. It was years after that I was told of the terrible experience of John Taylor of Port-Eynon. He was working this hole and was convinced that he had a giant lobster. He spent a long time getting it out. To his horror it was no lobster that came floating from the hole, but the body of a poor sailor, one of the lads drowned in the wreck of the *Agnes Jack* in 1883.

Is the crabbing as good as it was? The general opinion seems to be that it is not. Too many people work the pools too often. Crabbers are no longer locals. You can easily slip down from Swansea by car to work the low spring tides and many of these

newcomers take undersized crabs and berried lobsters. It seems
a pity. These rock-pools of Gower, rich in sea-anemonies, rare
seaweeds, shrimps and darting blennies need the crabs and
lobsters to complete their delights. And what rich colours they
display when the sun strikes through the clear water held in the
white hollows of the limestone.

At dead-low water the crabbing grounds stretch away to the
west, well beyond Overton Mere, and except for two points near
the Horse Rock and Thurba, they fringe the coast almost to the
famous Crabart at Worms Head. But now we are talking
already about the Magnificent Five Miles—the best section of
the whole Gower coast. The time has come for us to step out
along the delectable path that leads from Port-Eynon Head to
the Worm.

If Cefn Bryn offers the finest ridge walk, this is unquestion-
ably the finest cliff walk. You can start it at Overton, the little
hamlet beyond Port-Eynon, well back from the cliffs. It was once
a secluded place with a few old farms and a village green around
a duck-pond—the 'ton' or settlement 'over' Port-Eynon. There
are now new villas and bungalows along the road, but Overton
still seems the real gateway to the cliffs. A grassy lane leads
westwards and opens out onto the cliff-tops; or you can cut down
the path that leads southwards onto Overton Mere. I think I
prefer this lower path. At dead-low water you get an astonishing
view across Overton Mere, where the limestone strata seem to
lie as regular as tram-lines. The path stays on the edge of the
lower rocks and you see plenty of evidence of the concrete-like
structure of the raised beach. A curiously square-cut cave
marks the impressive Overton Cliff. This lower path is a
romantic way in places, as it climbs over the spines of the high
limestone ridges, then down into the narrow cracks of the
'slades'. Just over three-quarters of a mile from Overton Mere
you come to the bone cave of Longhole, originally excavated by
Colonel Wood in the 1860s. Further exploration produced
evidence that man had occupied it in Upper Palaeolithic times.
Your path leads ever westward and in the spring the gorse is a
glorious yellow and a whole galaxy of flowers dapple the limestone slopes, from rock-roses to ladies' slippers and pink
centaury.

You look out to sea, and even on the calmest days you can
detect the sinister presence of the Helwick Sands by a line of
darker blue. Once the wind blows they break white with foam.

They run due west from Port-Eynon Point for five miles and the East Helwick buoy off Port-Eynon shows how narrow is the channel between the shoal and the shore. The western end is marked by the Helwick lightship which you can pick out on a clear day low on the horizon. The presence of the sands indicates that, for all its summer beauty, this is a cruel coast for ships, and among the rocks of this savage shore you can see below you remains of past wrecks. A ship's boiler is wedged in a crevice below the end of Common Cliff and once you pass it, you will see the line of the coast trending a little to the northwards, allowing you to sense the great cliffs ahead and see, in the distance, the strange, compelling outline of the Worms Head itself. Past cliffs and down gullies the path twists its way, and every cliff and slade has its local name—Red Gut, Kilboidy, Eastern Slade, Western Slade, Groaning Slade, the last one aptly named as you labour up it on a hot day.

And so you come to the showpiece of the walk, Yellow Top and the Paviland Caves after doing a narrow and thrilling 'cat walk' half way up the face of the rocks. The lower path is forced inland here for the cliffs now plunge sheer into the sea. But you can also reach Paviland from the main Rhossili road at Pilton Green. A sign points to a public footpath which leads down through the fields around the handsome Paviland farm, a holding which goes back to the first days of the Norman conquest of Gower when it formed part of one of the twelve original 'knight's fees'. The path comes out at the top of the steep little rocky slade that cuts down to the sea beside the cliff of Yellow Top, easily identified on the right by the yellow and orangey lichen on the upper rocks.

The cliff top itself is a place that can take you far back into the past. Here are the low mounds that mark the line of the defences cut across the promontory to make a small fort. There are several of these little promontory forts along this western part of the south Gower coast. Many of them were carefully excavated by Mrs Audrey Williams, before the last war. From the pottery and other finds, she was able to date them to the Iron Age B Glastonbury Folk around the first century B.C. What a hard life they must have led in these tiny settlements. They had a few huts of wattle, or perhaps of turf and stone on this exposed headland. They hunted and fished and kept cattle and sheep. And all the time they lived in fear of raiders by night and enemies by day. For this was the period of the warlike Celts, of the fighting aristocracy with their splendidly decorated swords and helmets, made beautiful by the skill of the La Tène-style artists. Little of this was likely to have come the way of the few dwellers in the lonely forts of the Gower cliffs. They only knew the dangers it brought.

And 200 feet below them, although they could never have had the remotest idea of it, lay hidden a far earlier human settlement, going back at least 18,000 years. This is the famous bone cave of Goats Hole at the foot of the great cliff of Yellow Top. It is not easy to reach. The safest plan is to wait for low water and scramble down the rocks at the foot of the little valley, and then across the area of tidal rock-pools and so on up into the cave. When the tide is in—and it seems to be in more often than not—the approach is much more spectacular: you walk on a sheep-path across the steep, grassy slope that forms the western side of the valley. Then carefully down a steeper, barer slope on to the top of the level rock that runs out towards the sea, under the big rock wall. You step across a narrow fissure that separates this level rock from the wall, with the sound of the sea roaring up at you through the crack at high tide. Then you do an exposed traverse upwards and around the corner which brings you out onto easier ground.

The traverse made a strong impression on all the excavators of Goats Hole. Professor Sollas, who re-excavated the cave in 1912 with important results, was never tired of relating its perils. I remember him as the Professor of Geology at Oxford around 1930 and he told me, with a chuckle, "I once got stuck on that cliff and couldn't move up or down. It's the only rock that has ever stumped an Oxford Professor of Geology." The truth is that, once again as at the Great Tor, you can do it easily if you know a little about rock climbing or have a steady head. The holds are real 'jug handles' and the traverse is enjoyable. If you are nervous on steep slopes, leave it alone and wait for the tide to fall.

When you reach it, the cave itself is not particularly large and there is a neighbouring cave that is even smaller. But Goats Hole impresses you by its setting. The cliffs soar upwards and you feel as isolated as if you were on a lonely rock in mid-ocean. Then there is its history. It was one of the first British bone caves to be explored seriously and it produced a sensational discovery that shook the whole scientific world of the time. The excavator was the Rev William Buckland. In 1823, when he started digging at Paviland, he was already a famous man, the first Professor of Geology to be appointed at Oxford and a future Dean of Westminster. He was a most attractive personality, full of buoyant enthusiasms, sometimes expressed with a gaiety surprising in a sober and highly influential clergyman. When he heard from Miss Talbot of Penrice and Lewis Dillwyn of Swansea about the discovery in a remote part of Gower of a cave full of bones, nothing deterred him from hastening to the spot. At Paviland he dug carefully, indeed far more carefully than was usual in his day, and he recorded his discoveries in detail.

His report was published with a delightful cross-section of the cave showing a gallant excavator perched precariously on a ladder in the middle of it. The excitement was intense when Buckland unearthed part of a headless human skeleton, with bones stained brick-red in colour, amongst other bones belonging to long-extinct animals such as the mammoth and the woolly rhinoceros. Buckland thought that the skeleton was that of a female and inevitably she was christened the "Red Lady of Paviland". There were other objects lying alongside the skeleton, including shells and a collection of small ivory rods. In addition, flint tools and scrapers were found and a skewer made from the metacarpal bone of a wolf.

Two great questions immediately demanded an answer. Who was the "Red Lady" and how did she come to be buried amongst the remains of long extinct animals? Buckland solved the first problem by suggesting that the lady had been buried in Roman British times. Could she have lived in the 'British' camp on the headland above the cave? She might even have been the priestess of the tribe, even a witch, and some of the bones found with her were for divination, as was common in Gower in early days. As for the bones of the 'elephants' and other extinct animals—well, there was always the Deluge. In 1823 Buckland published his *Reliquiae Diluvianae, or Observations on the Organic Remains contained in Caves, Fissures and Diluvial Gravels, and on other Geological Phenomena attesting the action of Universal Deluge*. These strange bones were not contemporaneous with those of the "Red Lady". They had been swept there by the vast, swirling floods of the Biblical Deluge.

It is easy to chuckle at Buckland at this distance of time but, in his day, the Deluge theory had not been completely discredited. He was a pioneer and pioneers are bound to make mistakes. When Professor Sollas re-dug Paviland in 1912, he

had behind him all the knowledge accumulated during ninety
years of archaeological advance. He had no difficulty in deciding
that the skeleton was not that of a woman but of a youth of the
Cro-Magnon race, the earliest recognizable form of modern man
as distinct from the Neanderthal type. The youth had been
formally buried, and perhaps his bones had been stained with
red ochre in some primitive life-reviving ceremony. This is the
earliest recorded burial in the caves of Gower.

Paviland is still important to the archaeologists of our own
day, for it has produced by far the most extensive series of flint
and other material. Up until 1960 it used to be thought that
man, in some form or other, beginning with the Neanderthal,
had lived here in Paviland and other Gower caves more or less
intermittently through the many fluctuations of the last
(Würm) glaciation. A pleasantly tidy timetable had been laid
down in which, in South Wales as in South-western France,
cultures succeeded each other steadily through 60,000 years,
starting with the Mousterian, through the Aurignacian and the
Solutrean, to the Cresswell culture, which in Britain corresponds to the continental Magdalanian. Now all is in the melting
pot again. The new methods of radio-carbon analysis have given
much more accurate datings, and Dr C. B. M. McBurney of
Cambridge and the Prehistoric Society have taken a long, cool
look at the old picture. They have carried out new investigations
at Cathole at Parc le Breos and re-assessed the Paviland finds.

As a result, a new picture of early man emerges in South
Wales and above all in Gower. Dr McBurney has shown that the
occupation of the caves was much less intensive than was pre-
viously thought. They may have been uninhabited over far
longer periods, and the small bands who were bold enough to
enter Gower when the ice allowed it, did not all come from the
classic areas of South-west France. They may have travelled
across the dry English and Bristol Channels from deeper in the
Continent. The sequence now seems to be as follows. The first
few arrivals of the Neanderthal race lived in Paviland about
70,000 years ago and left behind them their characteristic flake
tools. Then came a long period of advancing ice, when the whole
of Gower was denied to man. He next reappears about 30,000
years ago, coming from Central Europe and was of the modern
type. The 'industry' of these newcomers seemed to have combined the Mousterian and Aurignacian traditions and even
anticipated the Solutrean of South-west France and Spain. Our

red-ochred youth of Paviland would have belonged to this race, about 18,000 years ago. Again man had to retreat before the ice, and did not come back to Gower until after 13,000 B.C. when we meet the Cresswellian culture. But Dr McBurney points out that this culture did not necessarily come directly from France. To me, all this points to one unwelcome conclusion. We are never likely to discover in the Gower caves the sort of thrilling cave painting they found in France and Spain. There will be no Gower Lascaux. Our early men were from the duller areas of Central Europe!

I am almost tempted to return to the good Dean Buckland! And to Kit Morgan in his *Wanderings in Gower*, with his vivid description of the Red Lady of Paviland, witch-like and leaping from crag to crag screaming maledictions from the highest rock. Although Mr Morgan would not earn many marks from conservationists or from members of the Gower Society for the following, now notorious remarks, on Paviland.

"It is glorious to be here in merry June! No end of sport can be had—hundreds of gulls and cormorants build their nests here. It is really worth a day's journey to have a few hours fun on these rocks ... but the sportsman must be here before the end of June—taking with him plenty of ammunition and not forget a few bottles of stout."

Happily there are still plenty of cormorants around Paviland and the great cliffs further west, with their young in June clustered on the rocks at the edge of the waves, black-suited and looking like deacons in a group gravely discussing a sermon after chapel. Or suddenly changing character as they spread their dark cope-like wings to dry—miniature Count Draculas!

Beyond Paviland the coastline maintains its splendour, and it is good to know that much of it is now safely in the hands of the National Trust. There are exciting rock formations like the curious, triangular rock of the Knave and the impressive overhang near Deborah's Hole. This small bone cave is easily entered, and produced the usual Pleistocene fauna and some worked flints. On past Red Chamber, and the narrow gullies of Foxhole and Butterslade, to the impressive limestone prow of Thurba Head. This is probably the most precipitous of the Gower headlands. It really does seem to drop nearly 200 feet sheer into the sea. It guards the eastern side of Mewslade Bay.

Mewslade runs down from the hamlet of Pitton on the main Rhossili road. The old Great Pitton Farm was one of my pleasures in my camping days. Fifty years ago the great kitchen was unchanged, with the marvellously hospitable Beynon family entertaining you as you sat in the inglenook by the deep fireplace with a hanging forest of hams overhead. Old Mr Beynon knew all the Gower stories and had a deep passion for music. His son Gwyn had the right singing voice to go with the stories and his daughters supplied a beautiful chorus. The fire blazed in the same place as it had done for over two hundred years. I do not think Mrs Beynon ever let it out.

The path runs down the slade alongside the high limestone wall and the crags guard it on either side. Then suddenly you come to the bay, one of the most dramatic in all Gower. Thurba Head rises sheer from the sands, and westward are the equally impressive slabs of Jacky's Tor. At low tide you can walk from Mewslade past Jacky's Tor then on under the towering crag and razor-edged ridge of Devil's Truck and the imposing rock towers of Lewes Castle, into Fall Bay. Tears Point guards Fall Bay to the west and its slope seems gentle and kind after the succession of limestone pinnacles and sheer rock that lift up so boldly from the sands of Mewslade and Fall. No wonder that this is the rock-climbers' favoured spot in Gower. Here is Gower's rock scenery at its stunning and most accessible best. The bathing is good too!

But when the tide comes in, the sands at Mewslade and Fall disappear completely. They are lost to the bather for at least two hours around high tide. In winter, the strong south-westerly winds drive in the Atlantic rollers and Mewslade fills with flying spray and the thunder of the waves.

And all the while, awaiting us around the corner of Tears Point, is the climax of the Magnificent Five Miles walk, the Land's End of Gower, Worms Head. The Worm as everyone calls it in Gower is one of the most remarkable headlands in Southern Britain. If you see it from the coastguard's station on the point, or better still from high up on Rhossili Downs, Worms Head lives astonishingly up to its name. It really does look like a vast serpent, coiling its way out to sea and rearing its huge head as it makes its final plunge westward. No wonder the old seamen, seeing it rising high above the waves as they came up-channel, called it the Worm (O.E. *Wurm*—dragon). And the resemblance is increased when the wind drives in from the west, making the spray leap up from the blowhole on the Outer Head and sending out a strange, hollow, booming sound that can even be heard in the village of Rhossili itself. "The old Worm's blowing, time for a boat to be going", the old Gower fishermen would say.

You look at it and you feel an irresistible urge to walk out to the very furthest point, but there are one or two dangers on the way. At high tide the Worm becomes an island, but about two and a half to three hours after high tide, the ebbing waters begin to leave bare the Shipway, the channel between the Worm and the mainland. It is a rough but practical crossing and you must remember that you only have roughly five hours on the Worm itself. So go across as the tide ebbs. Too many people have found themselves marooned on the headland, for once the tide turns and begins to come in, it does so at a surprising speed. The same warning applies if you go out after crabs or lobsters onto the long spur of low-lying rocks away out beyond the Shipway and again exposed at low tide. This is the Crabart, a great crabbing ground, but for experts only.

Once across, you find yourself on the biggest of the three sections or humps of the Worm, the flat-topped Inner Head. The grass here used to be close-cropped when the farmers kept sheep on it, the only section of the Worm used for this purpose. The grass had a great reputation for producing specially tender mutton, and the Talbot family of Penrice used to graze a flock on the Worm between September and March. Mr Jack Bremmel remembered that one was killed every week for the Talbot table, and a local farmer had the job of going over between tides every Tuesday to bring it onto the mainland, where it was collected by a castle servant. It was killed at Penrice if the family were in residence. If they were at Margam or London it was sent to them, live, in a specially made travelling box. The Talbots declared that there was nothing to equal "Worms Head mutton", as it had been fed on grass salted by the sea winds. Today sheep graze again on Inner Head and the wheatears nest in season in the salt-sprayed grass.

You make your way from Inner to Middle Head over a section of rough rock where you should take a little care, although there is no real difficulty. Towards the end of the Middle Head, a little off the path, you will find a sort of natural balcony with a grand view out over Rhossili Bay and the sea birds screaming and nesting below. You cross from Middle to Outer Head over a huge natural arch of limestone, the Devil's Bridge.

The Outer Head is a place apart, a rare patch of the earth's surface, full of wild air, the crying of the gulls and the thunder of the sea. The strange, tormented hissing and booming from the Blow Hole is always in your ears, and you remember the words of the old traveller Leland, writing in the days of Henry VIII, about the wonderful "Hole at the Point of Worme heade, but few dare enter into it, and Men fable there that a Dore withein the spatius Hole hathe be sene withe great Nayles on it: but that that is spoken of Waters there rennynge under the Ground is more lykely".

At the very end of the Worm, the cliff plunges sheer over a hundred feet into a sea that never seems to be still. In May and June the ledges are alive with breeding birds—razorbill, guillemots and kittiwakes. And on a ledge about fifteen feet above highwater mark, right under the final precipice, is a bone cave, but you have to be a bit of a climber to reach it. The scramble can be dangerous if you have had no experience on rocks. Yet excavators have dug here and uncovered the bones of mammoth, rhinoceros, reindeer and cave bear. The passage goes deep into the rock, and when I crawled in it (and never dared to go to the end), I thought again of old Leland's story of a vast, secret passage running all the way under the sea from a valley in Carmarthenshire.

"There is also a Hole by the Heade of Wendraith Vehan, where men used to enter in, and there they say by spatius Waulks, and that thens gouithe one way under the Ground to Worme hedde, and another to Cair Kennen Castle."

Worms Head is now a Nature Reserve and visitors should be aware of the treasures of bird life and flowers it holds. I was glad to see that the climber's guide book declares that "no climbing should be done; any attempt to do so would bring down a storm of protest from all naturalists, the Gower Society and other watchful bodies. . . . Something should remain sacro-sanct."

Amen to that! But those who walk out to the end of the Worm usually go there in the right spirit. Even the organizers of the astonishing mass picnic of Bethel Sunday School, Llanelli, to Worms Head in 1854 sensed that this was an occasion which demanded a certain amount of reverence. The excursionists marched to the docks to the singing of the chapel choir, and embarked on two vessels captained by members of the Sunday School. The sea was calm and they landed safely on the Worm.

They said prayers for their deliverance from the terrors of the deep and then tucked into the huge hampers they had carried ashore. Meantime they found that the tide was going down, so the whole four hundred of them scrambled over the rocks of the Shipway and marched, singing, along the cliffs to Rhossili village. The Rector saw this astonishing invasion coming from afar and ordered the church bells to be rung in welcome. It was long remembered in Rhossili that the village well was drunk dry.

Back from your own excursion onto the Head, you follow the path of this singing Sunday School for a short mile along the cliffs to Rhossili village, and all the way, as you walk on the springing turf, your eyes are turned to the north. You are now overlooking the full sweep of Rhossili Bay. Some people claim that this is the finest unspoilt stretch of sands in Southern Britain and when you see it from the cliff-top as the tide goes out, you can well believe it. The sands run in an arc three miles long from Worms Head, on under the steep slope of Rhossili Downs out to the islet of Burry Holms. They are wide, unsullied and fringed by the white rings of the waves.

The keen fisherman will look down on them and remember that this is a great bass-fishing area. The Welsh record bass of 16lb 3oz was caught on Rhossili Sands by George Micklewright. There is exciting fishing also from the ledges that were carved out of the rock on the headland in the old quarrying days. The rock platform just around the northern corner from the coast-guard station is known as Kitchen Corner. Here a keen fisherman from Swansea, Mr. Coonan, built himself a small hut, and a davit from which he could launch a small boat in calm weather. He was a purist and would only take bass on a fly-rod. These bright, glittering fish shoal around the Worm and the Helwick Sands, and there are big ones about. The fishing regulars who frequent the Rhossili ledges talk of the "Monster of Kitchen Corner", a mysterious fish that snaps all tackle and then disappears in a dark swirl of water. It may not be a bass at all but rather a giant conger eel. Although the Welsh record for conger eels stands at 39lb, far greater monsters are known to exist around the Welsh coast. Conger eels of over 70lbs haunt the conger holes near the hulk of H.M.S. *Warrior* in Milford Haven. Why not a similar monster at Kitchen Corner? Or is it a fish or a marine beast as yet 'unknown to Science'?

I must ask that Master-fisherman of Wales, Clive Gammon.

He lived in Swansea and is a world-wide authority on all matters connected with the angler's art. He has just published his *Angling Guide to Wales* in which Gower sea-fishing has a high place. When I look out over the wide waters of Carmarthen Bay and the Bristol Channel from the coastguard's hut on the point near the Worm, I remember the roll-call of exciting fish Clive recited, including tope and shark, all to be found by an expert off the Gower coast. Even a huge sunfish was once sighted here by a fisherman who was looking straight down from the Rhossili cliffs. He reported that the sound of it grinding its teeth was like that of a cow chewing the cud!

But fishermen's tales are bound to come to mind as you walk along these cliffs and see, ahead of you under the shadow of the Downs, the little village of Rhossili itself, the most westerly village in Gower. Rhossili is the *ultima Thule* of the peninsula. It must have been fantastically lonely in the days before the motor-car. Nowadays it is much more accessible, since here the south road comes to an end and there are car-parks near the church and opposite the Worms Head Hotel, which is perched boldly and comfortably right on the edge of the cliffs. In spite of this, Rhossili still retains the strange feeling of being right at the end of the road.

As you drive to it through Pitton and Middleton you notice that even the trees have given way to the wind. In the old farmyard opposite the church there used to stand a 100-year-old oak which had only succeeded in growing in the face of fierce winds by lying on its side! It was proudly known as the Last Tree in Gower. Now, only the stump remains. This Rhossili landscape is spoke-shaved by the winter gales. Yet it is fertile withal. The early conquerors found it desirable, and the Lords of Gower had some of their own domain lands at Rhossili. The old medieval system of farming has still left traces in the strips of cultivated ground between Rhossili village and Worms Head. This area is known as the Viel. It is excellent for early potatoes, and, by ancient custom, it is divided carefully every year between the farmers, just as it was back in the Middle Ages.

The church of St Mary the Virgin stands firm as a rock against the winter gales. It seems a symbol of Rhossili, with its thick walls and saddle-roofed tower. The inner entrance to the church is protected by the porch and displays a fine twelfth-century Norman doorway. Within all is simple and white-washed, but there is one moving memorial on the wall. It is to Petty Officer

Edgar Evans who died with Captain Scott on the tragic journey back from the South Pole. He was a Rhossili man, and Scott picked him out for the Polar party because of his exceptional toughness and his skill in handling equipment. He died in harness, pulling the sledge until he dropped from utter exhaustion. The memorial is in white marble and somehow it brings into the church the chill of those vast, icy Antarctic wastes. You sense again the dauntless courage of the man, born in this little village, who pitted his life against their challenge.

When you come out of the church—and indeed wherever you are in Rhossili—you are drawn to that incomparable landscape composition of the Worm, the Downs and the sweeping sands. The cliffs on which Rhossili stands are 200 feet high and are a fine viewpoint, yet the view from the top of the Downs is even finer. You climb up by an obvious track through the gorse and the bracken to the Beacon, the highest point in Gower at 632 feet (193 metres). It was the old custom of Rhossili folk to take a stone up with them whenever they climbed the Downs to add to the Beacon. Could this ritual have some long lost pagan significance? In any case, all danger of paganism was exorcized when a quantity of the stones were carted down again to build Pitton chapel.

There are plenty of other stones scattered over the Downs, however, that take you far back into the mists of history— cairns, round barrows and oldest of all, the Swines Houses or Sweyn's Houses (O.E. *how*—a mound). They lie a little down the eastward side of the ridge about half-way along it, and are megalithic tombs of the same date as Arthur's Stone, around 2500 B.C. They are sadly ruined, however. Could Sweyn, the Dane whose name was attached to them so much later, be the same man commemorated in the name of Swansea? The ridge runs for over a mile, sloping gently eastwards down to the lonely farms of Kingshall and Sluxton, but plunging steeply to the west and the sea. The northern end of the Downs rejoices in the name of Bessie's Meadow. Who was Bessie, I wonder? She is as great a mystery to me as the Benjy of Benjy's Leg, near Eynonsford.

The view from the ridge of the Downs is splendid, as you might expect. All the now familiar landmarks are grouped below and around you, with the Worm snaking its astonishing way out to sea and the Atlantic rollers breaking white onto the curving sands.

Your visit to Rhossili Downs may coincide with one of the
meetings of those remarkable enthusiasts the hang-gliders.
With what might be described as artificial wings, these bold
experts take off—or rather run off—from the summit of the
Downs and float out on their wings high over the sands. This is a
sport requiring high courage and expertise. Rhossili has become
a major centre for the hang-gliders. The winds sweep in at a
steady rate and lift in a wave over the Downs. An expert can
take advantage of this to launch himself confidently into space.
It is a strange experience to be walking, for example, near the
cliff edge near Rhossili Church and suddenly see someone
floating past you out towards the Worm. Not all experts get as
far. But there have been aces of the hang-gliding game who
have launched themselves off Rhossili Downs and floated out as
far as the Worm itself. Immediately below and 500 feet down,
standing in the narrow glebe-land fields that fringe the shore, is
the one solitary house facing this whole wild stretch of sea and
sand. This is the Old Rectory. At the time when the living of
Rhossili was combined with that of Llangennith, the church
authorities felt that it was convenient to build the house
half-way between the two. What the poor Rector, or more important the poor Rector's wife, first felt when they saw it is not
recorded. It is half-way all right, but to what? No road reaches it
and the Rector had to travel on horseback or to walk. On winter
nights the full roar of the Atlantic gales comes howling around
the chimneys. No wonder some of the earlier occupants of the
Rectory became, shall we say, slightly eccentric!

When I first came to Rhossili at the age of ten they still talked
about a previous Rector who never talked to anyone in the
village. The only time they heard his voice was at Sunday
service. One day the postman met him in the street and offered
him a letter. The Rector turned and walked the whole, long way
back to the Rectory and then turned, took the communication
from the tired postman who had followed him, bowed gravely
and then disappeared into the house without a word. I confess I
would get slightly eccentric, too, if I had to spend a winter in the
Old Rectory. I need hardly say that it has the reputation of being
haunted.

I never found out the exact form of the haunting. One person
who stayed in the house, after the Church authorities had
wisely built a new Rectory near to Rhossili Church, told me that
on a certain winter's night "something very unpleasant indeed

comes out of the sea and comes into the house". Another story suggests that you can suddenly walk into a cold pool of air in the corridor and hear a low voice in your ear saying, "Why don't you turn around and look at me?" No one has ever dared. And so the stories accumulate and are likely to continue as long as the Rectory stands. There is no need to believe them, but who could resist telling or listening to them once you have seen the site of the Old Rectory. Besides, even the sands have their ghost at Rhossili.

There are surely ghosts among the sand-dunes, too. Between the present Rhossili village, perched on its cliff-top, and the Old Rectory at the foot of the Downs lies a stretch of dunes known as the Warren. In 1949 two skeletons were found here and in 1980 a careful archaeological 'dig' uncovered the remains of a 'lost village' complete with church. This had clearly been a substantial settlement but at some time in the thirteenth century it had been suddenly overwhelmed by a tremendous sand-storm. The walls have now been re-covered for preservation. We can only speculate on the chance that other 'lost villages' lie buried under the sand-dunes that occur in so many places around the Gower coast.

Now Rhossili Sands are a lee shore. In the days of sail you would be driven remorselessly onto the sands by winter gales, if you were not certain of your whereabouts. The bare ribs of the wreck of the *Helvetia*, cast away in 1887, still stick up from the sands near the cliffs of Rhossili. The tragic wreck of the *City of Bristol* left iron plates in the sands, still visible at low water near Burry Holms.

But besides wrecks, the wide sands of Rhossili hold mysteries, and above all, buried treasure. One of the great excitements of our young days was to go to the edge of the water at very low tide and try our luck at 'digging for gold', for who knows—one day the treasure of the famous 'Dollar Ship' may be uncovered again. Twice in the nineteenth century, Spanish coins of the early seventeenth century were dug up in quantities on Rhossili Sands. The first discovery was made in 1807 when the excited diggers got over 12lbs weight of Spanish dollars, with the date of 1625. Then the sands closed over the site. But Rhossili folk knew roughly where it was and handed on the knowledge. In 1833 four local men noticed an unusual shifting of the sands near the spot of the first find. They set off hurriedly for the beach and started to dig. Strange to say, they immediately lifted spades-full of dollars. Unfortunately for them, the tide started to come in. They dug frantically, but the wealth within their grasp washed off their spades. At last they gave up the struggle, yet they marked the spot firmly as they thought. They stuck a quarry bill in the sands, with a string to it and a bit of cork as a buoy. Unfortunately, when they came back next morning their bill and buoy were gone.

The story of the discovery of the dollars, however, spread like wildfire. Soon Rhossili Sands looked like Ballarat in the gold rush, with people from all over Gower, and beyond, staking out claims, quarrelling and fighting. The lord of the manor, Mr Talbot of Penrice, waived his rights to the find, and as a result, many poor labourers in West Gower got a very welcome windfall. Great ingenuity was displayed in order to beat the tides. One family called Bell came down from Swansea with large circular tanks of sheet iron, in which they worked desperately as the tide rose. The dollars were mainly of silver. There were dollars, half-dollars and pieces of eight. In addition to the dollars, two iron cannon were recovered, together with leaden bullets and parts of an astrolabe, the old type of navigational instrument used for taking the altitude of the pole star.

Some built houses out of the loot, and the Dollar Cottage still stands near the church at Llangennith. Others sold them at a very low price, thinking that, if the digging continued, they would become a drug on the market. One farmer took a sackful into Swansea. He reached the town, unharnessed the horse from the cart and took the sack away under his arm to the bank. But a keen-eyed neighbour of his from Llanrhidian spotted that there was a hole in the sack. As soon as the farmer had disappeared his neighbour made a careful search in the straw at the bottom of the cart and was rewarded with a tidy pile of dollars which represented a small fortune to him. Most of the dollars were melted down. And soon the sands closed in again, and no more dollars have ever been found.

Where did the 'Dollar Ship' come from? There was an old tradition in Gower that there were actually two ships wrecked on Rhossili Sands and that they carried the dowry of a Spanish princess who was to be married to an English nobleman. Others have suggested that the dowry the vessel was carrying was really that of Catherine of Braganza, who became the Queen of Charles II. There is no reliable evidence for this, and no record of the dowry ships being lost. Besides Catherine was Portuguese not Spanish. A few years after Catherine's marriage we have a record in the State Papers dated December, 1666. A Mr J. Man, an official, reported the wreck of "a Phyal vessel laden with wine, sugar and Brazil wood, on a sand ten miles off Swansea. The men are Portuguese and cannot speak English. Hoped to have saved the vessel and refused to save good, so all are lost." But Rhossili is twenty not ten miles from Swansea, and the record makes no mention of treasure. So the "Phyal ship" can hardly be the Dollar Ship.

But there may have been other wrecks of Spanish or Portuguese ships on the Gower coast of which no record exists. Rhossili could be a death-trap in the winter gales, for the old sailing ships of the seventeenth century had no way of accurately determining longitude, and galleons and warships struggling for home could make extraordinary mistakes in their position. After all, did not Sir Cloudsley Shovell perish with a whole English fleet in 1706, when his pilots completely missed the wide mouth of the English Channel and piled all the warships up on the cruel rocks of the Scilly Isles. The waves of the Atlantic pound Rhossili Sands and they wait to give a savage welcome to any poor mariner who is off course. Not every wreck would get reported immediately in the seventeenth century. There were plenty of Gower folk who would see to that! And prominent among them in those days was Mansel of Henllys, from that curious and reckless area around Llanddewi which, as we have seen, specialized in the nurturing of wild characters.

So I am inclined to believe the Gower tradition that there *was* another wreck. The story is firm on the point that a galleon was driven ashore some time in the reign of Charles II and that the wicked Mansel of Henllys beat the lord of the manor to the wreck, broke into it, got an immense amount of dollars and then disappeared. The story may be a little rocky here, for it seems that the wicked Mansel actually cleared off to Ireland to dodge his creditors. No matter. All the old Gower folk knew that his spirit haunts the sands, driving in a black coach, drawn by four grey horses. The Spectral Chariot of Rhossili Sands!

You walk along the edge of the waves at low tide out over the vast expanse of sand. In October, when all the visitors are gone and the winds start whipping white the tops of the long Atlantic rollers beating against the shore, you can feel very lost and lonely here. Only a few bass fishermen shivering as they brave the weather, and the mists forming along the top of the Downs. You look back to this bracken-brown high land dominating the bay. You pick up the traces of the smugglers' cellar behind the Rectory, discovered long after the smuggling days were over, when a chance heavy storm drove the stream that hid it down through the roof and scattered the stones over the hillside. You look at the spot where the last smugglers were surprised by the Revenue men on 16th February 1805, and fled leaving 101 casks of brandy, gin and rum littered over these very sands. And surely, somewhere at hand, must be the spot where the dollars were discovered. There are many ghosts on Rhossili Sands.

The flocks of oyster-catchers run piping before you along the sea-edge towards Burry Holms. A stream flows out from the Burrows that succeed the high hill of Rhossili Downs and makes a shining patch of water on the face of the sands. It has the strange name of Diles Lake. Now Diles Lake has always seemed to me the coastal boundary between south and north Gower. One side of Rhossili Bay always seems to belong to the south for you reach it from Rhossili village, the end of the south road. On the other side of Diles Lake the sands belong to North Gower, for you reach them from Llangennith, the terminus of the north road. Rhossili and Llangennith may once have shared a Rector between them, but Llangennith 'oxen' were not always so welcome at the Mapsant in Rhossili. We cross the wet sands of Diles Lake and enter North Gower.

6

The North-West Corner

Llangennith does not quite give you that end-of-the-world feeling you get from Rhossili. The village stands back from the sea—behind the wide expanse of sand-dunes that form the Burrows. It is perched on the col between Llanmadoc Hill to the north and Rhossili Downs to the south, and the land to the west slopes down to the sands over the flats of Llangennith Moors. You feel that Llangennith belongs to the land rather than the sea. This is farming Gower and the 'Llangenny Oxen', as the old folk called the inhabitants, had nothing to do with the seafaring and oyster-fishing that went on in the villages of the south coastline; but, make no mistake, when Llangennith folk heard of a wreck, they were on the spot as fast as any Port-Eynon 'crow'. Llangennith is also at the end of one branch of the north road and so it is the right point to begin our exploration of North Gower.

As you come over the hill down into it, you see at once that old Llangennith is a typical Gower Anglicana village. It is compact, with everything grouped around the village green, the old church and, of course, the pub. It has grown a little in recent years with villas along some of the lanes but the heart of Llangennith still remains in this tight little settlement around the village green. This is how it began in the early days of the Norman conquest and this is how it has remained.

So first to the church, dedicated to Gower's own saint, St Cenydd and, therefore, very properly, the largest in the peninsula. I agree that this is not much of a boast, since Gower churches are generally tiny compared to churches elsewhere. Llangennith Church was constructed on the site of the sixth-century priory, founded by the saint himself, which was destroyed by the Danes in A.D. 986. The priory was refounded probably by Henry de Newburgh after the Norman conquest of Gower and its revenues granted to the Abbey of St Taurinus at Evreux in Normandy. It was thus what was known in English medieval law as an 'alien priory' and its revenue was usually seized by the king whenever he went to war with France and then returned to its French owners when the war ended. All very civilized! However, Henry V needed money badly indeed for his French invasion and in 1414, the year before Agincourt, he seized the revenues of all alien priories, this time for good. Later, out of the Llangennith money, he granted a pension of £20 a year to a faithful knight with the improbable name of Sir Hortonk van Klux and there has been some speculation that the lonely farm of Sluxton, between Rhossili Downs and Hardings Down was originally Kluxton and is thus connected with this curious warrior. In any case, by 1442 pious King Henry VI was building All Souls College as a memorial to those who had fallen in the Hundred Years War. Llangennith came in handy for raising cash to endow his new foundation. He handed over the priory to the Master and Fellows of his new college, who held it until 1838. The glory of the old priory faded for ever.

But the old church still stands with its massive tower, complete with the Gower saddle-back roof and its lancet windows. Inside, you are confronted with the usual thorough 'restoration' but there are some points of interest still left untouched. In a niche on the south side of the nave is the effigy of a knight, with the lower part of the legs cut off to fit the statue into the opening. The old Llangennith folk used to call it the "Dolly Mare" and, as at Oxwich, this gives a clue to the knight's identity. He is one of the de la Mare family who held land around Llangennith and the style of his armour dates him to some time before A.D. 1307, when it became customary to mix mail and plate-armour. The old assumption that knights depicted with crossed legs, as is the unknown de la Mare, were Crusaders is extremely doubtful.

There are three carved stone coffin lids set in the west-end wall of the nave. Two show simple crosses and are probably from the graves of former priors. The third is more intriguing. It bears a complex interlaced pattern and is decidedly pre-Norman. Tradition maintains that it marked the grave of the holy St Cenydd himself, perhaps in that earlier monastery which was destroyed by the Danes. Now who was St Cenydd and what do we know about him? After all, he was Gower's only saint and thus demands our pious tribute to his memory as we stand before his coffin lid. The old medieval life of him was retold from monkish sources in the fifteenth century by the dull but learned Capgrave in his *Nova Legenda Angliae*, printed in Latin and published by Wynkyn de Worde in 1526. It is full of marvels and strange delights. These old Celtic saints seem curiously sympathetic and their lives, as related by the old monastic hagiographers, are almost as much tales of magic as of religion. Rome looked a little askance at them; perhaps they never measured up to their exacting standards of painful martyrdom for the Faith. In fact, precious few seemed to have been interested in martyrdom at all. They all seemed to live contentedly at prayer on some island, fed by kindly sea birds, or in a romantically placed cell, where they were happy to perform a miracle or two to oblige their visitors; and some traces of pre-Christian ritual, of ancient Celtic beliefs still lingered unreproved around their dwelling places. The old Celtic saints, in their kindly way, did not want to hurt their pagan neighbours' feelings too much!

The life of St Cenydd is a classical example of the pattern. He was born, so the legend relates, of royal stock, the son of Dihocus, a prince of Brittany; but as the tactful translation printed by the Rev J. D. Davies puts it "by a most unnatural sin". And here the kindly cleric adds a footnote, which has a certain charm for modern readers. "I need scarcely remind those who are acquainted with the Latin tongue that a literal translation of the text in this place is hardly possible". In truth Dihocus had seduced his own beautiful daughter and had made her pregnant. On Christmas Day King Arthur was holding his court in Gower and he summoned his vassals to meet him. Among them was Dihocus who brought his daughter with him. She gave birth to her son among the tents a mile from the palace of King Arthur but, as a sign of the unnatural sin of his conception, one of Cenydd's legs stuck to his thigh. The Prince, anxious to hush up the scandal, ordered a Moses-like cradle of wicker work to be made in which the baby was placed and cast on the turbulent waters of the little River Lliw, which flows into the bigger River Loughor. This stream swiftly carried the frail bark out to sea but as it drew near the dangers of Worms Head, the sea birds flew to the rescue. They lifted the boy from the waves, placed him on a safe rock on the Worm, stood around him in great flocks and "kept off the wind and hail and snow, with the shelter of their wings". On the ninth day, an angel of God descended and placed a brazen breast-shaped bell in the infant's mouth through which he was miraculously fed with "the sweetest savour of infantile nourishment . . . for in Welsh it is called to this day Cloch Tetham, this is being interpreted the Titty Bell. But the secretions which childhood naturally discharges in its retirement, he never did, for he was fed with a most subtile food, which had no secretion."

The birds and the wild deer were determined to look after him. When he was unexpectedly found by a kindly farmer and taken home to his wife, the gulls tore all the thatch off the farmer's roof until little Cenydd was taken back to his cosy nest on Worms Head. There, a doe politely filled the Titty Bell with her milk. Clothes were no problem. "The clothes in which he was wrapped adapted themselves to the circumference of the boy, according to his size and increasing measure, just like the bark growing round a tree; neither were the little clothes affected by any decay." As he grew older an angel looked in at regular intervals to complete his education.

At eighteen, he was ready for the saintly life. His angel directed him to the spot which is now the village green at Llangennith, where a stream sprung out of the ground to refresh him. Could this be the old village well, which is still crowned with a great slab of hard Old Red Sandstone rock carrying faint traces of a cross? Opposite this Cenydd constructed his rude hut, "and in the oratory built there, a heavenly host very frequently met him and conversed with him". His fame spread throughout Gower and beyond, and his Titty Bell had surprising power. One touch of it forced an evil doer to repent and give him the power to skip across the waves into exile with St David in Pembrokeshire. The good saint used it to restore stolen booty and to convert thieves. He became the friend and ally of St David and his leg was temporarily cured by a miracle to allow him to take part in an important religious conference. "Leaving the earth however to receive rewards in heaven, he departed on the calends of August."

A modest saint was St Cenydd, a kindly man spreading a quiet happiness around him. Somehow he suits Gower. And he would have turned a blind eye to the splendid saturnalia that was celebrated in his name every 5th July right up to the turn of the century. This was the renowned Llangennith Mapsant. Most Gower villages had their Mapsants or festivals on their saint's day. Rhossili's for example took place in the winter on 12th February, Llanmadoc's on 12th November. Everyone agreed however that, for sheer carefree exuberance,

Llangennith Mapsant took the palm. But then, Llangennith men were always famous for the way they enjoyed themselves. This was the place to come for cock-fighting, prize-fights, dances and 'bidding' weddings. A fine independent lot were the 'Llangenny oxen'. So much so, that when the Government introduced daylight saving during World War One and clocks had to be put back one hour, Llangennith held a public meeting in which it was decided not to accept the new law straight away but to give it one month's trial.

At the Mapsant the booths lined the village green, the fiddles played outside the "Welcome to Town" public house, there was endless dancing at the King's Head and everyone consumed enormous quantities of ale and 'whitepot'. Whitepot or 'milked meat' was a mixture of flour and milk and other ingredients, boiled together in commemoration, so they said, of the milk left by the kindly hind in St Cenydd's Titty Bell. All Mapsants had something special to eat. Llanmadoc had its pies, made of chopped mutton and currants; Rhossili had a kind of plum-pudding known as "Bonny Clobby".

In addition a wooden cock, dressed up in ribbons and supposed to be a representation of the birds that fed St Cenydd, was hoisted up to the top of the church tower and when the tower was repaired in 1888 the holes for the pole were carefully preserved and are there to this day. Three days the jollification lasted until the whole of north-west Gower was exhausted. "Aye, boy," Phil Tanner used to tell me, "Three days to die happy, then three weeks to come back to life."

Which brings me to the second of Llangennith's famous men—after St Cenydd—Phil Tanner, Gower songster extraordinary. Phil would never have claimed to be a saint. Far from it. He was a glorious enjoyer of life who lived for the day. But good fortune had given him a fine tenor voice which remained as clear as a bell until the day he died in 1950 as a noble singing patriarch of eighty-eight. He was the perpetual embodiment of the Llangennith Mapsant! He came from a family of weavers when the mills used to turn merrily along the brook that flows down from Rhossili Down, past Coety out to the sea at Diles Lake. But Phil was never a real weaver. He tried his hand at everything, even inn-keeping, but what he lived for was singing. He became Gower's greatest and best-loved folk singer, the man who knew all the songs and was indispensable at every 'bidding' wedding. In a Gower 'bidding' wedding, the guests would contribute money which was then returned when they, in turn, had a wedding in the family.

For days before the event, Phil would walk around the parish carrying a staff decorated with red, white and blue ribbons and chanting the invitation to the wedding. I remember that he could repeat the traditional words perfectly even when he was eighty-five. What a picture of old, vanished Gower he could re-create, as he sat on the bench outside the King-s Head on a warm summer evening, with his sheep dog at his side and a glass of ale in his hand, calling on us to be attentive with an authoritative "Order, order, gentlemen", and "Down, bitch, quiet", to the dog.

> I'm a messenger to you and the whole house in general
> To invite you to the wedding of Morgan Eynon and Nancy Hopkins
> The wedding which will be next Monday fortnight
> The wedding house will be the Ship Inn, Port-Eynon,
> Where the bride will take breakfast on plenty of good beer, butter and cheese,
> Walk to Port-Eynon church to get married, back and take dinner.
> Then I'll see if I can get you some good tin meat and some good attendance;
> And whatever you wish to give at dinner-table the bride will be thankful for.
> There will be a fiddle in attendance for there will be plenty of music there and dancing if you'll come along and dance. There'll be fiddlers, fifers, drummers and the devil knows what besides.
> I don't know what. There'll be plenty of drinkables there, so they tell me, but that I haven't tasted.
> And if you come to the wedding
> I'll do all that lies in my power that evening if required,
> To get you a sweetheart, if I don't get drunk.
> But the bride is wishful you should come or send.

Phil had a splendid white beard, eyes that twinkled and a wicked wit. "I see, boy," he said to a friend of mine who was arranging to sail for France after his wedding, "you're like the gander; you take your honeymoon on the watter." And his infectious chuckle would fill the whole King's Head bar. What a repertoire he had! Songs galore, but I do not think many of them were indigenous to Gower except the "Gower Reel". Phil could set our feet tapping when he gave us the reel as "mouth music"—"I'd sing the reel if we didn't have a fiddle". He picked up songs wherever he found them. I remember one which must have come from Ireland which was a great favourite of Phil's, with a splendid, swinging tune.

It was back in Tipperary I was born when I was young,
That's the reason why I've got the Blarney on my tongue.
I was the image of my daddy, even the Doctor did allow
And the girls all came to kiss me—Oh, I *wish* they'd do it now.

Chorus
How I wish they'd do it now. How I wish they'd do it now
They would tickle me down all over. Oh, I *wish* they'd do it now!

There were others that were deeply moving and which seemed perfect on those quiet summer evenings it was still possible to get in the late 1920s at Llangennith, when the air was warm and there was no sound except Phil's clear voice singing "The Sweet Primroses". He would clear his throat, call "Order, order. This music is serious", and ring out the first lines:

I must go down to some lonely valley
Where no man on earth there may me find
Where the pretty little song-birds sit tuning their voices
And always blows there, a most healing wind

("Down, bitch. Drat her, what's the matter with her? She was musical enough, boy, as a puppy.")

Stand back, young man and don't be so deceitful
For 'tis you're the cause of all my pain.
'Tis you who have made my poor heart to wander
And for to cure it now, 'tis all in vain

Then there were what Phil called "the naughty ones", only to be sung in male company, for Phil had a Victorian sense of propriety and would offend no one. And after all, how bucolically innocent was all his slight bawdry; "The Ballad of Ha-penny Park" for example with its chorus:

Where a halt was made, and a game was played
And Moll a shilling took!

As for the "Gower Toast" Phil always reserved this for "no ladies in sight". These are permissive days I know but no-one, I hope, will now take offence if I do not print it all but simply add the first line to my picture of Phil, in his coat of Gower-woven tweed and his thick socks—"No need to boast about 'en, boy.

Gower socks stand up for they-sen"—lifting his glass and giving
the company a glorious, all-embracing wink as he began

Here's to the maiden, bright with honour,

The rest shall be uproarious silence.

Phil died a few days after happily celebrating his eighty-
eighth birthday in 1950 at the Glan-y-Mor Home in Penmaen in
his beloved Gower, happy and singing to the last. He rests in
Llangennith Churchyard. Maybe there was not so much difference between him and St Cenydd after all. They would have
understood each other.

Phil was a wonderful link with Gower's past—with Gower in
the nineteenth century—but there is one product of Llangennith that can take us further back still. In 1784 a Mr
Leyshon Rogers of the parish began to keep a commonplace book
full of curious details of wages, valentines, witchcraft, cock-
fights, medical recipes and a host of other matters. As you look
through it, you realize what a gulf is fixed between life in the
country then and country life today. No cars, no electricity, no
telephones, of course but even more astonishing, no doctor. The
first resident practitioner in Gower was Mr Daniel Davies of
Reynoldston, who did not settle in Gower until 1816. The few
great landowners might be able to send to Swansea for a doctor
in an emergency but even the moderately well-off, like Mr
Leyshon Rogers, had to fend for themselves when it came to
treating themselves or their cattle. Mr Rogers had no great
command of the English language but that makes some of his
entries more pleasing. Some of his medical remedies seem truly
heroic.

"For the shortness of Breth and heft in the Stomeg, take Brimstone
powdered and Honey and mix in a glass of Brandy. Drink it in the
morning fasting and rest one morning. . . .
    To keep of any Disorder from any person and to make ye Blood to
Surkylate, is to take 1 quart of Decoction of Bark and to mix 1 Pint of
Brandy with it, and then to drink a glass full every night, and
morning fasting, as long as it do hold."

There are some more sinister entries under the title of "For
the art of unwitching, or unlucky people, the fable I heard, so
that I wrote."

"If you think that you have anything that is witched take some
May Tree and beat whatever cattle or anything that you

think is witched all over first, and boil some of the may tree in milk, then give two hornfulls for some few days, till the witch comes to say God bless them. . . .

If a witch be coming to the door, take a birch broom and put a cross in the door, then the witch cannot come into the house till the broom be tuk out of the door."

But the pleasantest entries are the Valentines that Mr Rogers kept handy for all occasions. I wonder if he used a new one every year and with what results!

> You are the one and only one
> And I am only he,
> That doth love one and only one
> And you my dear is she.

> My dear and better pray read this letter,
> And on the writer some pity take,
> You may have richer but not have better,
> I could my dear die for your sake.

And a last one, which has a poetic touch Phil Tanner would have enjoyed. I regret I never asked Phil for a Valentine. I am sure he might have remembered this very one:

> Streams of pleasure, rivers of wine,
> Plantations of tea and a young girl to mind

From the front door of the King's Head Inn, now pleasantly modernized and from the seat Phil Tanner used to occupy, you look out over the village green and the church towards the sea. This is the northern end of Rhossili Bay and you go down to it through the narrow lanes and out onto Llangennith Burrows. Behind you the land slopes up towards Llanmadoc Hill with a scattered farm or two and some standing stones, difficult to find amongst the fields and, it must be confessed, too many caravan parks only too easy to find. Some of the caravans spill onto the sand-hills but as soon as you walk past them you enter the wilder world of Llangennith and Broughton Burrows.

This is a very curious and surprising corner of Gower—for a corner it is, where the peninsula takes a sharp turn to the north-east and the wide Burry Estuary begins. Burry Holms is the small, rocky island that marks the point of the turn and behind it lies this strange triangular wilderness of high sand-hills, fringed by limestone cliffs on the north-east side. The walk around it is a walk of discovery. I enjoy it best when I start from the Broughton Bay end. You seem to come out of caravan land quicker if you keep to the high dunes and you get a view down over the sands of Broughton Bay, framed by Prissen's Tor to the right and Twlk Point almost below you.

How tempting look the sands of Broughton Bay and how sternly you should resist their temptation! You are now in the area where the waters of the Burry inlet meet the main sea and currents swirl close inshore at certain states of the tide. Broughton Bay bathing can be dangerous for the rash and inexperienced. From Broughton—pronounced locally as "Bruffton"—you follow the coast round to Burry Holms. At low tide you can walk along the sands. In fact, at low spring tide you can walk the whole way from Rhossili, through the sound between Burry Holms and the mainland, past Broughton Bay right up to Whitford Point entirely on sand. And a noble walk it is. But this section of it, between Twlk Point and the Holms is a delight in itself. The limestone cliffs are not amongst the highest in Gower—they rarely exceed 100 feet but they are backed by the high dunes of the Burrows and hold some curiosities.

Around the corner of Minor Point you enter Bluepool Bay. It is only a bay at low tide. The Blue Pool itself is a circular rock pool at the foot of the cliffs which is a splendid bathing spot when the tide is out. At high tide it disappears in the wash of the waves. In my childhood days we dived into it with a sense of adventure, for locally it was reputed to be bottomless. Alas for romance, accurate soundings proved a depth of a mere fifteen feet. On the western side of the bay there is a fine natural arch known as the Three Chimneys and near it, on the Blue Pool side, a remarkable discovery of gold moidores and doubloons was made around 1800 when John Richard, a fisherman, and his wife noticed something glittering in the crevices of the rocks. They found a great quantity of these pieces. Years later other searchers found gold doubloons on this very spot and recently skin divers have picked them up from the sea-bed. Clearly more than one 'Dollar Ship' has been cast away on this coast.

Just to the west of the Three Chimneys is the curious cave of Culver Hole. It is a total contrast to its better known namesake near Port-Eynon. The Llangennith Culver Hole can only be approached at low tide so there is always a danger that you might be cut off when visiting it. The entrance is a mere slit in the limestone which gives you no idea of the size of the cave behind it. You creep along a narrow passage until a big chamber opens up in the rock. It is quite dark so you need a light to visit it. It is a bone cave, a real hyena's den, but even more surprising was the discovery of the bones of over thirty individuals and broken pieces of cylindrical urns of the late Bronze Age, around 1000 B.C. It is hardly likely that this strange cave would have been used as living quarters. It was more probably used as an ossuary, where a small immigrant community buried their dead. It was also the spot where smugglers hoped to stow the last cargo of brandy run in Gower. The customs officers, however, foiled the attempt and seized the whole cargo.

About four hundred yards further on you come to the Spaniard Rocks—again a rocky point with memories of romantic wrecks—and you look across to the little island of Burry Holms. Holm comes from the old Scandinavian word, *holmr*, meaning an island, and it is well to remember that Burry Holms is an island when you visit it, for, as on Worms Head, unwary visitors who walk over to the islet on the sands sometimes forget that the tide comes in!

Burry Holms has a strange, lost atmosphere all of its own, a feeling that you are back in a remote past. Here are the ruins of a small medieval chapel where no doubt people came on pilgrimage to a shrine of St Cenydd. The kindly Gower saint seems always present here, as the gulls breed and rise in a white cloud from the rocks in early summer although the small automatic lighthouse has gone and flashes no longer as the dusk falls. The flowers are a delight and the sea cliffs glow with rarities in summer time. An earthwork consisting of a single bank and ditch bisects the island and dates from the Iron Age. From the highest point you can look out over the white horses breaking on the dangerous bar of the Burry Estuary. Beyond is the low line of the Carmarthenshire coast stretching around into Pembrokeshire and Tenby. And to the south, Rhossili Downs and the incomparable sands sweeping around to the Worm itself.

You cross back to the mainland and walk through the high dunes towards Llangennith. This is typical dune country and Gower has many examples from Broughton Bay right around the south coast to Pennard. Mr G. T. Goodman has compiled a complete list of the plants you meet as you move inland from the sea.

First come tough plants that can stand up to any amount of salt spray and even occasional flooding by the sea; the sea rocket, the prickly saltwort and their like which fix the drifting sand. Then the sea couch-grass takes over and, as Mr Goodman points out, creates a line of flattish circular mounds which gradually come together and make a jumping-off ground for the familiar marram grass that builds up the high dune ridges. As you go further back from the sea these dunes become covered with various mosses, creeping fescue, dewbury and even bracken. I always feel that, once you come to the bracken you are out of the real dune country. But on the stabilized dunes and in the green hollows between them grow plants with those intriguing names that are a delight to the non-botanist like myself. Mr Goodman and his colleagues may know them by their scientific titles but I revel in names like viper's bugloss, traveller's joy, hairy hawkbit, bloody cranesbill and evening primrose. They are all there at your feet as you thread your way through the high dunes behind Burry Holms and emerge at last out of the sandy maze to look back to Llangennith, on its green slope between its guardian hills of Rhossili Downs and Llanmadoc Hill.

Llanmadoc is Llangennith's nearest neighbouring village. As the crow flies it is only about a mile and a half away but that agile bird would go straight over the 605 feet (186 metres) high summit of Llanmadoc Hill to get there. The road has to be more circumspect; it curves back around the estern side of the hill to slide steeply down past Stormy Castle into Llanmadoc. The keen walker however should follow the crow, for Llanmadoc Hill, like all these Gower hills and downs, is exhilarating walking rich in burrows, cairns and a great Iron Age fort. Again, it is geologically an upsurge of Old Red Sandstone from underneath the limestone that covers most of Western Gower. The moorland comes right down to the road that drops into Llangennith. Opposite rises Hardings Down, just over 500 feet (157 metres) high and showing two prominent Iron Age earthworks. The open ground along the Llangennith road is known as Tankeylake Moor and the story goes that the holders of the Bulwark Fort on Llanmadoc Hill met the occupants of the Hardings Down Fort in a furious battle on this very spot. The Bulwark's leader, one Tonkin, was killed and so fierce was the slaughter that the blood rose above the warriors' boots. It is strange how these stories about savage battles totally unknown to recorded history persist, not only in Gower but in other parts of South and West Wales as well. Are they faint recollections of some real struggle retained for thousands of years in the folk memory, or were they later inventions to explain the presence of these mysterious earthworks? And we shall never know if the unfortunate Tonkin ever existed. "Old, unhappy, far-off things And battles long ago" as W. Wordsworth wrote.

You leave Tankeylake Moor and climb up along the paths that lead easily through the bracken to the summit ridge. The wild ponies wander before you; or can you call them wild any more since many of them are adepts at coming down to the edge of the main road and begging for titbits from the visitors in their parked cars? The hill is full of the song of skylarks in the spring and the fresh wind blows in from the sea as you walk. Along the ridge you come across the fragments of a Cist Vaen, a small coffin-shaped structure which once lay under an earthen burrow. There are Bronze Age cairns scattered here and there and, on the eastern end of the hill, an impressive maze of high banks and ditches known as the Bulwark. It is now a little difficult to make out the exact plan but there seem to be three lines of defence each entered by a separate protected way. It is a typical late Iron Age fort, the second largest in Gower, for the first place is taken by the great entrenchments at Cil Ifor Top which cover nearly eight acres.

But the Bulwark is impressive enough and you can picture the local tribesmen hurriedly driving their cattle behind the palisades that crowned the high banks as an enemy approached. They must have been occupied when the Romans advanced into South Wales. Did the legions have to storm them as they pushed their way westwards through the land of the Silures? If they did, the old Celtic defenders must have seen their fate advancing towards them over a long distance, for the Bulwark and Llanmadoc Hill look out over the whole northern line of the peninsula. As you stand on the ramparts you can see, at once, the extraordinary contrast between the southern and western coast of Gower and its northern side.

The whole northern coastline is dominated by a vast marshland which stretches out in a maze of water-channels and glittering pools towards the sands of the Burry Estuary. It goes under different names as you travel eastwards—Cwm Ivy Marsh, Landimore Marsh, Llanrhidian Marsh, but by whatever name you call it, a true salt marsh it is, on which the cattle and sheep graze, ponies roam and the tide creeps in along the 'pills' or channels through which the little streams of North Gower struggle out towards the sea. The marsh birds call amongst its loneliness and the wild duck know it in winter. There is a cliff-line here, although you might never suspect it. The 200-foot marine peneplain that forms such an impressive white limestone fringe to the south coast drops steeply down to the marsh. Long ago, as the ice melted back, the north and south coasts must have looked exactly the same. But for thousands of years the Loughor River has been pouring down its sediment on to the northern shore of Gower. The land has crept out from the cliff edge, which is now left buried in trees, with only an occasional crag breaking through; and the marshland is still growing and creeping out towards the far sands of the estuary.

From Llanmadoc Hill you will see the western boundary of this salt-marsh country, the mile-and-three-quarters-long spit of dunes and pine woods called Whitford Point. It is a strange, lonely place, with the sands and marsh on its eastern side and the sea to the west. On the map it looks like a rhinoceros-horn sticking out of the head of Gower! This is the country that now lies before you as you go down from the Bulwark through the bracken and come out at Llanmadoc.

Llanmadoc is a strip of a village, running along the road called by the delightful name of Rattle Street and dropping down Frog Lane to the nearby hamlet of Cheriton. Along the road are the pub and the chapel and at the top are the church and the older houses grouped around an embryo village green. The church is tiny, the smallest in Gower and dedicated to St Madoc. The present building is thirteenth century, with the usual embattled tower with a saddle-backed roof. It has been most extensively restored but still retains a Norman font and a Romano-Celtic tombstone which was discovered built into the wall of the old Rectory. It is now placed in the window sill near the pulpit. It dates back to the fifth or early sixth century and the inscription reads "AD VECTI FILIUS IGVANI HIC JACET"—"The stone of Avectus [?] son of Iuanus. He lies here". A strange voice reaching us from the long distant past of the Dark Ages.

An even rarer find from the same period was made at Parc-yr-Odyn (The field of the kiln) near Cwm Ivy. A farmer ploughed up a curious old bell, rectangular in shape and with traces of some bright shining substance attached to it which was probably gold. It closely resembles in shape some of the ancient, elaborately decorated bells from Ireland, where sacred bells were carried by many of the old saints. The mind immediately turns to St Cenydd and his Titty Bell. Could St Madoc have had the same thing? And did St Madoc ever really come to Gower? Although the Welsh knew him as Aeddan Foeddog, son of Caw—and the Foeddog was eventually contracted into Madoc—Aeddan Foeddog was really St Aidus, an Irishman in origin. Perhaps the old bell ploughed up at Llanmadoc could have been St Cenydd's? As I peer at it, in its case in the National Museum of Wales in Cardiff, I like to think so, whatever sober historians might say. When you come to the Dark Ages it is surely permissible to speculate and dream!

Llanmadoc was also one of the few Gower churches which retained traces of medieval wall paintings. Somehow I can forgive the drastic restoration of the church for it took place with the approval of the man who I have had great pleasure in quoting and reading during the whole time I have been preparing this book. I almost feel I know him personally though he died at the age of eighty-one in 1911 after a long, busy, happy life. He was the Rev J. D. Davies, Rector of Cheriton as well as of Llanmadoc.

He was an Anglo-Catholic, deeply interested in ritual but in so many other things as well, and was the historian of West Gower to whom all subsequent writers must go. He has collected all the stories, verified all the documents; sometimes to the terror of old Miss Talbot who lent him rare manuscripts from the Penrice archives and once found them scattered all over the Rectory floor with the Rector crawling happily amongst them to verify an obscure point of genealogy. He built the present Rectory across the road from the church, with its high roof and overhanging eaves. There he was visited by the Rev Francis Kilvert who has left us a vivid portrait of the Rector in his diary. Kilvert came to Llanmadoc just after the Rectory had been rebuilt and did not approve of it. He felt it was a "bare, unfurnished ugly barracks" while Mr Davies, with his close shaven head and somewhat seedy black coat looked like a Roman Catholic priest. "He took us into the churchyard but let us find our own way into the church which was beautifully furnished and adorned but fitted up in the high ritualistic style. The Vicar said that when he came to the place the Church was meaner than the meanest hovel in the village."

But Kilvert was, nevertheless, charmed with the man once they went inside the Rectory.

The Vicar invited us to join him at his luncheon to which we added the contents of our own picnic basket. He had a very good pie to which we did justice for we were all very hungry with the sea air. We were waited on by a tall, clean old woman with a severe and full cap border who waits on Mr Davies and is so clean that she washes the kitchen floor four times a day. She used to wash her master's bedroom floor as often till he caught a cold which frightened her and she desisted.

We suggested that she might be of Flemish blood which would account for her cleanliness. The idea had never occurred to Mr Davies and he was much struck by it. The house was thoroughly untidy and bachelor-like and full of odds and ends. The rigging of a boat stood in the hall for the Vicar is a great sailor and sails Carmarthen Bay in a boat built by himself. A quantity of pretty fretwork and carved work also stood about in the hall and the rooms and miniature bookcases and cabinets for drawing room tables made by himself and sold for the benefit of Cheriton Church Restoration Fund. He is very clever and can turn his hand to anything. Besides which he seemed to me to be an uncommonly kind good fellow, a truely simple-minded, single-hearted man.

The Vicar's handiwork can be seen, not only in Llanmadoc Church but in Cheriton and Llanrhidian as well.

One constant visitor to Llanmadoc in recent times might have puzzled the good vicar if they had ever met. This was Ernest Jones, the disciple of Sigmund Freud and his biographer. Jones was a Gowerton man, who occupied a high and important place in the early history of psycho-analysis and whose heroic efforts succeeded in saving Freud from the vengeance of the Nazis by bringing him to England. He had his holiday home here in Llanmadoc for many years. As you walk through Rattle Street and Frog Lane you can easily see why the great psychoanalyst enjoyed coming here. He would not be bothered with a single patient amongst the contented folk of Llanmadoc! I reckon old Phil Tanner had the last word about psycho-analysis when he told me once with a wink "There's nothing wrong with any man that a pretty gal and one thousand pun a year wouldn't cure at the drop of my hat."

From the little green before the church there are two lanes you can follow. One leads down a green hollow, past the farm of Cwm Ivy and out onto the salt marshes and Whitford Point. The other passes the church and the vicarage and stays on the higher ground. It curves round the north-western flank of Llanmadoc Hill and approaches Broughton Bay from the north side. The road is narrow and it also gives access to caravan sites so it gets cluttered up in the summer. But you have the steep bracken-covered slopes of Llanmadoc Hill rising behind you and the sea in front. Right under the steepest slope of the hill is the old farm with the strange and romantic sounding name of Lagadranta. Once again it is a case of an English corruption of a Welsh name. Lagadranta is none other than Llygad-y-nantai, the eye of the streams.

Looking at the position of Lagadranta under the steep prow of Llanmadoc Hill and imagining its isolation before the caravan parks arrived, it is easy to understand that it was one of the last places in Gower frequented by the Verry Volks. One morning the good wife of the farm was visited by an old woman who asked for a loan of a sieve. The housewife declared that she did not have such a thing but the old woman knew better. "I'll take the one you have there over the vat straining the hops." The housewife now suspected that she had to do with one of the Verry Volk, for it was well known in old Gower that the Verry Volks used sieves "for to sifty gold". She gave it willingly to the old woman. Some days later the old woman brought back the sieve. "Since you were so good as to lend it to me, the biggest cask in your house shall never be without beer." She then walked towards the well and disappeared into it.

All was well for many weeks. Lagadranta revelled in free beer. Now one of the conditions laid down by the old lady of the Verry Volks was that on no account should the housewife tell anyone else, but the housewife was a woman with a woman's one frailty—she couldn't keep a secret. She gossiped with a neighbour whereupon the magical beer supply immediately dried up.

This little north-eastern corner of Gower was evidently a favourite haunt of the Verry Volks. Not far away, at the foot of Cwm Ivy Tor, is a pleasant stretch of green sward which was well known as the fairies' dancing ground. It was, however, very dangerous to interfere with them when they were enjoying themselves in Cwm Ivy. A Llanmadoc man was imprudent enough to step into the ring when they were dancing and was immediately run through the foot with a fork. He limped home in agony and consulted a wise woman. She told him that his only chance was humbly to beg the Verry Volks' forgiveness and then put his foot back into the circle. Whereupon it was immediately healed.

Leaving Lagadranta—and offering a quiet tribute to the Verry Volk—you go down through the caravans to the wild, still unspoilt Broughton Burrows and over the dunes to the sea. Llangennith and Llanmadoc share Broughton Bay between them since the parish boundary runs right out from the middle of the sands to the sea-edge, yet it is curious that no continuous lane goes around the base of Llanmadoc Hill to unite the two places on this westward side. Lagadranta looks to Llanmadoc and the farm next to it, Delvid, looks to Llangennith and only a footpath joins them. This time we will turn north on Broughton Sands.

Two limestone outcrops come down to the sandy dunes. The first is Prissen's Tor, once marked on the map as Spritsail Tor but the Llanmadoc people have always called it Prissen's. High up on the tor are two small caves linked by a tunnel. They were discovered during quarrying operations, which accounts for the smooth slabs at the cave entrances. We sometimes forget how many of the steep cliff faces we admire in parts of Gower today were artificially produced. Time has soothed the scars into beauty. This Prissen's cave was the usual hyena's den, full of miscellaneous bones but there were also fragments of very much later Roman pottery. After Prissen's comes Hills Tor and the higher ground takes a definite turn. From now on it runs east, to form the rim of Gower that looks out over the salt marshes. At Hills Tor, of course, we are still on the sea side of the great low-lying spur of Whitford Point.

This remarkable stretch of dunes and pine plantations runs north for two miles out into the Burry Estuary. It is now a nature reserve and part National Trust property. It is a wild, lonely place. I like to walk out to the point first on its sea side, looking out at the endless expanse of sandbanks that are exposed at low tide. Vast flocks of oyster-catchers run piping through the shallows for this is a great place for birds. Strange pieces of flotsam and jetsam can get cast up on the sands. I have only one lament. Today this treasure trove has become far too commonplace. We are in the plastic age and this unpleasant dandruff, combed out of the falling hair of our overmechanized civilization, is all too prevalent on Whitford Sands. Gower, alas, is not alone in this.

But the sea, the salt air, the exhilarating sense of space and clear skies are still there as you walk. At the very end of the point, well out on the furthest spit of sand, is the old Whitford lighthouse. This is an elegant cast-iron tower, 44 feet high which stands 20 feet above the water at high tide. It was built in 1854 as the coal and tin-plate trade developed out of Llanelli and Burry Port on the Carmarthenshire side of the estuary. It was certainly needed, for the channel is constantly shifting and the bar into Carmarthen Bay is a welter of white water when the wind drives in from the south-west. Yet the worst shipwreck disaster in these parts occurred on a totally still January night in 1868. Eighteen to nineteen vessels, all sailing craft between eighty to 400 tons burden and loaded with coal, had been towed out of Llanelli by the steam tugs. They cast off and rounded Whitford Point, aiming to clear Burry Holms with the ebb tide. But the wind died away completely, the tide turned and between nine and ten that night disaster struck. A remarkably heavy swell, totally unperceived by the ships when they rounded Whitford Lighthouse, was now running in the channel. It tore all anchors loose, lifted some ships up and down with such force that their bottoms were stove in. The floodtide gained in strength and drove many of the unfortunate colliers onto the rocks at Broughton Bay or dashed them against each other. Within an hour sixteen of the eighteen boats were total wrecks. The strange thing is that this terrible scene was taking place without anyone on shore being aware of it. The night was so quiet and still that no one thought of danger out at sea.

Next morning the inhabitants were horrified to find the whole coast from Whitford Sker to Burry Holms littered with broken spars, the shattered hulls of the ships, ropes, ship-stores, vast quantities of coal and the lifeless bodies of the poor sailors who had been drowned. These were piously buried in the churchyards of Llanmadoc and Llangennith. The Rev J. D. Davies records a strange story of that night.

The choir of the Parish happened on the evening in question, to be holding their weekly practice in the church, when suddenly an indescribable scream of terror was heard in the churchyard, as of one in the last extremity of mortal fear. I immediately ran out to see what was the matter, and saw a young lad, whom I knew very well, standing in the middle of the walk, not far from the porch, with his face not only blanched, but actually distorted with fright. "What is the matter, my lad?" I said. "Oh," he replied, "I saw a man without his hat come and look in at the window." I brought the poor terrified lad into the church, where he remained some little time before he came to himself. It was currently believed that what he saw was the

apparition of one of the poor seamen who was drowned, as it was just
about the time when the wreck took place.

The Whitford Light was disused in 1933, but the tower, with
its elegant iron balconies, is still intact, and due to the efforts of
the yachtsmen of Burry Port, has been put back into action
again. Once more the warning light shines out over the winding
sand-banks of the Loughor Estuary. You feel very lost and
lonely when you stand beside Whitford Lighthouse, although
you can see the big power station at Burry Port looming up
across the sands away on the Carmarthenshire side of the
estuary. In the old days, before they dredged the channel up to
Llanelli, it was possible to cross the estuary by a path through
the sands. John Wesley was guided across it from Pembrey
when he came to Gower. It was a tricky way through sand-banks
and quicksands and Wesley was thankful to reach the Gower
shore safely. Today you would be utterly unwise to attempt such
a thing. The tide comes in swiftly and you can find yourself
isolated on an ever-decreasing bank of sand before you know
where you are.

When you walk around the flat sand of the point to the eastwards you come to the part of Whitford Sker known as Berges
Island. When you look to the east from the dunes of Berges
Island you start to get the feel of the great expanse of the salt
marshes that now stretch before you. The change from the wide
seascapes on the west side of the point is notable and exciting
above all for bird lovers. It is here that you get, for the first time,
a taste of the quality of the bird life of the estuary and
the marshes. You must come at the right season, of course,
and February is one of the great months here, although a raw
day out on the Sker will also give your face something to
remember.

Great murmurations of starlings cross from the Pembrey side
to Gower in the early morning. Dunlin, sanderling and knot
teem along the shore. The wintering geese fly in, with chevrons
of the white-fronted variety together with the commoner Brent
geese, in flocks forty-strong. The great northern diver can be
seen here and duck in plenty, mallard and teal and hundreds of
wigeon. But amongst the rare visitors like the black-throated
diver or the great crested grebe a mystery bird arrives and has
been recorded on occasions all through the year. This is the eider
duck.

Now the mystery about the eider duck is simply this—since 1900 it has been reported all the year round in the Burry Estuary but it has never been seen to breed there. It breeds in Scotland, the Farne Islands, Northern Ireland even in Brittany but never in Gower. And yet it is always there, and even goes through its moult in Gower and has its full breeding plumage in spring. But yet no one has ever reported it breeding on the estuary, even though naturalists have kept the most elaborate watch on it. Very strange indeed. No wonder the Gower Society adopted this attractive but mysterious bird as its emblem.

Amidst the flights of birds, you walk back to the mainland along the spit of Whitford Point. A special path has been carefully marked out by the Glamorgan Naturalist Trust through the pine plantations which brings you back to the little cluster of houses that is Cwm Ivy, below the cliff rim. You have to leave your cars here when you visit Whitford and no one who loves the country will object to that. Eastward from the path, before you come to the Forestry cottage, a low embankment cuts off the Cwm Ivy section of the marsh from the outer salt marsh, here known as the Grooze. You can use this dyke as a footpath to get back into the exit point of the Burry Pill and so up again onto Frog Street. I would never walk along the foot of the escarpment past Tulpin's Well if I were you. This is one of the squelchiest patches of Gower, and although the Verry Volks have been reported around the muddy waters that seep out from the densely wooded cliff, I would most certainly leave it to them.

Back safely from Whitford Point and Cwm Ivy Marsh we walk down Frog Lane and reach the little hamlet of Cheriton. Here the longest stream of West Gower, the Burry Pill, at last reaches the sea, or rather wriggles out onto the marshland. The little stream flows out of the woodlands past the attractive church with the ancient Glebe House standing close by.

Cheriton Church in its tree-surrounded churchyard is generally accounted the most beautiful in Gower. It is dedicated to the old Celtic Saint Cattwg. There are no aisles or transepts and the embattled, saddle-roofed tower stands between the nave and the chancel. As the tower stands in the middle, there is no chancel arch but the two arches of the tower with their clear-cut mouldings and corbel shafts make an elegant frame as you look towards the altar. The choir stalls, the altar rails and altar, even the chancel roof were all carved by the Rev J. D. Davies in light-toned wood as a labour of love for the church he served so well.

The churchyard looks peaceful today but in 1770 it was the scene of a wild riot over a land dispute. The fighting factions, it is hardly necessary to say, were two rival branches of the boisterous Lucas family, on one side the Stouthall branch, on the other the Horton Lucases, who were descended from the wild Port-Eynon Lucases of Salt House notoriety. Apparently a Manorial Court was held in Cheriton to discover who had the title to the Lucas lands in the parish. Both sides however were Lucases and therefore were not disposed to worry too much about the law if it went against them. The lands were given to the Horton lot, whereupon the Stouthall branch rushed to the attack. Anne Williams, the Rector's daughter, was then living in the old Great House overlooking the churchyard. Her mother, however, was a Stouthall Lucas and her uncle, also a Lucas, was a clergyman living in the village. Anne was horrified as she looked out of her window to see her whole family, as it were, in bloody battle before her. That curious legal compilation, the 'Lucas Annotations' once again forgets all its lawyer's jargon and gives almost a T.V. commentator's description of the event.

"The scene is before her and she sees again her kinsman John Lucas of the Great House, Horton and Port-Eynon, very stalwart and powerful, standing upon the tomb with his father behind him calling unto their followers around them, forcing their kinsman and his men over the banks, even into the river, whence they ran along the bed thereof under the ford. John Lucas the younger saying unto her as he pursued, 'Uncle is in Church, Anne, don't cry', whereby his assurance of safety of her father who, being clergy, he locked in the Church, it being offensive to shed blood in sight of clergy." After which delicate respect for the proprieties, John Lucas proceeded to beat the living daylight out of his adversaries, one of whom was killed. No wonder the Stouthall branch heir, also a John Lucas, when he came into his estate, felt bound to build that civilized mansion which is the present Stouthall. He had to prove that not all Lucases were of the Port-Eynon variety!

The Great House, from which poor Anne Williams watched the riot, has been pulled down. It once belonged to a branch of the well-known Cradock family whose head, Sir Matthew Cradock, was Steward of Gower in 1491 and again in 1497 in the reign of Henry VII. But the Glebe House, now Glebe Farm, still overlooks the north side of the churchyard. It dates from the fifteenth century and was probably one of the houses built in Gower by the Knights of St John. The tall chimney, on the churchyard side, was supposed to be a 'Flemish' chimney, proof of the presence of the Flemings in Gower. It is in fact, a rather typical medieval chimney and seems to suit the old house very well.

The road climbs up out of Cheriton and runs for a short mile behind the rim of wooded limestone cliffs fringing the marshes until it drops down into the little hamlet of Landimore. Landimore was a place of importance in the early days of the conquest and was one of the original 'knight's fees'. It stands on the edge of the great saltmarsh and a road goes down through the white-walled houses onto the wide levels. You can park your car and walk along the track that skirts the marsh underneath the line of wooded cliffs called Tor Gro. This is probably the best place to study the old shore line that, beneath its green covering of small trees and brambles, corresponds to the sea-girt shore of the south. This rim of white rock ends westwards in the bolder cliff of North Hill Tor or Nottle Tor, which marks the point where the Burry stream swings out from its valley near Cheriton onto the flat land and so to the estuary.

Nottle Tor was quarried in the old days and possessed an extensive cave in which the young men of Cheriton, Landimore and Llanmadoc ran to hide when the man-of-war's boat bringing the press gang was spotted coming across the estuary from Llanelli during the Napoleonic Wars. On the land side it bears the ditches of a promontory fort of the Iron Age.

Just before you reach the spot where you park the car, marked by the notice that Landimore Marsh belongs to the National Trust, you can climb easily up the steep grassy slope that guards the village. The limestone rocks break through and it is a fine viewpoint over the salt marshes. I usually find a group of keen bird watchers perched here on week-ends, as the long skeins of duck move across the sands and flats and the herons stalk among the pools. Do they come over from the heronry at Penrice, I wonder?

A little further east, looking down on Landimore from the edge of the steep slope, are the scanty remains of Bovehill Castle. They are covered in such a tangle of brambles, ivy and small trees that it is difficult to make them out from below, but you can push in through the bramble thickets and find yourself among the empty walls with a deserted cottage close at hand, buried amongst nettles and thorn bushes. A forlorn, abandoned place yet it was once the seat of the important knight, Sir Hugh Jonys. In the fine memorial brass to his memory which survived the blitz in St Mary's Church, Swansea, he is described as a Crusader and indeed he received the honour of knighthood at the Holy Sepulchre at Jerusalem on 14th August 1441. He became Knight-Marshal of England and was rewarded for his services by the grant of Landimore from John, Duke of Norfolk, who was then the Lord of Gower.

The gallant old warrior settled down snugly at Bovehill, which he made into a fortified manor-house in the style of the day. You can still find traces of the trench he made for the lead pipes of his water supply from a well on Ryer's Down. Later on Bovehill passed into the hands of Sir Rhys ap Thomas, the supporter of Henry VII who seemed to have become possessed of half the castles of West Wales as a reward for helping the Tudors to the throne. Then it fell into decay and now it is a mouldering pile of abandoned walls. So passed the worldly pride of the Jonys.

A short mile eastwards from Landimore you come to the far more impressive remains of Weobley Castle. Again a fine site on the high land looking right out over the vast salt marshes. Weobley is a fortified manor-house in essence, but there were earlier fortifications here before it was enlarged in the fifteenth century. The Department of the Environment has done its usual excellent job of guarding and restoring the ruins. You can trace the Great Hall and the courtyard with the houses for the little garrison. From the time of the first conquest of Gower to the fifteenth century Weobley belonged to the de la Bere family and it was Sir John de la Bere who was in residence when in 1406 Owain Glyndwr and his followers swooped down on Gower and carried fire and sword through the peninsula. Hardly any of the Gower castles escaped serious damage. Sir John sent out piteous appeals for aid to the garrison at Swansea but those unhappy soldiers had far too much on their own plate. Glyndwr and his rebels swarmed all over the countryside—Sir John was compelled to see his castle severely smashed.

From the de la Beres it eventually passed like Landimore into the hands of that ever-ready castle collector Sir Rhys ap Thomas. Then later on it was no longer required as a lordly residence. It gently decayed into a farm. In its last years it came into the Mansel family's hands and it was Miss Mansel Talbot of Penrice Castle who handed it over to what was then the Ministry of Works.

The new farmhouse stands near the castle and from it a track, marked "Private", leads down the steep dingle and out onto the salt marshes. The American Army used the marshes as a firing range during the War, and constructed this long causeway out over the flats ending in a look-out perched on the outer sands. It has, at least, been a help to the present farmer of Weobley Farm, Mr Pritchard. Recently, I stood with him beside the walls of Weobley Castle looking out over the salt marsh. He was trying to spot where his sheep had got to. One of the major channels called Great Pill runs out near Weobley and the sheep tend to go out beyond it, for the sweetest and newest grass seems always to be at the outer edge of the marsh. The Great Pill can fill up fast behind them. On spring tides the water comes in an astonishing distance. It covers the marsh completely and washes up into the fields.

The horses and even the cows know all about the dangers of the advancing tide. They sense it coming and retreat in time. The sheep, apparently, are not so intelligent. Although they can swim, they supinely allow themselves to be cut off by the tide and drowned. So Mr Pritchard drives out on the causeway, continually sounding his motor-horn. The sheep recognize the sound as a danger signal and retire in a big flock along the causeway to safety.

From Weobley the road goes eastwards to the road junction of Oldwalls. There are some fine 'standing stones' hereabout, particularly the great menhir called Mansel's Jack or Samson's Jack in the fields near the farm of Manselfold. For the moment you turn away from the sea and the marshes to look once again at the long central ridge of Cefn Bryn. We are back under its influence and for the next few miles eastwards it fills the southern horizon. At Oldwalls, too, the direct road from Llangennith comes to join the road on the rim of the marshes which we have been following ever since we left Llanmadoc. This road comes out from Llangennith and skirts the foot of Ryer's Down to pass through the hamlet of Burry Green.

I have always liked the look of Burry Green for there really is a green here, wide and untouched, and the houses are grouped on its northern side with a few whitewashed farms on the south. Among them is the pleasantly modest little chapel of Bethesda.

This was one of the many built through Gower in the 1800s by the money and influence of the remarkable Lady Barham, who lived near at hand in the mansion of Fairy Hill. Lady Barham was a most unlikely figure to find in Gower, busy completing the work of evangelizing the peninsula begun by John Wesley. She descended on it almost by accident. She was the daughter of the Baron Barham, formerly Sir Charles Middleton, who was First Lord of the Admiralty at the time of Trafalgar. She had long frequented the evangelical circles around the Countess of Huntingdon and Wilberforce and was a friend of Hannah More and George Whitefield. She was at Bristol on her way to stay with friends at Taunton when she received a note saying that they would not be ready for her for a fortnight. She decided to spend the interval at Swansea. She took a trip into Gower, immediately declared it an evangelical desert and settled at Fairy Hill with the intention of completely revitalizing the whole area. This she proceeded to do with furious energy and an aristocratic determination to get things moving in a big way. Gower was ripe for her advent.

Wesley, as we saw at Oxwich, had stirred up interest but his converts were still small and scattered groups. Hywel Harris and his Welsh-born missioners had also made forays into Gower but were never really happy there. Hywel Harris consoled himself in 1742 with the reflection that, at Newton, "many open rebels seem as melted as wax". He also made the long but unrewarding journey to 'Rose Scilly'. But many of his followers found Gower stony ground. Of Lunnon they wrote, "They are very dead there", while Penclawdd was "a dark pagan place". Lady Barham's money and energy soon changed that. She vigorously supported her missioner William Griffith who became known as the Apostle of Gower. The little chapels sprang up all through the countryside; Bethesda at Burry Green was the pioneer in 1814, then came Bethel at Penclawdd (1816), Trinity at Cheriton (1816), Paraclete at Newton (1818), Emmanuel at Pilton Green (1821) and Mount Pisgah at Ilston (1822).

Not everything went as smoothly as Lady Barham might have wished. There came a moment when she insisted that her secretary, the Rev William Hamilton, be inaugurated as a minister and this led eventually to a break between her and the Welsh Calvinistic Methodists, with the result that many of the chapels she established eventually went over to the

Congregationalists. William Hamilton is buried under the pulpit at Paraclete in Newton and the story was chronicled by the most unlikely religious historian in the whole range of ecclesiastical research—none other than Dylan Thomas. Dylan's mother's sister was married to the minister of Paraclete and when he began his career as a journalist, Dylan used the chapel records to write one of his earliest feature articles which appeared in the *Herald of Wales* in 1932. The imagination boggles at the idea of a possible meeting in the Elysian Fields between Lady Barham and Dylan Thomas.

There is no question who would have converted who! Lady Barham was undoubtedly an imperious figure. Behind Bethesda Chapel on Burry Green an outside flight of steps leads up to a gallery where Lady Barham had a special, high-backed pew for herself and the household of Fairy Hill. She was carried to chapel over the muddy fields in a sedan chair borne by two stalwart rustics. If she disapproved of a sermon she had no hesitation in leaving half-way through by the outside stairway and have herself carried back to Fairy Hill.

Fairy Hill was originally one of the Lucas's houses known as 'Peartree' and lies in the narrow valley of the Burry stream. We have been meeting the Burry Pill at its mouth at Cheriton; we have already visited its source near Llanddewi. From Burry Green the road follows its middle course to the south and forms one of the few north-south links in Gower. The stream curves around the western edge of the Cefn Bryn ridge and was big enough to turn several mills along this section. They are still there although all are now disused. Near Fairy Hill, too, is the curiously named Cadiz Hall. For years I had assumed this house must have been named after the great Spanish port and commemorated the part played in the Earl of Essex's great expedition against Cadiz in 1596 by Robert Mansell, of the Penrice-Margam family. He was knighted for his bravery and afterwards rose to high office under James I, becoming one of the leading figures in naval affairs and being appointed Vice-Admiral of England in 1618. His portrait hangs in the picture gallery at Penrice Castle although it has been so thoroughly repainted that we can hardly claim it as a true picture of the man once described by a leading authority on the history of Glamorgan as "probably the ablest and most distinguished public man whom that County has produced". I would like to think that he once resided here in the heart of Gower.

Once again, the hard facts of history destroy romance. Cadiz is simply a corruption of Cady or Cade, the name of a family established in Gower in the Middle Ages and who had a holding near here on the slopes of Cefn Bryn.

The Burry stream does, in fact, form the western boundary of the long Cefn Bryn ridge. The main road eastwards from Burry Green crosses its waters at the wooded hollow of Stembridge, then runs for a mile and a half to Oldwalls. At Oldwalls you are again aware of the presence of Cefn Bryn—you cannot really escape it when you are in Gower. This time it is the northern slope that you see, brown and bracken-covered. The moorland actually comes down to the main road a little further on at the farm of Cilibion. All the fields hereabout once belonged to Neath Abbey. The old Red Road from Reynoldston which crosses Cefn Bryn links with the north road near Cilibion. They also used to call the Red Road the Coal Road, for this is the way the coal carts used to creak across the ridge bringing the coal from Penclawdd to South Gower.

This northern side of Cefn Bryn is criss-crossed by paths all of which get very boggy in winter. Near the junction of the Cefn Bryn road and the north road is the fine Bronze Age tumulus of Pen-y-Crug and also one of the largest stretches of water in inland Gower, the Broad Pool. Again, this is not saying much. Gower lakes, like Gower churches, are tiny. They would probably be regarded as glorified ponds anywhere else. But Broad Pool charms, not by size but by site. It is on the edge of a wide sweep of the commons of Cefn Bryn. The wild ponies haunt it, the herons stalk along its banks on the days when no tourists come and the duck know it well in the winter.

Broad Pool is a bit of a mystery for at first sight it is not at all obvious from where the water comes or why it should stay in the pool. Not far away, the Old Red Sandstone appears to form the back-bone of Cefn Bryn but Broad Pool is on the limestone. The answer seems to be that the water is held up by a thick layer of glacial boulder clay which has subsided into hollows dissolved in the underlying limestone. Broad Pool is a Nature Reserve and is rich in insect life, including several species of dragon-fly. The microscopic fauna is also notable. One problem has become acute in recent years, however. The fringed water lily (*Limnanthemum*) has invaded the pool and this pushful newcomer has spread inordinately until it seems to have taken over half of the two acres of water available. It produces an attractive flower for a short period but that seems all the good I can say of it. I have no desire to see Broad Pool smothered with the stuff.

Loitering besides Broad Pool and looking out over the wide spaces of Cefn Bryn, I have rather overrun myself. I have come a mile too far along the north road from Oldwalls. But this is the last time we shall be visiting Cefn Bryn and it seemed right and proper to enjoy the wide sweep of Gower's special moorland before tracing the northern shore-line eastwards to the point where the peninsula merges in the mainland and the real 'Welshery' begins.

We return, therefore, to the signpost that points down to Llanrhidian. Llanrhidian is the last village of Gower Anglicana on this side; the last village on the limestone and the last that looks out onto the salt marshes. It is, therefore, a bit of a turning-point in our survey. It is also a village of charm and character. Of course, like every village in Gower it has had new housing thrust upon it and some of that housing, like the row of new red-roofed villas opposite the village green, seem less than tactful in fitting into their ancient setting. But, on the whole, Llanrhidian still feels a village which has kept its heart and pride. The one street tumbles steeply down the hill to the marshes and the church is tucked under the wooded slope broken by the high outcrops of limestone. The village green lies before the church and it is also on a slope. Two mysterious and very large stones stand on the green on either side of the path that leads to the church.

The upper stone is a slab of quartz-conglomerate from Cefn Bryn and is curiously shaped, with three short stumps sticking out of the top. Iron staples were embedded into the stone. It has been suggested that it could be all that remains of an old Celtic wheel cross, of a type which was common in Wales in the tenth century A.D. The top could have been knocked off by Puritans during the Reformation and the staples inserted long after-wards, when the old stone was used as a sort of village pillory. This pillory suggestion has been queried on the grounds that this stone was probably put in its present position around 1820 and pillories were abolished by law in 1816.

We know a little more about the erection of the lower stone, which is a block of limestone. A vivid entry in the parish register describes the scene "on the 8th day of April, 1844, a very large stone weighing nearly 2 tons raised on its end a short distance from the 'Welcome to Town' public house. 10 to 12 men volunteered to do it—1 pint of beer each". Then again, "on this day, the Churchwardens and the Minister, with the assistance of some twenty strong hands—and double the number of shouting boys—the large Lime Stone was erected on End with no little difficulty." The great stone stands there firm to this day but where did it come from? Was it originally one of those menhirs or standing stones resembling Samson's Jack? Manselfold Farm is not so far away. Or could it have been part of some now-destroyed vast stone alignment dating back to around 3000 B.C. Both of the Llanrhidian stones are standing puzzles; but then, Llanrhidian seems to specialize in puzzling stones.

In the porch of the church is the strange, carves stone known as the Leper Stone. This is a massive, coffin-shaped stone bearing grotesque and simplified human figures and animals on one face, which was dug up outside the porch of the church in the nineteenth century. The animals look like bears with paws held up, and the stylized human figures may represent Mary and St John at the Cross. Or they may be figures from Viking history, for the late Professor Nash-Williams identified the stone as a 'hog's back' similar to those found in Northern England and dating from the tenth century. The animals look like bears with paws held up, and coffins containing the relics of a saint and were favoured by Vikings after they had been converted to Christianity. But what is this 'hog's back' doing in Llanrhidian? There are none in Ireland and this is the only one in Wales. Did a wandering Viking bring one down with him or even instruct a local craftsman to make him one according to the pattern he dictated? We must add the Leper Stone to the other mystery stones of Llanrhidian.

The church itself is dedicated to both St Illtud and St Rhidian. It has a strong, battlemented tower on which stands a block of masonry said to be used for carrying a beacon fire. Within, the altar has been carved by the Rev J. D. Davies, while Mr Fleming, a well-known antique dealer whose ancestors came from the village, has presented some valuable painting to decorate the choir. It seems all the more tragic that Llanrhidian Church, in common with so many Gower churches, has now to be kept locked against vandals. It is one of those churches which invite you to meditation, built as it is in the shadow of a beautifully wooded cliff and with so many relics of the remote past placed all around.

There is one old building in Llanrhidian which is always open—at the correct hours, of course. This is the quaintly named Welcome to Town inn. The Welcome to Town seems to have been a typical Gower title for inns. There was once a similarly named inn at Llangennith, kept by Phil Tanner's wife, which displayed the notice "Call Softly, Drink Soberly, Pay Freely, Depart Quietly". When I was a small boy I thought that the Llanrhidian Welcome was really named The Welcome to Town Gentlemen but I am sure I mistook the position of a very necessary notice in close juxtaposition to the inn sign.

The Welcome still lives up to its name, and the old house with its sloping roof at the back has always been a centre of the local life. Here the Gower United Association for the Prosecution of Felons used to hold its annual dinner. These associations were common in remote rural areas before the beginning of a regular police force. The country gentlemen and the substantial farmers offered rewards for the apprehension of criminals on an agreed scale. For burglary, house-breaking, highway or footpath robbery the Gower Association paid five guineas; stealing farm animals got the informant the same amount. "Milking any cow or robbing what is commonly called a Rabbit Warren"—two guineas. The last case dealt with was a case of sheep stealing in 1856, but the Association went happily on its way for the next thirty years enjoying the annual dinner at the Welcome to Town, until in 1892 there were only 6 members left. They had a last splendid tuck-in, and when they had paid the bill declared the Association disbanded with a balance in hand of 2½d.

So ancient an inn is bound to have a ghost and the Welcome to Town has its resident apparition. He seems to be quite harmless. When you look into one of the front rooms you may see a coachman dressed in Regency style sitting quietly in a chair—and then he vanishes! I have a theory that he must have been waiting to take someone home after an unusually hearty dinner of the Gower United Association for the Prosecution of Felons!

From the Welcome to Town the road drops down towards the marshes past the Nether Mill. The mill no longer works full time and one of the great millstones leans against the wall, but the inscription on the slate plaque still records with pride

Built in the year 1803 at the
Sole Expense of Wm. M. Evans, Gent

John Beynon ⎫   William Edward ⎫
            ⎬   Masons   ⎬   Carpenters
Evan Jenkin ⎭   George Evans   ⎭

It is over 170 years since the old mill was built by the men whose names are on the slate, yet the walls still look solid and beautiful. The mill pond is still there with a flock of the whitest-imaginable Aylesbury ducks and the miller's son still lives in the farmhouse and his garden is bright with flowers. Although the great wheel was dismantled he still grinds flour on the mill.

The road winds on and out to the marshes. In fact you can walk along a path that skirts the whole edge of the marshland to Landimore, with a fine view of Weobley Castle perched on its high ridge to the west. The lonely looking buildings you come to at the road's end before the path begins are the former woollen factory of Stavel Hagar. Woollen weaving was a widespread industry in north Gower in the old days, before big scale mechanization killed the small water powered factories. The Tanners were the most famous of the Llangennith weavers and the Dixes of Stavel Hagar were the pride of Llanrhidian. The looms at Stavel Hagar were not dismantled until 1904 and one of the Dixes, Harriet Dix, lived on in the house until 1950. Here they wove the red shawls or 'whittles' and the 'minka', the coarse striped flannel that all miners and tin-plate workers insisted on having for their working shirts as an act of faith. Out from Stavel Hagar the salt-marshes stretch to the horizon. The marsh birds give their lost, piping calls. It seems a lonely place today now that the cheerful sound of the looms is stilled.

When you look out over the flats as the winter mists gather, you can believe the tradition that a galley called the Scanderoon Galley once got stranded in the mud between the complicated channels of Leason Pill and Golbut Pill. It carried gold in riveted containers. All the gold was salvaged except one container which sank into the mud. Many years later a Llanrhidian man suddenly became rich and he could never explain the source of his wealth. In the 'sixties of last century a pilot crossing the marsh to board his boat noticed a gaunt timber outline of a large ship sticking out of the mud of Leason Pill. Was it the Scanderoon Galley? Will the tide expose it again? The Scanderoon Galley is north Gower's reply to Rhossili's 'Dollar

Ship'. Out on the marshes, with the mists closing in, you can believe anything.

But here, as you leave the salt marshes, you are on the edge of another dividing line in Gower. Within a few miles, changes occur that are not marked on the surface of the ground but which are nevertheless important. Underneath, the limestone gives way to the Millstone Grit and the Coal Measures, and the English language starts to retreat before the Welsh. You are in the north-east borderland between Gower Anglicana and Gower Wallicana.

7

North-East Gower

Most Gower visitors, after they leave Llanrhidian, feel that they have 'done the tour' of Gower. They will drive back to Swansea along the main north road. They will pass some of the places we have already visited—Cilibion with their last close view of the moorlands of Cefn Bryn, down into the hollow at Llethrid where they cross the Ilston stream, then over the breezy expanses of Pengwern and of Fairwood Common to rejoin the south road above Killay and the spreading suburbs of Swansea. But if they look westward as they return across Fairwood, they will see a dark line of high ground, speckled with woods and hidden patches of gorse and reeds, with farms and lonely houses perched on the skyline. This is the edge of north-east Gower, the unknown Gower that lies between Fairwood and the wide sands of the Burry Estuary. The tourists tend to leave it on one side and, on the face of it, they may be right. The north-east corner hides many of its attractions. They are there however, and no one can claim that he knows his Gower unless he also knows the land between Fairwood and the mouth of the Loughor river.

As soon as you come up the hill from Llanrhidian you are on the western edge of it, and before you is the rounded hill that I regard as the starting point of the change, Cil Ifor Top. It is the first up-swelling of the Millstone Grit and it is crowned with the impressive earth ramparts of Gower's biggest Iron Age fort. It covers an area of nearly eight acres and is thus bigger than its nearest rival, the Bulwark on Llanmadoc Hill. It was probably constructed around 100 B.C., but as with all the other Gower earthworks, we know nothing of its real history. We can only conjecture. Clearly it must have been a place of importance to the men who built it, for they put a vast amount of labour into its construction, and when the ramparts were crowned with palisades and the complex entrances fitted with great timber barricades and pointed stakes, Cil Ifor would have looked a formidable place to an attacker. And who actually used it? Did the territory of the fierce fighting tribe of the Silures, who gave the Romans such trouble to subdue, extend as far west as Gower? If it did, Cil Ifor might well have had to be stormed by the Romans as they advanced into West Wales. After all the Roman camp of Leucarum (Loughor) is only five miles away. We can only speculate, and such speculation is frowned upon by archaeologists and historians. We can however outflank the defences by taking the road marked Welsh Moor.

This leads through a wide common tucked away amongst small woods and farms. Its very name indicates that we are here on the borders of Gower Wallicana. The farm names, too, are mixed. Welshmoor Farm is near Llanelen, Gower's Load next to Caecenwyn; but the Welsh names predominate. Llanelen Farm is an intriguing place. You reach it down a typical Gower lane, off Welsh Moor. I last walked down the lane in late spring when the hedges were a tender green and a mare and her long-legged foal went clattering away ahead of us to the farm buildings, so solid and white-walled. This is how an old Gower farm should look. I was on the track of a Gower mystery. Just beyond the farm, so they say, is the site of a long-lost medieval village and church with a strange, romantic history. Llanelen once had a chapel of ease, and there are records showing it still in existence in the time of Edward VI. After that, church and village disappeared from history. Grass grows over the site of the church and the cottages, with scattered stones here and there. A great yew tree 500 years old alone marks the spot. The story goes that a ship came ashore on the high tide, and the survivors staggered through the darkness and up the steep slope to Llanelen. They were welcomed but gave a tragic return for their hospitality. The ship's crew carried the plague. In a matter of days the villagers were all dead. Llanelen never recovered. The ghost of a lady in white haunts the place where the village now lies in ruins, weeping for the fate of Llanelen, and it is deemed extremely unlucky to touch what remains. A farmer from Wern Halog, just below Llanelen, once took a stone from the church, but it rolled around with such fury that he had to return it.

I walked out beyond the farm through a small wood where the trees had been cut. It was ghostly enough, but where were grassy mounds that marked the church? I wandered around and could see nothing—and no sign of a 500-year-old yew tree. But I had not walked far enough. The yew tree is there all right, and in 1975 the Pendragon Society began excavations and turned up the walls of the church and some of the old houses. Another of Gower's 'lost villages' had been found. The church might even have been built on a site that goes back to the Dark Ages. Even when recovered, Llanelen remains to puzzle us.

But I had a fine view out from the brow of the hill of mystery, from Cil Ifor Top to the west, out over the marshes to where a long spur jutting out to the sands marked the hamlet of Crofty and the beginning of Penclawdd. Penclawdd is the biggest and most important place in this north-east corner of Gower, and the two roads that lead to it from Llanrhidian were below me as I looked: a direct wide road from Cil Ifor and a secret winding road along the edge of the salt-marsh. I know exactly which one to follow. The direct road is for the man in a hurry in his car. The road on the edge of the marsh is for the walker and the happy loiterer, who enjoys space and birds calling and the feeling of the salt wind blowing in from the distant sea.

This is the eastern end of the great expanse of salt-flats that has been with us all the way from Whitford Point along the whole of Gower's north coasts, for at Crofty a spit of land runs out along which you can by-pass the channels and flats of the marsh and walk out directly onto the actual sands of the Burry Estuary. As a result, this is the point from which the cockle-pickers follow the tide out to the biggest cockle-beds in Britain. Penclawdd, around the corner from Crofty, is usually credited with the cockle industry, but most of the pickers come from Crofty and nearby Llanmorlais.

The pickers are women and they are reputed to be the toughest in Wales. They have to be, for they go out in all weathers. They gather at Salthouse Point in Crofty and move out in a long procession over the sands. In the old days they drove their donkeys before them, laden with panniers' and I remember watching them and thinking that they looked like an Old Testament tribe on the march over the desert sands. Nowadays they use little flat carts drawn by ponies, for lorries or light vans crush the cockles. It takes a good hour to reach some of the outer beds, crossing channels called '*Gwters*' by the cockle pickers. They know them all by name—Gwtwr Fach, Gwtwr Fawr, Gwtwr Cefn Sidan, and the Grwnshirs river, and at some of them, they have to float their carts over.

The cockles are gathered with a short rake and sieved to ensure that the smaller and immature ones fall back into soft sand, for the cockle has to be given time to grow. It begins with a brief free-swimming stage and then settles down in the sand to develop. It feeds on minute organisms in the water and moves about the sands with its 'foot'. You can tell the age of a cockle by the rings on its shell; it adds two in its first year and one for every subsequent year. A cockle can live for six years, but it is a very lucky cockle that reaches the age limit. It has any amount of natural enemies including the gulls, starfish, sea-urchins and plaice. And of course, the cockle-pickers.

It is back-breaking work and sometimes the tides can bring danger. There have been drowning tragedies on many occasions in the past. But there is a great spirit of comradeship amongst the cockle women; they know they are a very special breed and are proud of it. I sensed this when, just after the war, I talked for the BBC with Mrs Morfydd Jones of Penclawdd, and she gave me a vivid account of her adventures.

> Cockling nearly caused the death of me a couple of times, then. The first time was when I was fifteen. As soon as I left school I had a craving to go with the cockles. Mother said "No", but I borrowed a donkey and went out with two friends. But we misjudged the tides coming back and got caught in one of the pills. My two friends managed to wade across, but I was behind with the donkey. Suddenly I was swept off my feet. I could hear my friends on the bank saying their prayers out loud for me to be saved. I just managed to cling hold of the neck of the donkey when he lost his footing too. The poor dab was already weighed down with our two hundredweight of cockles, but he swam like a Trojan and dragged himself and me onto dry land. I had swallowed so much water I was more dead than alive when they took me home. My mother was wild of course, and it was good-bye to the cockles for a couple of years. But the call was too strong in the end.

The cockle-woman of the past were famous figures in Swansea Market when I was young. They almost had a regulation dress for coming to town, with red and black stripes, black and white aprons, grey plaid shawls and flat straw hats with raised brims on which they balanced a wooden pail of cockles while they carried two large baskets on their arms. What figures they had—like Grecian goddesses! You could trace them moving through the crowd by the pails floating overhead. They came in by the early morning train for the Saturday market and returned by the 2.30, to be met by their husbands at Penclawdd Station. The Penclawdd husbands called the 2.30 train "The Relish" for they knew that the women would always bring back something tasty for supper after a successful day's selling.

Before the train ran to Penclawdd the cockle women used to walk the whole seven miles into Swansea balancing their wooden pails on their heads. They would walk barefooted to save shoe-leather and at a spot on the Gower Road, half a mile after they had passed Killay, they would wash their feet and put on their boots to march proudly through the town. The spot is still called Olchfa (Welsh—the washing place) and today a new modern, comprehensive school stands there, also with the name Olchfa. What a change in seventy-five years!

There have been great changes too, in the way the cockles are processed. The boiling has been mechanized, many of them are tinned. New problems now confront the industry. The yield is dropping, in spite of planting new beds with young cockles from East Anglia. There has been talk of overfishing. Some people put the blame on the oyster-catchers. They say that great flocks of them are increasing in the estuary and that the only way to save the cockles is to shoot the oyster-catchers. Official permission has been granted to thin out the oyster-catchers—to the fury of the conservationists. The controversy continues and someone like myself, who is charmed by the oyster-catchers but who appreciates the needs of the cockle-gatherers, can only hope that in the long run, they will be able to co-exist. And that the cockle industry will recover its former glory.

Penclawdd, at one time, had other interests besides cockling. It is on the south crop of the coalfield and had several collieries; some of the workings went under the waters of the estuary. The pits have been long closed and gorse and bushes are clothing the old coal-tips. The village also had a copper-works back in the eighteenth century and its products were put to strange use. The copper was brought from the Parys Mountain mines in Anglesea and made into small pieces shaped like horseshoes. These 'manillas' were used in West Africa to buy slaves. The little village is quiet now and can look picturesque when the high tide floods up to the waterfront and the small boats rock on the still water. Penclawdd had to have a waterfront, for in Welsh, Pen(y) Clawdd simply means top of the dyke.

A road climbs steeply up the hill behind it to the hamlet rejoicing in the name of Blue Anchor, after the well-known inn. This has been modernized and extended but when I first knew it, it was a great place for Penclawdd wedding receptions. I remember hearing the landlord confide in me as I watched the guests enjoying themselves from the safety of the bar. "Don't say anything, but it was she proposed to him. No, it's not so uncommon here, boy. In Penclawdd the women rule. Well they earn the money, don't they!" I'm still wondering if that is true!

This hinterland of Penclawdd has a character of its own. It used to be semi-industrial, when small collieries were still viable. You come across ivy-covered ruined mine-shafts and small overgrown tips but there are farms as well, interspersed with little patches of commonland. It is high ground. The ridge known as Mynydd Bach y Cocs, (the Little Mountain of the Cockles) is over 400 feet and gives rise to the Morlais stream which flows north to leave the hills near Llanmorlais and enters the sea at Salthouse Point. On the edge of this secluded area, just off the road from Fairwood Common towards Cilonnen, is Gellihir Wood, part of the Naturalists' Trust Reserve in Gower. This patch of woodland only covers seventy acres but it is very important as it shows exactly what an untouched piece of Gower wooded country looked like before replanting or cutting. It is covered with ash and elm in its northern sector and with birch and oak on the south. It is very quiet as you make your way along the damp, soggy paths through the trees. A grey squirrel shot up a tree ahead of me, swift and vivid. Dare I say I was sorry to see him? When I was young the charming red squirrel was the king of the Gower trees. Clearly our native squirrel has had to retreat in Gower before the grey invader. Wales used to be one of the last strongholds of the red squirrel but now only a few areas in North and Mid Wales remain to him. I wonder if there are any stray survivors left in Gower.

Of the larger animals, the badger is still surprisingly common. There are sets, not only in places like Gellihir Woods but along the cliff-tops as well. Let us hope that this splendid creature can still hold his own in the crowded Gower of the future. Sometimes it seems as if all hands are against him. I can never forget my surprise and delight, while driving alongside Gellihir Woods—many years ago I'm afraid—to see what looked like a large old English sheep dog lolloping along the lane ahead of me. Then his head turned and I could see that unmistakable long line of white fur fringed with black from the brow down to the pointed muzzle that marks Old Brock, as they called the badger in Gower. He did not seem to worry. He trotted along as if he owned the place, came to a hole in the hedge and disappeared. I felt I had been privileged to see him.

I have never seen the next largest of the Gower mammals, the otter. I have got no recent report I must admit, but I am told that this most graceful and sinuous creature can still be found along the Ilston stream and maybe along the Burry Pill. After all, there are plenty of brown trout in Ilston, and the sewin, or sea-trout, come up the Burry River so an otter would have quite enough to eat. And I cannot think that he would ruin valuable fishing, for inland Gower is hardly a fly-fisher's Mecca. Like the badger, I hope that there will always be a place for him in Gower. I am not worried about the fox. That cunning rascal can be relied on to survive anything. He is as bold as brass and will even raid the dust-bins in the Swansea suburbs.

Perched on the highest point of the central ridge is the scattered village of Three Crosses. There is still a village green here, but you are now well out of the atmosphere of agricultural Gower. This was once mining country although all the pits have gone. Yet there are still memories of the time when even this north-east corner was part of rural Gower. Just along the road from Three Crosses is the hamlet of Poundffald. The very name indicates that this is a mixed up area between Gower Anglicana and Gower Wallicana, for what is '*ffald*' but Welsh for pound. So Pound—Pound it is! And there is still an old pound there, the enclosure where they used to put the strayed animals of the village; only today it has been incorporated in the buildings of the pub as a cellar. The pub is a warm friendly place, with a lounge and bar that glitters with brasses. Opposite are the big outbuildings of the farm and a glimpse of the Loughor Estuary beyond.

In Three Crosses itself, the most prominent building is the Congregational Chapel, Capel y Crwys, one of the oldest chapels in Gower and a name famous in Nonconformist history. From the green before it, the road runs north-east to drop down into the little village of Dunvant, which still maintains its individuality in spite of the steadily encroaching houses of the Swansea suburbs. Dunvant is an Anglicization of the Welsh "*dwfn-nant*" or deep stream, and you really are in a narrow valley here. It is interesting geologically, for the valley was cut by the overflowing melt-water which had been pounded back by the glaciers at the end of the Ice Ages. At the bottom of the valley is Ebenezer Chapel and the Post Office, and a little way up the hill back towards Three Crosses is the pub with the most amusing name in Gower. It boldly proclaims itself the 'Found Out'. It has been rebuilt, but the old pub was the place the

colliers used to slip in quietly for a pint on coming home with
their wages on pay day, and where the suspicious wives would
suddenly descend on them to make certain the wage packet did
not melt away in the '*cwrw*' or beer.

There are now few colliers left in Dunvant to be 'found out', for
all the local collieries are closed; but you will hear splendid
singing here on the practice nights of the Dunvant Male Voice
Choir. In fact little Dunvant may not look exactly like a
picturesque old Gower village, but it has produced musicians,
artists and poets to make up for its lack of architectural glory.
Ceri Richards, one of Wales's greatest painters was born here,
although when you see Dunvant on a wet day you wonder where
Ceri got his splendid colour sense from, for his canvases are a
riot of sensuous colour. John Ormond, now a producer with the
BBC in Wales, is a poet of importance and power and has drawn
much of his inspiration from his early life in Dunvant.

The road north out of Dunvant runs through the narrow
channel made by the glacial melt-waters to Gowerton, which I
regard as marking geographically the end of Peninsula Gower.
We are already well into Gower Wallicana, for we left English-
speaking Gower behind long ago at Llanrhidian. All the
villages in the north-east—Dunvant, Three Crosses, Penclawdd
and Gowerton—are basically Welsh speaking, or were until
recently. You will still hear Welsh being used in the shops and,
of course in the chapels. But industry not agriculture was the
foundation of most of these north-eastern villages, although the
collieries and the tin-plate works that were originally the cause
of their being, are now all closed. The site of the works at
Gowerton is now a grassy patch next door to the rugby club.
Gowerton belongs in mind and spirit to the rest of the old
commote of Gwyr, that inland, Welsh, mountain country which
we are going to explore in the last chapter of this book.

But Gowerton also faces both ways. Behind it are the slopes
that mark the 200-foot peneplain of Peninsula Gower. Before it
are the flats and marshes formed by the Rivers Llan and Lliw
that come down from the hill country to join the Burry Estuary
and the Loughor River. You look out over them and in the
distance is the higher ground of Loughor village with its
Norman castle and Roman fort. The long railway and road
bridges span the estuary and the high hills rise behind it. You
realize, as you drive over the levels towards Loughor that you
are leaving behind the Gower of limestone cliffs, the breezy

downs, the fortress churches and Phil Tanner's folksongs, of that strange amalgam of Welsh placenames and English inhabitants, of the wind driving in over Whitford Point and the Worm twisting out to sea from Rhossili Sands, all that has so delighted you in Peninsula Gower, Bro Gwyr—Gower of the Vales! At Loughor you enter a new land—Bryniau Gwyr, Gower of the Hills.

8

Postscript: Gower of the Hills

At Loughor this book should reach its natural conclusion. We have set out to explore the Gower Peninsula, but once you stand by the ruined stump of the Norman castle on the little hill of Loughor and look to the north, you realize that you are in a new land. The village of Loughor itself was once the Roman fort of Leucarum, guarding the river-crossing. Extensive excavations in 1982–83 revealed the importance of the site. The line of the ramparts has been traced and the foundations of some of the administrative buildings uncovered. The Normans followed the Romans and, with the nineteenth century, industry came to the area. But there is no question that, once you are at Loughor, you are well out of peninsular Gower.

The sea, which has been an ever-present background so far in these pages, now fades from the picture. True, the Loughor Estuary still winds northwards into the hills, but high tide makes it look like a magnificent lake rather than a part of the wild sea. In the background rise the high moorlands behind Pontardulais. They are on an altogether bigger scale than the friendly downs of Cefn Bryn or Llanmadoc Hill. Industry shows its presence in a way we never noticed in our wanderings around Penrice or Rhossili. There are still coal mines at work at Bryn Lliw, and at Abernant. Tin-plate is still manufactured at the great works near Llangyfelach, Velindre forms part of the giant combine that has swallowed the scores of minor plants which had given birth to villages like Gorseinon and Grovesend.

The chapel not the church is the centre of their village life and the Welsh language the basis of their culture. This was the area that was first swept by the last great Welsh religious revival. Indeed, it was at Moriah chapel at Loughor that the young revivalist, Evan Roberts, started this celebrated spiritual fire-storm. "Gower of the Hills' is a country where the little '*eisteddfodau*' used to flourish, where the colliers took pride in their brass bands, where the male voice choirs were the glory of the villages and where rugby almost had the force of a religion. There have been changes in recent times. The hold of the Welsh language is not so strong as it was, although strenuous efforts are now being made to encourage Welsh speaking. But the countryside is still deeply Welsh in feeling.

All this sharply divides the two Gowers. It is indeed remarkable that two tracts of land so different in character should have remained administratively united for so long. Political convenience was no doubt the reason for preserving the boundaries of the ancient Welsh commote of Gwyr long after the peninsula section had become completely anglicized. This Welsh section of Gower is not 'tourist country' like Gower Anglicana. In character it is part of the industrial world of the South Wales coalfield and thus deserves a book to itself. But it is still legally part of Gower. So, to end our Portrait, let us look at one or two of the curiosities of this 'Gower of the Hills'. We might tempt the tourist, on his hurried way westward to his holidays on the distant Pembrokeshire coast, to make a short detour to the moorlands.

The main road swings around Swansea on its way west and from Llangyfelach to Pontardulais the hills that you see to the north are well over the 1000 foot mark. The village of Llangyfelach lies at the point where the by-pass returns to the main road, near the high modern slab that houses the Drivers' Vehicle Licence Directory. The Swansea suburbs are now spilling over the hill towards it, but Llangyfelach Church still keeps its curious separate tower, while the nave holds a slab with an early Christian inscription and one of the few memorial brasses in the area. Opposite, the big Velindre Tinplate Works dominates the whole landscape.

At Penllergaer—the old home of John Dillwyn Llewelyn, the pioneer of electric telephonic transmission and one of the first early photographers—the road turns and runs through Pontlliw to Pontardulais. At Pontardulais you are once more on the official boundary of the seigniory of Gower. The estuary of the Loughor ends here. "The Bont", as everyone calls it locally— 'pont' means bridge in Welsh—also marks one of the Roman crossing points. A Norman motte and the old church of St. Teilo lie close to the river's edge. St Teilo is, in fact, out on the marsh and you reach it by a footpath from Pontardulais. It has been sadly neglected but there are now hopes of a restoration. Near this point the new motorway crosses the Loughor. Pontardulais

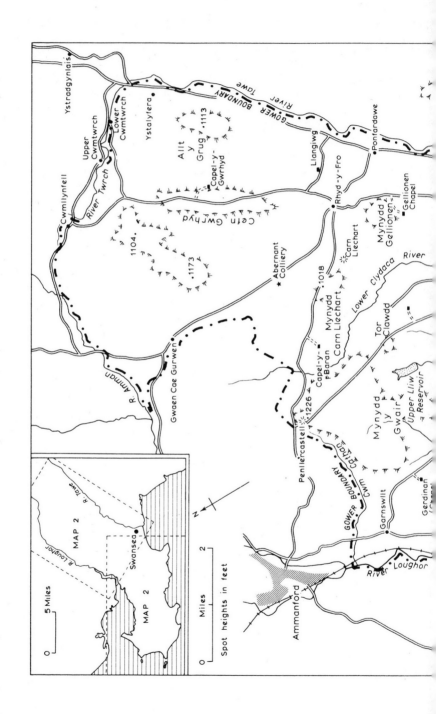

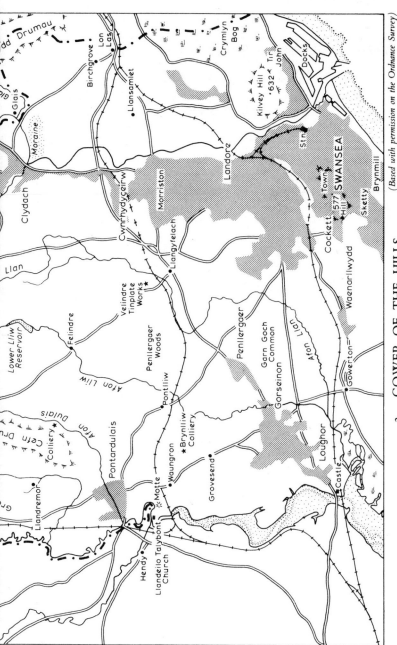

2. GOWER OF THE HILLS

(Based with permission on the Ordnance Survey)

is a typical Welsh industrial village, but it has always been a notable cultural centre and a fountain-head of great choral singing. Visitors were warned, however, as they drove down the long main street on Sunday, that at the time of writing, the bridge at Pontardulais marked the boundary between wet Glamorgan and extremely dry Carmarthenshire. We waited for the 'referendum' to see if this part of the 'Bont' remained dry. It went wet!

The River Loughor winds north from Pontardulais through a green valley, but at Garnswllt the Gower boundary cuts back from the river into the hills. A lonely road runs up Cwm Cathan high over the moors to the little village of Felindre and can give you a taste of the quality of these hills—with their little chapels, lost on the edge of the open country, and the sheep farms tucked into the high hollows. You can also reach Felindre direct from Pontlliw or Llangyfelach. The *'felin'*, or mill, is still there near the banks of the Lliw as it bursts out of a miniature gorge, and on the slope behind it, around a sharp bend, you come to Nebo Chapel. In the churchyard stands the Felindre Murder Stone. It was put up in 1832 and the inscription, which is increasingly hard to read, runs as follows:

To Record Murder

This stone was erected by General Subscription
over the body of Eleanor Williams aged
20 years a native of Carmarthen living
in service in this hamlet of Llangyfelach
with marks of violence upon her person
who was found dead in a well by
Llwyngwenne Farmhouse then in the occupation
of Thomas Thomas on the morning of Sunday,
December the 9, 1832.
Although
The savage murderer may escape for a season
the detection of man yet doubtless God hath
set his mark on him either to time or eternity
And
The cry of blood will certainly persue him
to a terrible and righteous judgement.

Some lines in Welsh follow which are almost too worn to read.

These co-called murder stones were not uncommon in South Wales at this time, and in parts of England as well. The motive behind them seems to have been a hope of bringing the murderer to justice, either by self-confession or by new witnesses coming forward.

Behind Felindre the River Lliw cuts back into the moors which rise northwards towards their highest point. You can reach this delectable area by complicated lanes that run east-wards out of the village or more easily by driving north from Llangyfelach. Your road takes you up over the wide spaces of Mynydd y Gwair—in Welsh, the mountain of hay or perhaps of the high pastures. High and open it certainly is, as you drive in a strangely straight line, past the earthwork of Tor Clawdd, to Penlle'rcastell—'the summit of the place of the castle'. Walk over to the complex of mounds and ditches that is all that remains of this old stronghold, which the Welsh called Castell Meurig. It was probably a Welsh not an English castle in origin, for it is right in the heart of the 'Welshery'. History is generally silent about it. Castell Meurig was too remote to attract much attention, but what a view the castle defenders must have had from the battlements!

This is the highest point in 'Gower of the Hills', at 1,226 feet. Here, in the heart of the high hills, is the one spot where, on a clear day, you can see over the full extent of official Gower. Southward is the flash of the sea and the line of Cefn Bryn and Llanmadoc Hill running out into the winding Loughor Estuary. Eastward lies the deep trench of the Tawe and the dark moun-tains of the central coalfield, Gower's barrier to the east. All the landmarks are here. Close at hand the lonely little valleys curve up towards you—the Lliw with its reservoirs and the upper Clydach with its woods and farms. The hump-backed hill of Mynydd Carn Llechart runs out as a spur from Penlle'rcastell, bearing the ruins of a strange megalithic tomb dating back to 3000 B.C., and the little chapel of Capel-y-Baran on the edge of the moorland. There is something deeply moving about the survival of these modest houses of worship in lonely, wind-swept places. Further away, on Mynydd Gellionen behind Pontardawe, is an even lonelier chapel, Capel Gellionen. Built into the wall is a replica of the remarkable Gellionen Stone. The original is now in the Royal Institution at Swansea. Who is the strange figure depicted on the stone wearing a sort of square cloak? From what period does he come—from the mysterious pre-Christian Celtic world or from the Dark Ages? No one is certain.

Chapels are not the only religious monuments lost amongst

these hills. Behind Rhyd-y-Fro the road twists upwards to Llangiwg. Here the thirteenth-century church huddles close to the rocky outcrop which once sheltered the cell of the holy hermit Kiwg. Kiwg's church was a great place of pilgrimage until the Reformation put a stop to all the old observances. But strange customs lingered long in these lonely places. In the late seventeenth century, the Rev Thomas Morgan reported of Llangiwg "at St Stephen's day people early in the morning beat one another with holly-sprigs till they bleed; maybe this has reference to the Proto-martyr's bloody death . . .". And again: "Corpse candles have been seen to go out of the houses at Llanguke, where people have been sick, and the party dying, the corpse follows the same way that the candles lead."

Behind Llangiwg rises the most northerly section of the moor-lands of Gower-of-the-Hills, Cefn Gwrhyd. It, too, has its lonely chapel near the point where the moor reaches 1,100 feet. In the valley that separates Cefn Gwrhyd from Mynydd Carn Llechart, and hidden from the surrounding hill country, lies the ultra-modern Abernant colliery, a bit of a showpiece for the National Coal Board. For the rest, coal has faded back from this corner of north-east Gower where once it was all-powerful. There is now no major colliery left among the old mining villages. Abernant has swallowed them all.

The border runs first along the line of the River Twrch, which flows down from the range of the Carmarthen Vans. These mountains lie outside the limits of Gower but they form a noble backdrop to the Gower scene. The summits reach 2,600 feet and break to the north in a wave of Old Red Sandstone cliffs and lake-filled hollows. The Twrch cuts down to join the Tawe near Ystalyfera. Here tin-plate works once flourished among the mines. All is changed but Ystalyfera is still intensely Welsh in feeling, proud of its choirs and bands.

The eastern boundary of Gower now runs along the River Tawe southwards towards Swansea. Swansea was our starting point and there it is fitting we should end. Again as you drive, you are passing through a valley that has lost most of its early industry. No coal is worked here and all the tin-plate works have gone. The inhabitants have found other sources of employ-ment and light industries have come into the area. Between Ystradgynlais and Pontardawe the Forestry Commission has reclothed the valley with trees and the old coal-tips are rapidly becoming green and melting back into the landscape. At

Pontardawe the site of the old steel works has been levelled and the whole valley now seems a vast green meadow. Industry returns when you reach Clydach. Here is the big plant of the International Nickel Company, known locally as "the Mond", from the distinguished German chemist Dr Ludwig Mond who played a big part in establishing it. His statue—depicting him looking impressively determined in a vast, wide-brimmed hat and leaning on his walking stick—stands at the work's entrance beside the main road. Behind the works a curious, high bank runs across the whole valley. This is the terminal moraine of the glacier that once flowed down the Tawe Valley at the end of the last Ice Age.

On the eastern end of the moraine is the village of Glais; although in this bottom end of the Swansea valley it is hard to distinguish where one village ends and the next one begins. The houses are all close together along the roads. But a mountain rises behind Glais called Mynydd y Drumau, and in a strange way, the actual boundary of the lordship of Gower and of the parliamentary constituency crosses the Tawe just above the moraine and runs up to the summit ridge of the mountain at 893 feet. This is the last chunk of upland Gower and, in some respects, it is the most odd and out-of-the-way corner of the lordship. It is also the last part of Gower we shall visit and the setting for the last Gower character we shall introduce.

This character is Gabriel Powell (1710–1788), the immensely powerful and forceful steward of the Duke of Beaufort from 1735 onwards and known as the uncrowned King of Swansea. Under Powell, Swansea became the classic pocket-borough and if any scheme did not suit the interests of the Duke, out it went! Between 1706 and 1764 Powell carried out a detailed survey of the seigniory of Gower, known ruefully to the ducal tenants as Gower's Doomsday Book. Such a man was not likely to ignore the preparations of a legal team from the Cadoxton Estate in the Neath Valley side of the mountain to re-survey the boundary of the manor of Kilvey, which since the Middle Ages had always been treated as part of Gower. The boundary line ran through the little Cyrnach brook which rose high up on Mynydd y Drumau and runs down to join the Glais stream, and so into the Tawe.

Powell and his men were early on the top of the mountain and met the Cadoxton pretenders coming up accompanied by ten small collier boys who were to be beaten around the bounds to make sure they remembered where the boundary stones were placed. But across the infant Cyrnach stood the formidable figure of Gabriel Powell. As the stones were placed mid-stream by the Cadoxton men, he and his minions flung them onto the far bank. The Cadoxtonians sought to outwit him by shouting to the boys to creep between Powell's legs and plant the stones in the middle of the stream. Powell simply yanked the lads away with one hand. So, slowly, they descended the mountain, with the Cadoxton men trying to get their lads into mid-stream and Powell flinging them contemptuously onto the bank. Inevitably Powell won. The boundaries of Gower today remain exactly on the line he defended.

Now, before us rises the dark mass of Kilvey Hill, towering over Swansea. We have completed the circuit of the noble and ancient seigniory of Gower. We began at Swansea and we have returned safely to our base. Thanks to Gabriel Powell we have travelled along the exact route of all who 'beat the bounds' of Gower, from Henry de Newburgh, the first conqueror 900 years ago, to myself at the tail end of the long procession of the many Perambulators of Gower.

So now Gower stands ready for your own Perambulation. May you find it unchanged, and as delectable a country as I, with the pardonable partiality of a honorary native, have lovingly depicted it.

Index